Published by Ingram Publishers

ISBN: 978-0-578-51791-9

"...an informative book, full of important information for those of us who want knowledge on Substance Abuse Disorder (SUD), and treatment approaches. Addresses Harm Reduction, the struggle to commit to either a Discovery or Recovery path, and resources available. Read this book, informative and concise packed with good learning." Diane Geiser MSW, LCSW, Preceptor Great Lakes Naval Hospital

"Falling Trees is a Must Read for a comprehensive history and understanding of the many aspects of addiction. The authors do an excellent job of intertwining a recognizable theme with data driven best practices for treating alcohol and drug addiction. One size does not fit all, and this theme resonates throughout the book along with practical tools for the professional. I was energized with this review and encouraged by the practical examples!! Vicki Wahler, MS LPC Gateway Technical College Student Support Counselor/Elkhorn/Burlington Campus

"Mark and Janet know exactly how to separate the trees from the forest, allowing the reader to gain a comprehensive perspective and find a workable pathway to overcoming substance abuse. An informative read for anyone desiring to take back control of their life or the lives of others." Brian McKenna, LCSW, CAADC EDGE Counseling Solutions

Acknowledgements

Janet

I would like to recognize the amazing accomplishment this book represents for my husband and partner of 25 years, Mark. When we started our journey together, we were young and fresh social workers working in residential treatment at the same facility. You have inspired my desire to learn and grow as a person and a clinician. Not everyone has an opportunity to share their life and work with the person they most admire. I feel grateful to have written this book with you and look forward to more shared adventures as we journey into the empty nest years.

My family has influenced some of the content in this book with their courage, compassion, and humor. I had the blessing of growing up in a family that loved one another and made the best of all circumstances. My mother and my late father were an example of commitment and grace under fire. Like all families, mine was not perfect. Through our struggles with illness, addiction, and domestic violence our family deals with difficulty with humor and compassion. The more difficult the situation, the more we laugh. Fortunately, I married a man with a family who also possesses the gift of humor and I am grateful for each of them.

Over my 27 years as a social worker, I have had the unique opportunity to be along for the ride with many individuals and families as they have struggled through mental health issues and recovery. The courage and resilience I have witnessed from my clients never ceases to amaze me. I am humbled and honored to have shared in some of their journey. It is my hope that this book reaches out to others who are hurting with a message of hope, compassion, and grace.

Mark

Janet and I have been talking about writing a book together for many years. The topics we debated writing varied from time to time. We even started on one book and family obligations, work, new ventures, and other priorities interfered with getting too far into our project. Many pieces in our lives have fallen into place for us to be able to give our book the attention it required. Falling Trees, Color Blind Scientists, and Addiction evolved from the many conversations we have had with each other and our clients. We both decided enough talking about it. "Let's just do it!" We put our heads down and started on our journey to publishing our first book.

Ideas began to flow and putting this book together became a reality. Initially, we believed we could accomplish this without any help. This would have been a **huge** mistake and not served our passion for writing this book well. There are many people involved directly and behind the scenes in turning this book into a reality. We first thought of importing photos to go along with our writing. Through our many discussions, we finally decided to use an illustrator finding an amazing young talent (thanks to our youngest son), Emily Cyr. Her creative illustrations and amazing ability to draw what was in our heads have greatly added to our book. She offers whimsical drawings to support each idea we are trying to convey.

When we researched topics on writing a book, a vast majority of experts recommended hiring an editor. Initially, we were reluctant to follow this advice. We were under the belief we could complete this on our own. It soon became apparent the experts knew what they were talking about. We realized we did need an editor. A good number of applicants responded to our ad. Melissa Anderson stood out over all the other candidates. Melissa has been an excellent addition to our team. She was knowledgeable as well as passionate about taking on the project. Her feedback was constructive and gentle. As our book evolved, we knew we hit a homerun in our decision to hire her. She guided us through this process with patience and excellent feedback. We have been very fortunate to find someone with her talent and personality.

This book could not have been published without the support we have received from our children. Each one of our three boys have offered their encouragement and feedback throughout our writing of the book. They have not only supported us, but each inspired us in their own unique way. They have always been in our corner and our biggest cheerleaders, though we don't think they would appreciate that characterization. Jacob has always had an amazing zest for life, talent, and ability for self-reflection that has inspired us. Daniel's early in life challenges taught him to be incredibly persistent for which we greatly admire him and the courage with which he conducts himself. Nate's optimism and drive to reach each and every goal even when it seems impossible causes us to believe that this too is possible. Thank you all for the joy and music you bring to our lives!

Of course, we cannot write a section of acknowledgements in our book without mentioning who pointed us in this direction in the first place. Janet talked about her family (whom I am grateful for their support to the both of us) in her section. My parents provided a great foundation for me to pursue my goals. They have offered encouragement and instilled in me independent thinking, risk taking, standing up for myself, and pursuing my ambitions. It is not a coincidence that all my siblings have their own businesses (as did my parents). I could picture my late father smiling in heaven and giving me a thumbs up. My brothers have been supportive throughout my professional career and I have never felt shy about asking their advice.

The start and completion of this book would have not been possible without my coauthor, Janet (my wife). She has provided much more than a co-author for this book. She has been my inspiration and role model. Janet has been patient and kind in her feedback. Insightful in her ideas and direction. Offered humor when needed, direct feedback when ideas were not falling together, and encouragement when I was getting frustrated with our millionth rewrite (maybe a slight exaggeration…only slightly) and insisted that we do it in a way that did the subject matter justice. Before I met Janet one of my coworkers gave me some unsolicited advice. Never marry someone in the same profession as you. This has easily been the worst advice I ever received. Among the many attributes she offers to me as a friend and wife, I receive a double bonus in her offering me professional feedback.

5

My former and current colleagues have offered help and direction in my professional life. When I first started out in the field, I had some excellent teachers to point me in the right direction. There are some of whom I still have relationships with. My knowledge about mental health and substance has been greatly reliant on their feedback and support.

Lastly, this book could not have been done without my clients. They have shared their success and failures with me. We have been to battle together in fighting addiction. There have been some casualties along the way as addiction is a powerful enemy. I have seen some of my clients lose their lives, wind up in jail, have families give up on them, take someone's' life, and lose in other ways to their battle with addiction. I have seen a great many more success stories. Families that have hung in there and getting a payoff of seeing their loved one remain abstinent from substances. Addicts that have turned around their lives and work at repairing the damage substance abuse has done. Alcoholics who have completely given up their drinking and courageously faced the challenges of building a sober life. I have always felt privileged in being allowed to be a part of someone's life when they are facing such a huge challenge in facing their addiction. I have learned a great deal from my clients and appreciate the trust they have given me. My hope this book will be able to offer those suffering from addiction the direction and support that will benefit them in their fight against addiction.

Falling Trees, Color Blind Scientists, and Addiction

by Mark Myers LCSW, CADC and Janet Myers LCSW

Emily Cyr, Illustrator
Melissa Anderson, Editor

TABLE OF CONTENTS

Authors' Forwards

Mark Myers, LCSW, CADC

When I first started out in the substance abuse field, I can confidently say it was not by design or by some calling, but more by chance. My first year of graduate school for social work we were randomly assigned field work placements. I was placed at the Edward Hines Jr. Veterans Administration Hospital. Five of us were assigned to the VA, and the first day a supervisor asked our group where we wanted to be placed. Not knowing what exact services were offered at the hospital, or where I would wind up, I anxiously tried to come up with a decision. Fortunately for me, she started from right to left and I was the last one on the left. I had noticed a sign above the entrance to a hallway with an arrow pointing to a Substance Abuse Unit. I am not sure how much time elapsed between me recalling that sign and being called upon by the instructor. When I blurted out my answer, the supervisor seemed pleased with my decision. Thinking back, I wonder if I had not noticed that sign, or if she had gone from left to right in her questioning, what direction my career would have taken. Nonetheless, from my first day in the unit, I started on my career journey.

At that time, the substance abuse unit was strictly for patients recovering from drug use. Some patients had abused both alcohol and drugs, but the substance of choice needed to be drugs. Those facing alcohol addiction exclusively were housed on another unit. Patients spent 48 days in the unit, where they received care and counseling from a mix of professionals and paraprofessionals (recovering addicts). While they also offered individual and family counseling, the primary focus was on group sessions.

The first days were a huge learning experience for me. I was taken aback by the patients' circumstances and I wondered to myself, "How could they allow their lives to get that out of control?" and "Why in the world would they keep making these choices?" As my time in the unit continued, I realized these questions did not lend themselves to easy answers. I learned how addictions consumed individuals. I understood that at some point it was the drugs making the choices, not the individuals. I began to understand what addicts were facing and what my role could be in facilitating change.

At the end of my graduate program, I was recruited to work with substance abusing teens at an inpatient substance abuse facility. My knowledge and understanding of addiction increased greatly during my time there. It provided a wonderful foundation and learning experience. I understood more about the havoc addiction creates in people's lives. I understood that people can lose a great deal from the challenges of substance abuse. I also discovered that people can stop using substances and return to happy and productive lives.

This facility followed what is known as the "Minnesota Model," which is based on the 12 steps of Alcoholics/Narcotics Anonymous. The treatment team consisted of a medical doctor, nurses, college degreed counselors, recovering individuals, and techs and aids. As great of a learning experience as this was, I soon realized that despite individual differences, most of the time we were making similar recommendations: complete the program and refer to a residential setting for aftercare. These recommendations were made regardless of the patient's previous treatment history, level of use, substance of choice, support systems, or motivation. When I saw individuals succeed, I felt that we were offering the right guidance. However, I also saw individuals fail in those settings and succeed in a less intensive setting. Some individuals dropped out of the program and moderated their use without any professional help. Still others never went into any treatment program and quit on their own. It became clear to me that substance abuse treatment isn't one-size-fits-all.

In graduate school, we learned as social workers to start where the client is at. I found this to be especially true in a substance abuse setting. I realized that not all people can benefit from or need long term professional care, and people stop using in all different sizes, shapes, and forms. Addicts and alcoholics face similar problems (their addiction) but their challenges and obstacles can differ. Their support and motivation will also vary. Each substance abuse problem is unique to the chemically dependent person.

The path to recovery is different for every person. What gets their arrow pointed in the right direction is not always easy to determine. Since I started working in private practice (over 25 years ago at this writing) I have learned that each journey is unique and special. When I meet with a client, I can never predict where our counseling journey will end. As confident as I am in my abilities, there are too many variables that can affect the outcome. I can offer tools, support, and resources for them to succeed, and most of them do, but I still must prepare them and myself for the reality that recovery is not always a given. Often it takes hard work and sacrifices. Sometimes it is hard for individuals to see the payoff.

Defining a substance use problem to individuals and families is not always an easy task for professionals. Opinions and experiences can vary from person to person and setting to setting. I describe the problem in these terms: if a tree falls in the forest and no one is around to hear it, does it make a sound? If someone has a substance abuse problem that has not come up on the radar, does that mean he or she does not have a problem? This is what motivated us to write this book.

Tina Turner sang a song called "Proud Mary." In the opening she says, "We're gonna take the beginning of this song, and do it easy. But then we're gonna do the finish rough." Well we are going to do the opposite. We are going to start out rough and work to easier. First, we present the challenges of addiction, how devastating and consuming it is for addicts and their families. Readers need enough information to know what they may be facing. Our last section discusses recovery aspects with actionable tools and advice for how to address addiction and the destructiveness it may have caused. Recovery will not be easy, and in fact, for some it can be extremely difficult. However, that does not mean there is no hope. Recovery is within reach for everyone.

Our bodies/lives look to find a balance. All systems work together toward this goal. Active substance abuse throws this balance off. Substance users system adjusts to the new norm. We adapt to a drug or alcohol using lifestyle. Once a person stops, their body establishes a new balance. If you are deciding to stop using, this book can assist you in understanding what you will be facing. Planning to address struggles along the way is also helpful. Although you may not control your addiction, you can take control of your life. Taking the necessary steps to plan your life and anticipate challenges in your recovery is a crucial component in recovery. The more you plan for in recovery, the more likely you will succeed.

Anyone facing, dealing with, or wanting to know more about addiction will benefit from this book. Not all chapters will apply to everyone. However, "knowledge is power," as they say. The more informed someone is, the better decisions they can make. By the end, you will not only understand the workings of addiction, but also be better equipped to reclaim a healthy lifestyle. We refer to real cases to illustrate our arguments. Names, circumstances, and other identifying characteristics have been changed to maintain confidentiality.

Janet Myers, LCSW, PEL

Mark and I often talk about what would have happened if one decision in our lives were different. We met when we were both fairly young clinicians in the mental health field working at a residential treatment center. His journey has in many ways been my journey after nearly 25 years of marriage. We undertook this project together because in both our private practice and our other work we have continually studied and recognized the impact of substance use on family members and friends of the user. We have witnessed the joy of individuals who reach out and accept the help of their loved ones as well as the difficult experience this can be for all parties involved. We have, unfortunately, seen individuals continue to use even when all of the pieces for their success have fallen into place.

One of the most frustrating parts of substance use for family members and friends is the thought "What is so bad in your life that you need to use?" "What have I done wrong?" "Did I cause this?" "If I just…I can make it better." We help families understand that the user's substance abuse is not about the family. Learning to set boundaries and allowing the user to experience the consequences of their use without rescuing or trying to "fix" them is a journey all its own. Loving someone with a substance use disorder requires much of a spouse, family member, or friend.

It is our hope that you will find here information, comfort, and support on this journey. Substance abuse can be overcome. We believe with all our strength that there is help, hope, and healing available. Thank you for picking up this book.

SECTION 1

Introduction: Falling Trees and Noises

If a tree falls in the forest and no one is around to hear it, does it make a sound? Intellectual debates on this subject have raged for generations. How you approach this question depends upon how you define it. Perceptually, if no one is present to observe the tree, it will not emit a noise. Sound is created when vibrations travel through air, water, or matter and enter our outer ear. From there, the sound travels to the brain, which interprets the input. If an ear is not there to pick up these vibrations, the argument goes, no sound is made. The opposing view maintains that the natural world exists apart from our perception of it. We do not have to perceive sound to know it occurs. We recognize that even when we are not looking directly at the sky, it is blue. This debate will continue, and a universal agreement will not be achieved anytime soon. Most likely, your answer depends on your own view on the question. Can something exist without being perceived?

Just as with the question of the falling trees, determining if substance use is a problem, for the most part, is defined by our perspective. For some, there is a clear line between a destructive and healthy relationship with substances. For others, it may not be so clear. For example, a husband may complain that his wife now makes a big deal about his drinking, but before they were married, they used to drink all the time. There was a change in circumstances (marriage, being older, or in this case a baby) which made previously normal drinking now seem like a problem. Or someone who lives by himself, drinks heavy and daily, and has undiagnosed health problems (he has not gone to the doctor in several years) may continue to drink with seemingly no problems. Or a woman feels it is unfair she is asked to give up her recreational marijuana use because of a positive drug screen at work.

For some there is a distinct line they cross that makes it clear their relationship with mood altering drugs is destructive. For others it is not so obvious. Experts may not always have the answers either. Professionals are affected by their own perspectives and orientations. Different providers use different methodologies. A patient can receive dissimilar diagnoses from multiple clinicians, even on the same day. Even if a decision is made to stop using, acknowledging the problem does not mean mission accomplished. This book will cover both dimensions of recovery, wanting to stop and being able to stop. In the context of this book, we define "substances" or "drugs" as any compounds with mood-altering properties, including illicit narcotics, legal drugs (prescription and over the counter), and alcohol. Also, names and identifying factors in the case studies we present have been changed to protect client confidentiality.

When does substance abuse become a problem? Our answer can vary enormously from family to family, community to community, or even culture to culture. The use of mood-altering substances dates back at least as far as the Stone Age. The discovery of beer jugs in Neolithic China confirms that fermented beverages existed 9,000 years ago (Gallagher and Hetherington, 2005, para. 3). Archeologists have confirmed that pre-Columbian Mesoamericans consumed hallucinogens at least as far back as 8,600 BCE (Carod-Artal, 2015). The Incas, meanwhile, are known to have chewed coca leaves (the source of modern cocaine) as a stimulant to help with high altitude living ("History of Cocaine," n.d., para 2). In Mesopotamia, ancient Sumerians grew opium at least as early as 3,400 BCE, referring to it as Hul Gil, the "joy plant" (DEA Museum & Visitors Center, n.d., para. 1).

In many cases, intoxicating substances played, and sometimes continue to play, a central role in religious, cultural, and spiritual ceremonies (Beyers, 2012, para. 1; Cleverskey, 2002, para. 3; Crocq, 2007, para. 4). People of many diverse cultures use mind altering substances to aid in their spiritual journeys, communicate with the dead (Botanical Shaman, 2018; Cleverskey, 2002), facilitate rites of passage (Gale, 2002), and even help in decision-making (Gale, 2002). Some Native Americans, for example, use peyote as part of spiritual ceremonies to the present day (Guarnotta, 2018).

Not surprisingly, alongside this long history of substance use, we also find many references to drug and alcohol abuse. From Noah's drunkenness in the Old Testament (Genesis 9:20-26), to Alexander the Great's possible death from alcoholism (Liappas, Lascaratos, Fafouti, & Christodoulou, 2003), to a surge in opium overuse starting with the American Civil War (Trickey, 2018), there are well documented negative consequences of intoxicating substances throughout history. As a result, entire societies and religions have at times shunned or prohibited their use.

The Temperance Movement in the United States for example grew in opposition to the negative social effects of intoxication and alcoholism. In 1774, Quaker Anthony Benezet published a book, *Mighty Destroyer,* detailing the ravaging physical and moral impact of alcohol abuse. In 1774, Benjamin Rush M.D., one of the signers of the Declaration of Independence, was one of the first to characterize alcoholism as an addiction that needed medical intervention in his *Medical Inquiries and Observations Upon the Diseases of the Mind* (Gold & Adamec, 2011). This opened up a new outlook on the treatment of alcoholism and ultimately substance abuse. By the 1830s, a large portion of Americans –

Protestant Christians in particular – advocated total abstinence from alcohol (The Editors of Encyclopaedia Britannica, 2018). This same movement eventually led to the Eighteenth Amendment and Prohibition in 1920 ("Roots of Prohibition," 2011).

Our attitudes toward substance use can and have changed over time. What we see as problematic now may have been viewed more favorably in years past, and vise versa. Sigmund Freud advocated the use of cocaine as an antidepressant (Valjak, 2017). It was even used as an ingredient in Coca Cola starting in the 1880s ("History of Cocaine," n.d., para 7). In the 1920s, the United States government started regulating more closely the use of substances and passed laws to prohibit the drug from being included as an ingredient. Marijuana, meanwhile, was classified as a schedule 1 drug in the 1970s, meaning it has high potential for abuse and no medical benefits. Currently, however, its popularity is trending upward and has recently been decriminalized or legalized in many states (History.com Editors, 2018). And of course, Prohibition was repealed in 1933, just 13 years after the passage of the Eighteenth Amendment.

Since societal and cultural attitudes vacillate over time, it is reasonable to expect that societal attitudes regarding substance use will vary as well. Our views also adjust as we develop a better understanding of how substances impact individuals and relationships. As medical science evolves, so have our positions on certain substances. Currently, alcohol use is largely accepted in our society. The U.S. alcohol industry generates $25 billion per year in revenue (Kell, 2017, para. 2), while Americans consume 2.5 gallons of alcohol a year on average (Beer by the Numbers, 2016, para. 2). For many communities, moreover, alcohol sales and manufacture is an economic lifeline (Kell, 2017, para. 2).

The line between substance use and substance abuse is further blurred by the fact that many mood-altering substances may have medicinal purposes. Certain components of the marijuana plant have been used to help with seizures, pain management, and side effects from chemotherapy (Zimmermann, 2017). Cocaine has long been used as a topical anesthetic (American College of Medical Toxicology, 2019, para. 4). Although not wholly accepted, as of yet, studies are also starting to show additional medicinal properties of other illicit substances. LSD may assist in the treatment of Post-Traumatic Stress Disorder (PTSD) (Jaslow, 2012), Ketamine (a short acting analgesic abused for recreational purposes) has been used to treat depression (Oaklander, 2017), and ecstasy may have anticancer properties (Freeman, 2011). Even moderate alcohol consumption has been purported as being beneficial for our health (Bachai, 2013; Mayo Clinic Staff, 2018c).

One might expect that nations with the highest production or consumption rates of mood-altering substances would also have the most serious social consequences. However, quantity and availability are only two factors to be taken into consideration. For instance, the Czech Republic has the 9th highest rate of alcohol consumption in the world ("List of countries by alcohol consumption per capita," n.d.) but ranks only 33rd in percentage of alcohol related deaths (MarketWatch, 2014). In Ireland, from the year 2000 to 2010 there was a nationwide drop in alcohol consumption (OECD, 2015), however, from 2004 to 2008, the number of alcohol related deaths increased (Reilly, 2011).

Drugs have similarly conflicting data. The countries that produce the most cocaine nationwide are not the top consumers of cocaine (Mattyasovszky, 2018). Columbia is one of the world's largest cocaine distributors, yet cocaine use is lower there than in other nations (Smith, 2017). Availability and consumption do not necessarily lead us to defining substance use as a problem. It is, however, usually a safe bet to state that higher consumption of a substance will lead to greater problems.

How societies have addressed treatment for substance abuse has likewise changed over time. There have been many interesting (and sometimes distressing) approaches to helping people struggling with addiction. Thankfully, the field of addiction treatment has grown and evolved enormously. In order to understand how we came to be here; we must first understand where we have been.

The word "addicted" comes from the Latin word *addictus*, meaning to devote or sacrifice. Shakespeare was the first to introduce "addiction" into English in his play *Othello*. The notion that addiction is a physical condition that needed medical intervention – rather than a moral failing – is a relatively modern one. Early treatments ranged from bizarre to cruel. Hydrotherapy was practiced in the 1700s, during which patients were immersed or sprayed in cold or hot water (Furman, 2017). In 1857, the New York State Inebriate Asylum was built as the first hospital for treating alcoholics. Although it eventually failed and was closed, it paved the way for the treatment of addiction in hospital settings (Simonson, 2014). In 1879, the Gold Cure was introduced as an alleged cure for alcoholism, an injection medication allegedly containing gold, strychnine, and alcohol (Feinman, 2018; Hickman, 2018). Later analysis discovered it contained ammonia aloin, cinchona, and over 25% alcohol. Still, the Gold Cure Institutes of Niagara Falls, New York lay the groundwork for recognizing alcoholism as a disease in the 1890s.

In the 1900s, treatments also included large doses of insulin (Pullar-Strecker, 1945), injections of blood from horses (Twining, 1916, p. 29), and even lobotomies (Bushak, 2015; White, 2014). In 1935, Alcoholics Anonymous (AA) was born, which changed the field of addiction treatment. AA further strengthened support for the disease concept, established the 12-step model, and based their treatment on alcoholics helping other alcoholics. There were other significant milestones in substance abuse treatment. *The Journal of*

Inebriety first appeared in the United States in 1876 (Weiner & Whitem, 2007). Preceding that was the *British Journal of Addiction*. They both viewed alcoholism as a disease.

Still it wasn't until 1952 that the American Medical Association (AMA) offered a definition of alcoholism. In 1956, the AMA supported treatment for alcoholism, although it stopped short of supporting alcoholism as a disease. In 1957, the Veterans Health Administration developed alcohol treatment units. Around the same time, therapeutic communities were becoming popular. The staff was largely recovering substance abusers. In 1971, the American Journal of Psychiatry published criteria for the diagnosis of alcoholism. The Joint Commissions of Accreditation (the organization in charge of accrediting hospitals) developed standards to treat alcoholism using criteria established by the American Journal of Psychiatry. Training requirements for paraprofessionals were however not clear or established. There were treatment settings that used recently graduated residents as their treatment staff. If a recovering staff member relapsed, they returned to the unit as a resident. Treatment centers frowned upon using medications for those experiencing dual diagnosis issues. Dual diagnosis, which will be explained in greater detail in later chapters, refers to someone who has both substance abuse and mental health symptoms.

In the early 1980s, substance abuse treatment was a booming industry, with treatment groups for women, LGBTQ populations, adolescents, and the elderly, to name a few. In 1989, Stanton Peele wrote a book critical of the recovery community called *The Diseasing of America* which challenged the idea of addiction as a disease and argued that moderation was possible. We can't determine if this book alone sparked the critical look at the recovery industry that followed, but it reflected a shift in how the addiction field conducted treatment.

Dual diagnosis has earned greater acceptance, as has treating coexisting mental health disorders with prescription drugs. Medications to aid in cravings and withdrawal for those in early recovery have become mainstream treatment. We also encourage individualized treatment approaches. Professionals are more willing to meet the client where they are at, in terms of recovery stage, and not where we want them to be. There has also been a shift towards more individual counseling as well as intensive outpatient and day programs. Another big change took place when insurance companies began covering treatment centers. The Mental Health Parity Act (1996) required health plans to reimburse for substance abuse. Managed care companies that oversee benefits for insurance companies increasingly required evidence-based treatment and provider accountability.

Treatment has evolved, and it is important to understand this evolution not only in the treatment field but in society. The history of substance, dark chapters and all, have helped shape the substance abuse field today. We benefit from years of experience to help us develop the best tools to help addicts and alcoholics.

Where doctors have seen a medical problem, governments see a social and legal one. Historically, governments have taken a legislative approach to responding to substance abuse. Yet, harsh or restrictive substance abuse laws sometimes have the reverse effect. Iran today has some of the strictest laws against substance trafficking and drug use in the world, including the death penalty. However, Iran was estimated to be home to 2.2 million drug addicts in 2016 (Bengali and Mostaghim, 2016). The United Kingdom has determined that strict drug laws are not effective (Travis, 2014), and despite regulations, the United States remains a leading consumer of cocaine and marijuana (Warner, 2008).

Prohibition in America did reduce liquor consumption in the initial year or so. But consumption eventually rose to about 70% of what it was before the law was passed (Miron & Zwiebel, 1991, abstract). Prohibition also gave rise to black market smuggling, gang violence (Roos, 2019), and fostered binge drinking, among other negative consequences (Lerner, n,d.). Similarly, when the U.S. Congress passed The Harrison Narcotic Act in 1914 (Wilson, et al.), which made it illegal for physicians to prescribe narcotics for the treatment of addiction (Harrison Narcotics Tax Act, n.d.), this only drove users underground (Brecher, E. M. & the Editors of Consumer Reports Magazine, 1972; Mudaliar, 2018, para. 8).

What then of the growing trend towards marijuana legalization? The concern with some is that legalization of drugs would increase use among the population. If drugs were legal, wouldn't more people use drugs? In 2001, Portugal made the radical move of decriminalizing personal possession for all drugs ("Drug policy of Portugal," n.d.). Over the next few years, not only had drug use decreased to pre-decriminalization levels, but cases of new HIV infections dropped and street overdoses decreased significantly (Szalavitz, 2009; Transform, 2014; Vastag, 2009). Furthermore, drug related crime decrease over time (Oakford, 2016), and drug induced overdoses were lower than the European Union's average in 2014 (European Monitoring Centre for Drugs and Drug Addiction, 2015, p. 80). This also took away a possible complication related to substance misuse: legal problems. In other words, many users who would have previously been sent to jail are now seeking treatment or are in recovery (Szalavitz, 2009; Vastag, 2009).

Perhaps we can view substance abuse from a more environmental or personal perspective. Our surroundings influence our behavior. A person acts differently at work than with friends. Humans are driven by the desire to conform. As our surroundings vary, this affects not only our perceptions but our behaviors as well. For example, Jerry is in a relationship where he and his partner are heavy drinkers. Once the relationship ends, Jerry may not have much insight or concern regarding his drinking. However, if his next relationship is with a person who does not drink alcohol, there may be significant conflict. The rules and perceptions can vary depending on circumstance. If Jerry enters a relationship with another heavy drinker, most likely, this individual would likely not see Jerry's drinking as an issue.

In a second scenario, Joan, a daily smoker of marijuana for years experiences no complications at work throughout her many years of employment. The company changes ownership and now requires drug screens. Overnight, her pot use, which was previously not problematic, is now viewed as a problem. In a third scenario, Devin grows up in a home where there is heavy substance abuse. His viewpoint will be substantially different than Annie's as she was raised in a substance-free home. However, if they wind up dating one another, they would not likely agree on what constitutes normal or typical substance use.

Unfortunately, experts may not aid us in understanding the nature of a substance abuse problem. In the United States, a recent study identified that approximately 5% of the population misused legally prescribed medications (Thompson, 2014, para. 5). U.S. doctors are also keeping patients on painkilling medication (opiates or narcotics) longer than recommended ("Painkillers Driving Addiction," n.d.). Furthermore, the number of people addicted to opioid prescription medication is greater than the amount of people addicted to heroin (Centers for Disease Control and Prevention, 2018). These figures are not solely the result of doctors overprescribing but do give us an idea of what role physicians may play in opioid addiction.

Obtaining a consensus on defining what precisely comprises a substance abuse problem and how best to treat it presents a substantial challenge. Cancer, heart disorders, and other medical conditions, for the most part, can be verified through testing that leads us to a diagnosis. Substance abuse concerns are not so easy to diagnose in some cases. Where does this leave us? It leads to beetles in boxes.

Chapter 1: Beetle in a Box

Ludwig Wittgenstein, a philosopher, introduced a query. A group of people who have never seen a beetle before are each presented with a box containing something, they are told is a beetle. Each person is then asked to describe what a beetle is based only on what they see in their own box. As a result, their description will be defined entirely by their own perspective (box) and they may even disagree with each other because they may all have different contents in their boxes. Each person's interpretation is valid, but also limited. We face a beetle in a box challenge in the substance abuse field.

People can and do view substance abuse problems from countless perspectives. It is difficult if not impossible to come up with a universally accepted definition for addiction. A recovering addict may have a different perspective than someone who has never been around substance abuse. A neuroscientist and a recovering alcoholic may also differ significantly when describing substance abuse because of their diverging viewpoints and life experiences.

Even health care professionals have differing views on precisely what constitutes addiction and substance abuse. The World Health Organization (WHO) defines an addict as someone whose use is harmful, has a compulsion to use, suffers withdrawal, and experiences progressive neglect of alternative pleasures or interests because of psychoactive substance use (The World Health Organization, n.d.). The American Medical Association (AMA), meanwhile, views addiction primarily as a bodily disease, and focuses more on the physical effects including enlarged liver, tremors, and pulmonary disease (Mersy, 2003). For the American Psychiatric Association (APA), "Addiction is a complex condition, a brain disease that is manifested by compulsive substance use despite harmful consequence" (Parekh, 2017, para. 1).

There are some generally agreed upon guidelines. To aid in clinical diagnosis, the APA produces a manual for mental health professionals called the Diagnostic and Statistical Manual which has seen many editions since 1952. The current version, the DSM-5, establishes ten types of Substance-Related Disorders:

- Alcohol
- Caffeine
- Cannabis
- Hallucinogens
- Inhalants
- Opioids
- Sedatives, Hypnotics, and Anxiolytics
- Stimulants
- Tobacco
- Other or unknown substances

A substance abuse diagnosis is made based on four criteria: impaired control, social impairment, risky use, and pharmacological criteria. Levels of severity are assigned as mild, moderate, and severe. Mild substance use disorder has the presence of two to three criteria, moderate range is four to five symptoms, and severe is six or more symptoms. Due to the nature of substance use, there may be some overlapping of categories and more than one diagnosis (American Psychiatric Association, 2013).

While this manual provides useful guidelines for defining addiction from a medical and mental health standpoint, we have found that for individuals defining addiction is often more complex. What we can say is that individuals will need to reach their own conclusions about their use or a loved one's use. We have included some helpful guidelines in coming up with your own definition.

In our experience, the following areas of concern indicate that a line has been crossed. Note that not all indicators need to be met to signal a concern.

- Unsuccessful at limiting use. This would include inability to stop when intended.
- Hiding use from other people.
- Using in dangerous or risky situations. (Drinking and driving, using at work).
- Suffering health, legal, or work issues related to use.
- Family expressing concern about use or asking person to stop.
- Preoccupation about using.
- Physical reactions (withdrawal) when use stopped.

- Major life areas negatively impacted by substance use.
- Relationships outside family negatively impacted by use.
- Compromising value system (lying, stealing) due to use.
- Feeling guilty about use.

The common thread is that at some point addiction becomes a destructive force in a person's life. Compulsion in particular is a good indicator that use is a problem. A compulsion exists when there is a great need to use a substance, decisions are made to revolve around use, and a great deal of energy is expended toward continued using. In these cases, activities and routines are centered around use, which further impacts a person's place of employment ("Alcohol & Drugs in the Workplace," n.d.), health (NIDA, 2017a), society (NIDA, 2017b), family, and can endanger their life (Hedegaard, Arialdi, Miniño, & Warner, 2018). An inability or refusal to change a behavior that is destroying lives – including that of the user themselves – tells us that there is a problem.

The longer the addiction progresses, the more substances become a part of their lives and the harder the choice of stopping becomes to the user. We want to present the challenges faced in recovery. It is important to understand how and why addiction takes over someone's life. Which brings us to a French guy named Buridan and his view on donkeys.

Chapter 2: Dying Donkeys

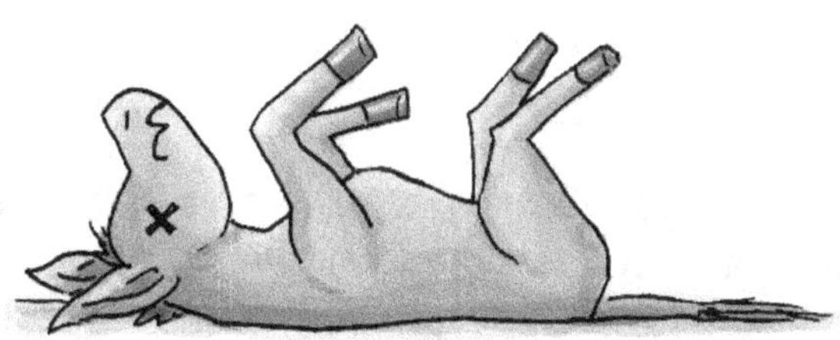

A 14th-century French philosopher, Jean Buridan, offered a paradox appropriately called Buridan's Ass. In this paradox, a hungry and thirsty donkey (ass) is placed in between a stack of hay and a pail of water. How will he choose which to approach first? The donkey will most likely go to whichever one of the two is closer. If the hay and water are of equal distance, according to Buridan, the donkey will be unable to decide which direction to go. Eventually, he will die of hunger or thirst due to his inability to decide between two equal options.

It's an absurd thought puzzle to be sure, yet the donkey's dilemma helps us begin to understand addiction. To most people, deciding between abusing drugs and abstaining from them would appear like a straightforward choice. The addict, however, experiences a comparable dilemma deciding between a substance that furnishes social lubrication, coping skills for stress, pleasure, and other perceived benefits, compared to the mounting costs associated with continuing use.

Addiction is usually the result of a series of choices, events, circumstances, and predetermined genetic disposition. A set of decisions leads to a lifestyle that becomes difficult to escape. At some point, an addict will realize that continuing to use, and the consequences associated with use, are inseparable. They cannot enjoy the benefits without also experiencing the repercussions.

Stopping substance use may be experienced by the user as something akin to loss. A theory advanced by Elizabeth Kubler Ross describes the stages of grief faced by someone coming to terms with a loss: denial, anger, bargaining, depression, and acceptance. These stages are not progressive, meaning everyone moves differently through each stage. Also, they do not have to experience all stages or stay in a specific stage for any length of time. Those dealing with a loss address these stages in their own unique manner. Similarly, users face stages in addressing their problem. The loss (or perceived loss) of a drug of choice usually causes addicts to:

- Deny that their use has become a problem.
- Become angry at the thought of having to give it up.

- Bargain with themselves or others to keep using.
- Feel depressed at the thought of giving up something meaningful to them.
- Finally accepting that they have a problem.

The hurdles to stopping use may result in a Buridan's Ass type of paralysis. Even though the benefits of quitting will enhance (and possibly save) their life, beginning that journey can involve huge obstacles and challenges. For some, this choice appears overwhelming.

If you reside in a house that no longer serves your needs, you must resolve to reconstruct it to make it more habitable. Every house will be unique. It will depend on individual personalities, family members, the current level of damage, and other factors. Those in recovery face similar choices. For some, they can make simple adjustments to achieve their goals. Others need to undertake a total teardown of the house returning to the foundation. Just as each house requires different renovations, each abuser/user must chart their own journey. Section two helps us understand the foundations of substance use. Section three contains tools to rebuild every life area affected by drugs and alcohol.

SECTION 2

Chapter 3: Spider in a Urinal

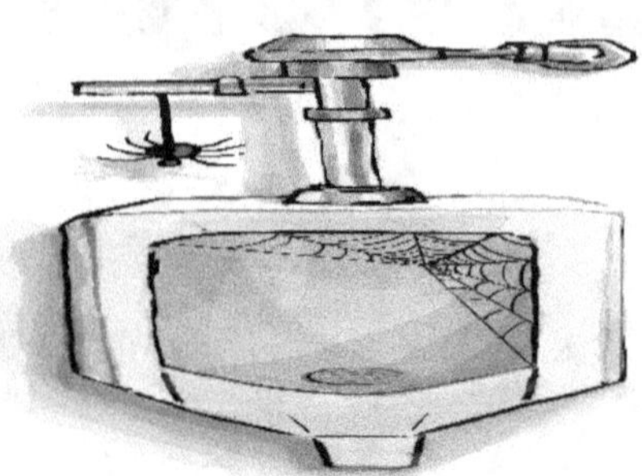

In his book, *The View from Nowhere*, Philosophy Professor Thomas Nagel proposed the following thought puzzle. One day, the professor noticed a spider in the urinal in the men's bathroom. He believed the spider was living a horrible life, being trapped in the urinal and getting urinated on every day. Out of kindness, the professor took a paper towel and moved it to the floor, where it did not move. The next day the professor found the spider shriveled up dead. This led him to question: was the spider better off in the urinal? Although the quality of life may have been horrific, the spider was still alive in the urinal. Which was a better position for the creature? Was it right for the professor to intervene? Despite our best intentions, interference can sometimes cause unintended harm.

Addicts face a similar challenge: "Am I better off if I stop using or keep using?" The user may believe change is impossible, or that quitting would make life even more difficult. Although they recognize that remaining inside the urinal (continuing to use) is a crummy existence. For those trapped in addiction, life in a metaphorical urinal can seem preferable to life outside. In this chapter, we will explain why it is so difficult for the chemically dependent to make these choices.

The reason substance use becomes problematic varies from person to person. Genetics, individual personality, environment, and life experiences all influence mental health and substance abuse problems. There is no one consistent determining factor that leads to substance abuse problems.

Some use drugs and alcohol regularly with few repercussions. Others experience problems with use, but they somehow stay under the radar (tree falling in the forest goes unheard). They make lifestyle changes that obscure or accommodate their addiction. Still others recognize that their use has crossed the line but become overwhelmed at the thought of stopping their substance use. No one sets out to have problems with drugs or alcohol. We have not yet met anyone who included substance abuse addiction on their bucket list.

Substance abuse is a progressive problem, and consequences associated with use develop over time. E. Morton Jellinek put forward one popular model of alcohol addiction in a 1946 essay called the Jellinek curve (Powers, 2015). His paper *Phases in the Drinking History of Alcoholics* revolutionized therapy for substance abuse in America at the time. He described the gradual course of alcoholism as a U-curve, with increasingly harmful use and decline on the left, and the up-hill road to recovery on the right, with rock bottom in the middle, literally the lowest point of the U. Once a person reaches the lowest point or "bottom," their recovery would entail working their way back up the curve. Many clinicians took the Jellinek Curve wholesale and believed recovery cannot occur until someone hits "bottom."

Two examples illustrate the usefulness and limits of the "hitting bottom" approach. One adolescent I was working with decided his "bottom" was when he was caught at school smoking marijuana. He was suspended (per school policy) for five days as a result. He was embarrassed when he discovered his teachers found out about his suspension. His parents were also angry and disappointed. For him, he had gathered enough information about his relationship with substances and decided to stop altogether. To cite a more extreme example, another individual spent 10 years in jail for killing his wife while in an alcoholic blackout. After his release from prison, he returned to drinking. Soon after, he took his own life. Along the way he had plenty of opportunities or "bottoms" that could have been the impetus to stop using. He did try on several occasions but was not successful. His "bottom" was the death of a loved one and suicide.

While many professionals continue to subscribe to the Jellinek curve, most realize we can offer help before circumstances reach such dire proportions. As we previously considered, there is still little consensus concerning the definition of substance abuse. Therefore, we can similarly expect many different approaches to treatment.

At some point, the abuser will experience the repercussions of their use. They meet their own spider and urinal. Unfortunately, they, themselves are the spider. As difficult as the life of an addict or alcoholic inside a metaphorical urinal may be for them, living without their drug of choice may seem like death. Their use becomes a priority. Leaving their addiction behind seems inconceivable. Let's consider why living outside the urinal becomes such an unthinkable alternative for the substance abuser. To live sober means relinquishing something important. Something exceedingly necessary to them (their substance of choice). By extension, eliminating the substance from their life means significant demands and adjustments once they cease to use. Most addicts and alcoholics understand that their present condition in life precludes them from experiencing freedom.

The abuser faces a demanding decision: do they sustain use and cope with the repercussions associated with using? Or, do they try to stop and deal with life without their substance of choice (**Figure 2.1**)? Abusers must reconstruct their lives to restore balance. To comprehend the difficulties involved in ceasing use, we will examine the factors which must be overcome to live life outside the urinal.

Figure 2.1

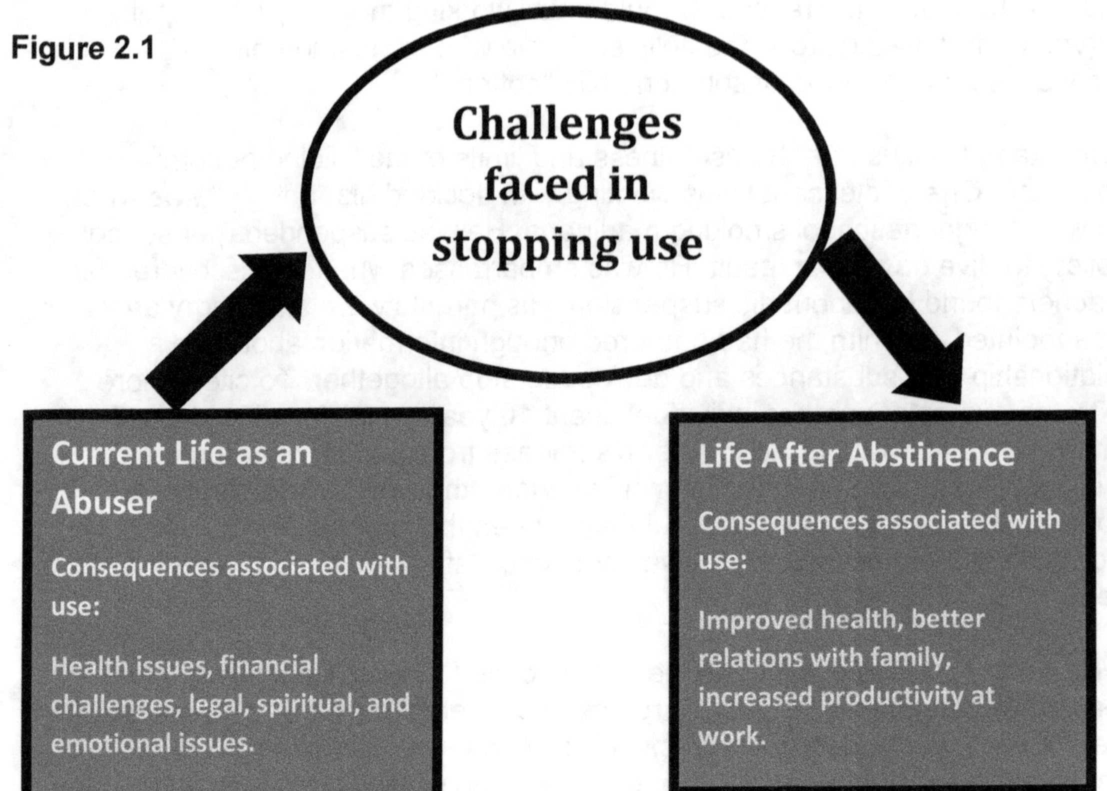

Chapter 4: Peers and Social Connection

The sense of belonging that comes with feeling accepted and part of a community is a basic human need. This need for social connectivity is hard-wired into our brains, and motivates people to conform, to an extent, to seek group approval. Our prehistoric ancestors would likely not have survived had they not banded together for survival, combining resources and working collectively as a community to hunt and to fend off predators and rivals. Although we are no longer hunted by saber-tooth tigers, that drive still remains. We are social creatures by nature and human connections support virtually all of us. By contrast, isolation and a lack of human connectedness can take a serious toll on our mental and physical health.

In the modern era, social connection poses a challenge. On the one hand, communication is easier than ever with social media and the internet giving us the capability to connect over a great distance. Yet these same technologies may be replacing more meaningful in-person interactions. After all, communicating by text, social media, or phone is usually more convenient than connecting in person, but there are usually more distractions and less available body language and verbal cues. A small part of our communication includes written or verbal (7%) interaction as opposed to nonverbal (93%) interactions (Tardanico, 2014, para. 4). Even with direct face-to-face communications we often miss much of what transpires. Is it possible that advancements in society contribute to more distance in our interactions? Are we losing out on the quality of interactions for convenience leading to feelings of loneliness? The advancement of technology may indeed be one reason that reported feelings of loneliness have increased over the years (Fottrell, 2018).

In face-to-face interactions, important communication is missed if someone is not picking up certain cues by the other person. For example, if you are on a date, and are talking about something, body language such as yawns and looking around indicate lack of interest in the topic. If a person seems interested, he or she would look at the signals they are receiving and keep that conversation going. Intonation (the tone, pitch, and cadence of our voices) is also lost in nonverbal communications yet can completely change the meaning of a sentence. A comment "okay, I made a mistake" can be an apology or a dismal. A change in tone could indicate a change in the direction of the conversation.

Missing these cues can also lead to misunderstandings. If a spouse discusses a touchy topic with his or her partner and misreads their partner's intonation, there will likely be conflict.

The way we interact also changes as we age (Cherry et al., 2011). Our level of engagement with others decreases. There are many factors that contribute to this such as lack of mobility, resources, and physical limitations. Concentration and memory are in decline and keeping up with changes or even the ability to keep up with current levels of technology are difficult. This makes it more difficult to keep in contact with family and friends.

Feeling lonely or isolated significantly affects both physical and psychological health. Loneliness may shorten one's lifespan, impact the endocrine system, and place one at higher risk for cardiovascular disease (Bhatti & Haq, 2017). Psychologically, loneliness can lead to feelings of isolation, rejection, and depression (Matthews et al., 2016). It can likewise affect someone's self-worth. Research has shown that the brain processes emotional pain, such as from rejection or isolation, and physical pain similarly (Weir, 2012).

Substance abusers find themselves in a lonely existence. They surround themselves with individuals who share their values, behaviors, and lifestyle. Conflicts may exist between group norms or expectations and an inclination to maintain use of a chosen substance. In that case, the abuser will hide their use, stop their use, or find a group more supportive of using drugs. Guilt and shame are more easily pushed aside to allow the use to continue.

At the same time, substance abusers often alienate those who do not share the same values regarding drug or alcohol use. This creates fewer supports down the road if the individual chooses recovery. Unsuccessful attempts and promises to stop use cause friends and family to distance themselves from the abuser. This leads to greater reluctance to offer support in the future.

All of society exists with sets of rules and expectations that ensure the future of that group. Social connections are comprised of different layers, each with its own experiences, expectations, and group norms (**Figure 2.2**). Social expectations further vary from group to group. For example, we act differently with colleagues from the office than with friends at home. The same pertains to a family or a bible study group. Unspoken rules exist that are specific to the group that helps establish expectations and behaviors. Degrees of intimacy shared within these circles dictate the level of disclosure in the group. Disclosure outside the parameters of that specific group can lead to embarrassment, isolation, and/or exclusion. For instance, if your work colleagues asked you what you did over the weekend, and you disclose too much information, you may be met with silence or awkwardness.

Figure 2.2

Connection Needs

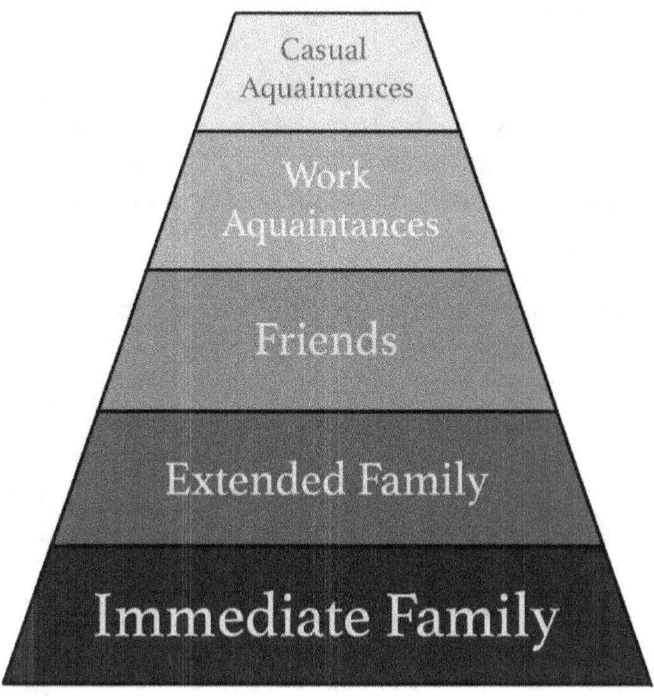

We are not always able to choose the groups with whom we associate. We cannot select what family we are born into. We often cannot decide with whom we work. Our relationships in each layer of our social connection can provide a degree of control within our social circle. The time spent or frequency of social contacts may or may not indicate the comfort level with that group. We spend most of our time at work, often more than with our own family. That does not mean we share the same comfort level with both groups.

Even if we do not feel 100% committed to a group, we will usually conform to the standards and expected behaviors within that group. Several experiments illustrate the extreme influence groups can have over individuals. In the famous Stanford Prison Experiment (Shuttleworth, 2008b), paid volunteers were assigned roles as either prisoners or guards. Very quickly, the participants adapted to their respective roles with prisoners becoming more submissive and guards more aggressive. With their newly granted authority, the guards resorted to cruelty and humiliation to the extent that the study had to be shut down early after only 6 days.

An earlier, more humane study known as the Asch experiment came to a similar conclusion about the power of group conformity (Shuttleworth, 2008a). Presented with questions, participants were guided to provide the wrong answer by having their peers intentionally select the wrong answer. The subjects (those not intentionally answering wrong) often answered questions according to how the group answered. There is little question that our social circles have a significant impact on our behavior and decision making.

For a successful recovery, an individual will often need to find a new social group that shares the same values. For abusers whose peer group is deeply involved in substance use, leaving this group can be a one of the biggest hurdles or causes of relapses. Leaving a group can understandably create feelings of isolation which can also lead to depression.

Isolation impacts recovery indirectly as well. For a person to make a commitment to abstinence is a big life choice which may generate apprehension or anxiety. Loneliness produces more anxiety. If being abstinent produces loneliness or isolation, the abuser may view stopping use negatively. This allows individuals to be more susceptible to the rewards perceived in using and encourages more difficulties in stopping use (University of Texas at Austin, 2018). Isolation generates its own feedback loop. Often individuals use because they feel lonely. Once users become enmeshed in this lifestyle, the fear of loneliness in turn makes it harder to leave.

Adolescents are even more at risk of choosing peers (and drugs) over loneliness. Peers are central to the life of a teen. The fear of social isolation may interfere with logical choices versus more rewarding (risky) behaviors (Albert, Chein, & Steinberg, 2013). Many adolescents also view teen drug and alcohol use as being more prevalent than statistics reflect. If someone asks them to change groups, they may feel skeptical such a group exists. Most using teens are skeptical there are other teens who do not partake in substance use. The belief is "everybody does it." Since the use is a perceived established norm within their group, it may be difficult to see their involvement as more significant than the average teen. An example of this is the Illinois Youth Survey, distributed in 2018, based on answers from adolescents in 2017. It found that 86% of 10th graders and 74% of 12th graders claimed they had not used marijuana in the last 30 days. However, when asked what percentage of students at your school you think have used marijuana in the last 30 days, 89% of 10th graders and 92% of 12th graders believed that at least 11% of the student body had used marijuana (Center for Prevention Research and Development, 2018, p. 14).

Since the adolescent brain is a work in progress (not fully developed until age 25), good decision making can be compromised. Teens are learning to navigate the adult world and a significant piece of this navigation is social. Peers become their reference points for the outside world. Adolescents further experience less confidence in leaving their using circle than adults and navigating the complexities of a new social group is likely to produce intense anxiety. If recovery does not occur in adolescence, the user who begins to use as a teen misses opportunities to learn how to socialize in settings without substances as a focus.

For example, Al is a 16-year-old who was heavy into smoking pot. He was arrested for breaking into cars. His probation sentence required him to remain drug and alcohol free. Now that he was being tested by the courts, his parents were giving him a hard time about his use, and he was close to flunking two classes in school (meaning he would have to go to summer school). Al acknowledged he was less motivated when he was high. He decided he wanted to give up smoking pot. Al did not want to change his friends as he felt they would be supportive. However, when he was with his friends, he found them to be unsupportive in his goal to stay away from marijuana. He found it more difficult to resist being around pot smokers. Al decided that since remaining pot free was important, it would be too difficult to be around his friends. He chose to socialize with a former group of friends who were not marijuana users.

Staying with a using peer group and remaining abstinent is not impossible. For most individuals in the early part of recovery changing peer groups is necessary for lasting abstinence. It is important to recognize this larger social picture when considering the role of community in recovery. Conversely, the positive effects of a supportive community can not only aid in early recovery, but allow you to feel connected and more positive overall (Lambert et al., 2013).

Chapter 5: The Brain, Survival, and Pleasure

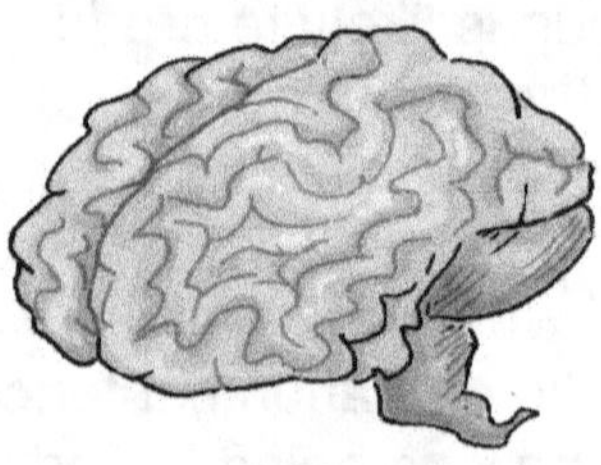

The brain makes up only 2% of our body weight. However, we devote 20% to 25% of the body's blood supply and about 20% of our oxygen to the brain (Alzheimer's Association, n.d.). A complex and vital structure, the nervous system (**Figure 2.3**) connects and functions together with the entire body to facilitate our survival.

Figure 2.3

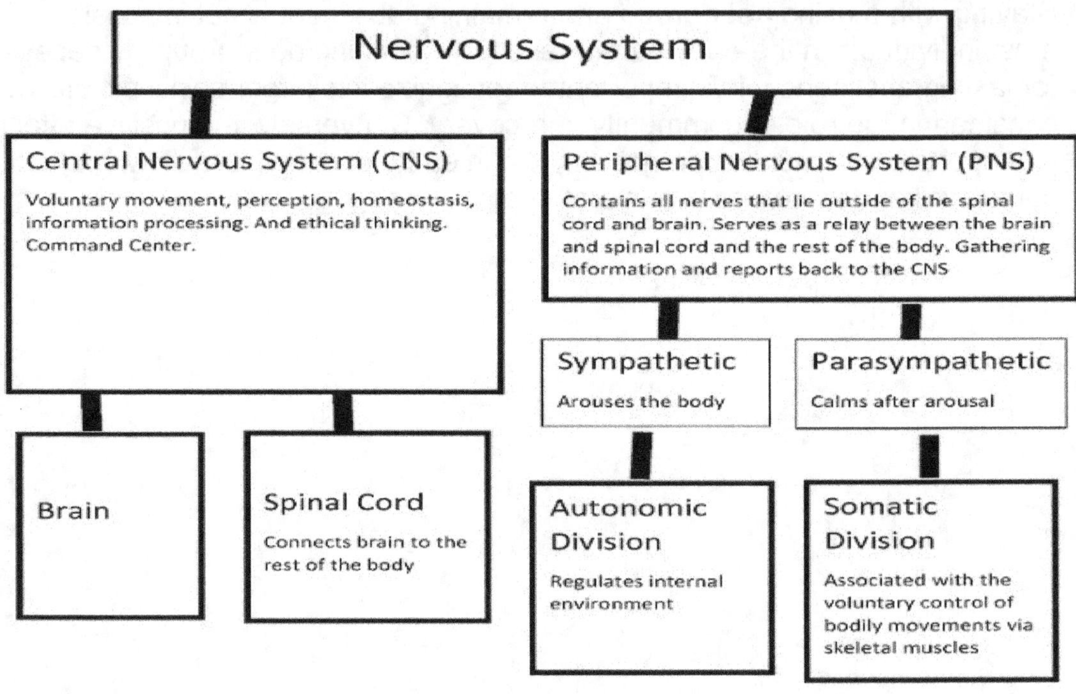

Our knowledge and understanding of the brain has exploded in the last decade. Advancements in science and technology have expanded our capacity to study and learn about how the brain performs. Before examining the impact of substances on the brain, we must first consider the most basic workings of the brain and analogous structures.

Despite the complexity of the brain, we view it as having one main job, survival. The flight, fight, or freeze response is an example. When we feel threatened, our brain kicks into survival mode and instinctually directs us to action (Cherry 2018; Selzter, 2015). This is essential to our survival as a species (Formica, 2009). Pleasure seeking activities are also hardwired into our brains. When we have a pleasurable experience, we are more likely to repeat an action. This is referred to as our reward circuit (Freeman, 2008).

Since our brain is the command center of our body, it has the responsibility of regulating the functions of body and mind. It connects our senses and works to ensure optimal functioning and survival (**Figure 2.4**). The brain functions as supervisor or boss, directing all employees to effectively work together. A great boss makes decisions based on input from his or her employees how best to address needs. As society has evolved, the demands on the brain have increased. It includes considerably more data to interpret with the flood of sensory information thrown at it today. Smartphones, advancements in technology, and inundation of news provide a challenge for our brain to sort through information and make decisions.

Figure 2.4

Brain-Body Connection

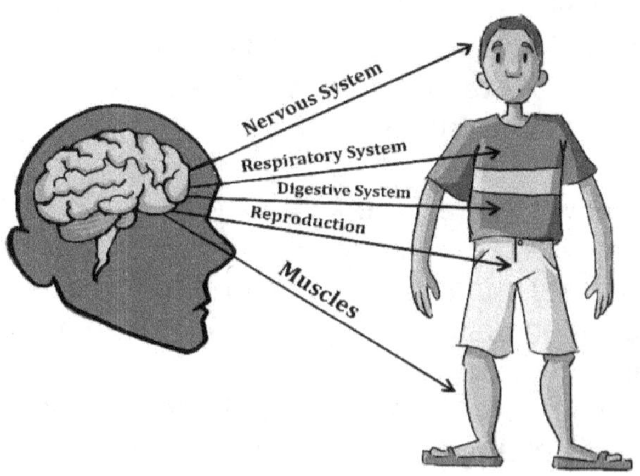

We possess approximately 100 billion neurons in our brain. They branch out to over 100 trillion synapse points (gaps where messages pass from neuron to neuron). These points are how messages are sent between diverse systems in the brain and body. Communication must cross over a tiny opening called the synaptic cleft or synaptic gap. Neurotransmitters are the chemical messengers that transmit messages from neuron to neuron. The neuron never directly connects with another neuron. Neurotransmitters flow into the synaptic cleft and bind to receptor sites on the target cell. Neuroscientists categorize neurotransmitters into two groups, excitatory and inhibitory. We base our decisions and actions on these two categories of neurotransmitters.

A common inhibitory transmitter is gamma-aminobutyric (GABA) which, when released, creates a calming effect. Excitatory neurons such as glutamate create the opposite effect. These neurons manage the flight, fight, or freeze response (Chudler, n.d.). For a neuron to fire and relay a message, sufficient amounts of the excitatory neurotransmitters must move past the threshold level. If there are more inhibitory neurotransmitters present, the action is prevented from taking place. Put another way, if we hit the gas pedal in a car, it will accelerate (excitatory). If we hit the break the car will stop (inhibitory). If we hit both the gas and brake at the same time, the pedal receiving more input will win out. (Do not try this at home!)

There are two possible outcomes once a neurotransmitter enters the synapse. Either it is reabsorbed back into the original neuron (reuptake) or broken down and reabsorbed. This is a dynamic process by which the body recycles or reuses neurotransmitters. The longer the neurotransmitter remains in the synapse, the more likely it will influence the next firing. It also allows the original signal to keep replaying if reuptake does not occur. A helpful analogy would be putting off cleaning our furnace vents. The longer we delay the cleaning, the more "gunk" (excess neurons) builds up and the less efficiently it runs. It can prevent us from ending one behavior and starting another. This affects the overall ability to send messages throughout our brain and body.

The knowledge of how the brain works has revolutionized our understanding of addiction. All drugs, whether prescription or nonprescription, impact our brain. Each category of a drug impacts the brain differently. The method of administration (how it enters our body), amount taken, the potency of the substance, tolerance level, and individual constitution will all be factors in how a substance affects a person. It is significant that our bodies adapt and respond to changes whether said changes are healthy or unhealthy.

Drugs either increase (agonist) the neurotransmitter's action or decrease (antagonist) its effects. They can make excitatory neurotransmitters more excitatory or inhibitory neurotransmitters more inhibitory. There are drugs that simultaneously produce excitatory and inhibitory effects. Drugs can also block the reuptake process, which prevents the neurotransmitters from being reused or eliminated. This leaves a greater concentration of the neurotransmitter in the synapse area. SSRIs (commonly prescribed antidepressants) also function in this manner. Keep in mind that the initial signal received does not stop until the neurotransmitters are reabsorbed or eliminated. This will create an overabundance of neurotransmitters in the synaptic area.

Although each drug may have its own unique high effects, all of them affect us by blocking the reuptake process, mimicking the effect of dopamine, or tricking our brain into releasing more dopamine ("How addiction hijacks the brain," 2007; Volkow, 2007). This creates dependency on the drug for pleasure experiences. Drugs can release anywhere from 2 to 10 times the amount of natural rewards typically experienced by the brain. The pleasure we experience from eating and even having sex can significantly fall short of drug-induced pleasure (Volkow, 2007). Studies in nonhuman primates have also shown that given a choice, test subjects will sometime choose drugs such as cocaine over eating (Nader, Czoty, Nader, & Morgan, 2012; Wake Forest University Baptist Medical Center, 2008).

Alcohol falls under the category of depressants. A depressant lowers neurotransmission levels. It is an inhibitor that slows down bodily functions such as breathing, heart rate, reaction time, and causes disturbed perceptions. Doctors prescribe depressants for sleep difficulties, anxiety, seizures, and muscle spasms (Konkel, 2015). In previous years, doctors prescribed them for pain, however this is no longer the established medical norm. Once a depressant enters your system, a neurotransmitter called gamma-aminobutyric (GABA) is activated. GABA's slows down bodily functions in an effort to keep our system in balance. If we get overanxious, the release of GABA restores the balanced state our bodies require. GABA also assists in promoting sleep. Conversely, researchers report individuals who struggle with sleep have less GABA than individuals who noted no sleep problems (Winkelman, 2008).

The effects of depressants taken for recreational purposes or from misused prescriptions include slurred speech, loss of coordination, slower reaction time, poor concentration, and disturbed perceptions to name a few. Long-term repercussions include the development of tolerance to the drug. The body shuts down its own production of GABA neurotransmitters to adapt to the depressant, and we become susceptible to withdrawal once the effects wear off. Withdrawal symptoms include feeling depressed or fatigued as well as sleep and breathing problems ("Depressants," n.d.). To avoid the uncomfortable or indeed serious effects of withdrawal, individuals require weaning off the depressant. Medical supervision for those who have used alcohol or depressants for a substantial period is essential. Determining dosage for prescription or over-the-counter medications is generally a simple matter when we know how much is being taken. Designer drugs and alcohol are exceptions. For alcohol, it is important to consider the amount and content of alcohol consumed. Each alcoholic beverage contains varied amounts of alcohol. For example, 12 ounces of Vodka will produce 12 times the amount of alcohol in our body than 12 ounces of beer (4% to 6% alcohol content) (Bryner, 2010).

Drugs falling under the classification of stimulants release excitatory neurotransmitters. Physicians typically prescribe stimulants for Attention Deficit

Hyperactive Disorder (ADHD), insomnia, and occasionally depression (The National Institute on Drug Abuse Blog Team, 2017). Since these drugs have a serious abuse risk, the medical profession has become more cautious in prescribing them. The effects of stimulants include rapid heart rate, rapid breathing, and increased blood pressure. Overuse of stimulants can lead to paranoia, psychosis, and heart failure. Stimulant use releases dopamine and norepinephrine, two neurotransmitters that also regulate mood and behavior. Dopamine, for example, also called the pleasure chemical, impacts our motivation and regulates the release of hormones in the pituitary glands. They believe norepinephrine to play a part in the fight, flight, or freeze response (Stannard, n.d.). The fight, flight, freeze response is our body's reaction to a threatening stimulus. (**Figure 2. 5)**

Figure 2.5

Within moments of receiving the stressor situation, the secondary phase of the General Adaption System begins.

1.) A small portion of the brain called the hypothalamus triggers the pituitary gland (located near the base of the brain) to release the hormone ACTH into the bloodstream.

2.) ACTH goes directly to the adrenal glands, which then increases the output of adrenaline into the bloodstream, as well as the related hormone, corticoids. This hormone brings the body up to an aroused state.

Within the first eight seconds, the bloodstream carries these stress hormones into every cell in the body.

At the same time, commands travel through the nerve system to alert the heart, lungs, and muscles to action. The muscles are more richly supplied with blood, causing tiny blood vessels to constrict and blood pressure to rise. The liver works harder to convert stored glycogen into glucose, which the brain and muscles will need in greater supply. Meanwhile, breathing becomes more rapid, increasing the amount of oxygen in the blood. This enables the muscles and brain to use the glucose more efficiently.

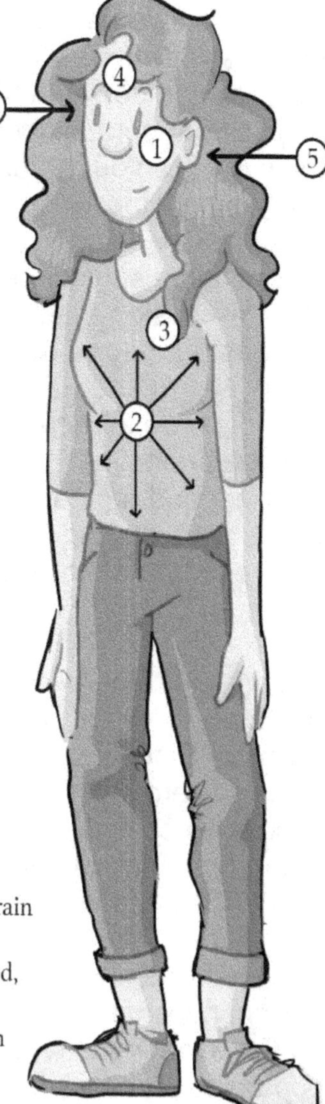

3.) The heart sends an abundant supply of blood to the priority portions of the body. The skeletal muscles brace, causing the necessary blood in the stomach to be reduced in favor of the high priority areas elsewhere. This can cause indigestion, and over a long period of time, ulcers.

4.) The brain prepares for violent physical action, which is why it's difficult to think effectively in the midst of a panicked state.

5.) Hearing may become more acute.

6.) Pupils of the eyes will dilate, making vision more sensitive.

The last category we will examine is opiates, prescribed mainly for pain. Prescription drugs that fall under this classification include morphine, codeine, OxyContin, Demerol, heroin, fentanyl, opium, and hydrocodone. Opiates' immediate effects include pain relief, feelings of euphoria, sleepiness, and drowsiness. When we feel pain our body naturally releases opioid molecules. This is our internal mechanism allowing us to continue to function or respond to painful stimuli. They bind to our receptors sending messages to block pain. This response attempts to keep our body in balance and functioning despite discomforts we may experience.

The brain functions on a reward system. We previously considered the importance of pleasure to our survival. If we feel pleasure during experiences, we are prone to repeat the action. When we eat, drink, have sex, and other activities, those activities stimulate our reward system. Once we experience these feelings, our brain makes a positive association between the activity and the feeling. Drugs not only allow us to bypass our normal reward system, they can dull or turn off this system. As a result, we lose our natural ability to produce these rewards. This is how an addiction develops.

There are many areas of the brain that substance abuse affects. Two specific systems most important to this discussion are the prefrontal cortex (PFC) and the limbic system. The PFC manages our decision making, planning, and memory (Neuroscientifically Challenged, 2014). The PFC allows us to make logical decisions and most of the time override irrational or impulsive decisions. The Executive Functioning area of the brain, the PFC is also responsible for paying attention, organizing and planning, and regulating emotions (The Understood Team, 2017). The PFC helps us plan out and orchestrate goal-directed activity and filter incoming information, as well as process working memory and short-term memory (Siddiqui, Chatterjee, Kumar, Siddiqui, & Goyal, 2008).

The limbic system, a more primitive structure in the brain, is described as our pleasure center or reward system. Overall, it supports functions such as emotion, memory, behavior, and motivation. Since many of our emotional responses generate in this area, the limbic system has the ability to take priority over other parts of the brain in some circumstances. The limbic system enables us to continue to survive as a species by rewarding actions geared towards survival and reproduction such as eating food, drinking water, social interactions, and sex which generally allows propagation of the species (Crossen, n.d.). Pleasure, as we said earlier, increases the likelihood of our repeating the behavior that creates the pleasure. The release of dopamine into the body reinforces the experience and encourages us to repeat the experience. We eat a piece of fruit; if we enjoy it, then our brain releases dopamine. That experience is encoded into memory. We remember it the next time we see fruit (memory encoding).

Drugs of abuse target our brain's same reward center. In fact, the amount of dopamine released is anywhere from 2 to 10 times more than natural rewards, even sex (Volkow, 2011). This is a powerful reinforcement that no natural reward could even hope to match. When the brain and body become reliant on a drug(s) over time, they allow the drug to take over responsibilities. An example of this would be the relationship between the limbic system and PFC. For individuals involved in using substances, the limbic system bypasses the PFC and makes its own decision when using drugs (Neuroscience News, 2016). They form a new pathway without including the PFC. This powerful ability to circumvent reason and logic that are the responsibility of the PFC leads to dangerous consequences. As substance use continues, this pathway becomes stronger. It is not a fair fight and often the drug experience prevails. This experience is likened to Bambi (the PFC) meeting Godzilla (the limbic system) (**Figure 2.6**).

Figure 2.6

Four additional areas of the brain are impacted by substance abuse. The amygdala functions as our built-in alarm system, responsible for emotions, survival, and memory. It can activate the fight, flight, or freeze response (**Figure 2.7**). The hippocampus or memory center of the brain provides contextual information to the amygdala. It aids in the long-term storage of memories, such as where we live, our address, and people we've met and places we have experienced. The hypothalamus produces many of the body's essential hormones, chemical substances that help control different cells and organs. The hormones from the hypothalamus govern physiologic functions such as temperature regulation, thirst, hunger, sleep, mood, sex drive, and the release of other hormones within the body. The hypothalamus generally focuses on maintaining balance or homeostasis. Lastly, the thalamus functions in the development and consolidation of long-term memories. It relays sensory information and motor signals to the cerebral cortex. It assists in regulating consciousness, sleep, and alertness. The thalamus functions as a switchboard operator, relying on information sent back and forth between various parts of the body and brain.

Figure 2.7

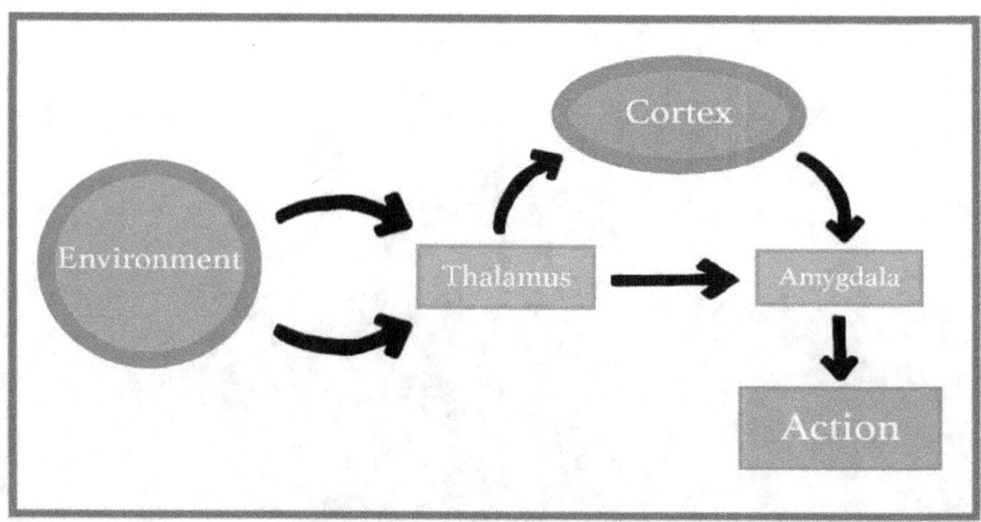

All parts of the brain, to some degree, play a role in our decision making. There is not one specific area of our brain that is solely in charge of decision making. All parts play a factor. Most of the decision making is done in the prefrontal cortex area but other parts of the brain influence that decision. For example, we previously mentioned that the amygdala will take over if a situation is seen as a threat, even if it may not necessarily be an actual threat. If I was previously beaten up by a young man in a red hooded jacket, I will have stored that memory in the thalamus, turning it into a long-term memory. Now if I see a young man approaching me in a red hooded jacket, I may perceive the situation as threatening and walk (or run) away. Any stimuli or activation in any one of these areas will factor into our decision making.

Drug use changes the preferred pathways in our brain (James, Charnley, Flynn, Smith, & Dayas, 2011). When drugs take over our system, they alter our natural dopamine levels and our ability to produce them. Drug use significantly increases our dopamine levels (Di Chiara & Imperato, 1988). The increased dopamine level becomes the new norm. Alcohol use meanwhile impacts our ability to interpret and respond to social signals (Parmet, 2013). Substance use causes a depletion of serotonin levels in the brain. It impairs our ability to wait and weigh our decisions. This increases impulsivity and poor decision making (Mechelmans et al., 2017; Worbe, Savulich, Voon, Fernandez-Egea, & Robbins, 2014). When we experience stress, the hypothalamus releases certain hormones allowing our brain and body to respond to the stressor. During the initial stages of withdrawal from substances, stressful situations are often relapse triggers (Horvath, Misra, Epner, & Cooper, n.d.).

Substance use impacts the hippocampus and short-term memory recollection (Watkins, 2018). As a result, it's difficult to remember things without the drug and its effect. The amygdala is also important in memory consolidation. Emotion-based memories will be especially strong. This creates a powerful connection to the drug and the effect it creates ("Structure and function of the brain," n.d.). Long-term alcohol use can further damage the prefrontal cortex (Alcoholism: Clinical & Experimental Research, 2008, para. 4). Memories associated with using experiences are referred to as addiction memory, and can create such a reward that they bypass the prefrontal cortex when a memory related to drug or alcohol use occurs (Hymen, 2005). Studies show substances such as alcohol impact the PFC's ability to carry out its responsibilities (Alcoholism: Clinical & Experimental Research, 2008, para. 7). Regular use of opiates also affects our short-term and long-term memory (Li et al., 2013). Long-term marijuana use impacts the hippocampus and memory processes associated with problem-solving (Depra, 2015). Our decision making becomes affected by long-term heroin use (Li et al., 2013). The tissue in the brain known as white matter is vital for communication between different parts of the brain. Heroin disrupts its integrity and interferes with our messaging system (Li et al., 2013). Long-term cocaine impairs our ability to handle stress or deal with changes (Srikameswaran, 2011). Stimulant use interferes with sleep and memory (Boutrel & Koob, 2004; Roehrs & Roth, 2015) which can also affect our consolidation of memory. Finally, they have found the thalamus plays an active role in drug users' cues or urges experienced in relation to drugs and alcohol (Huang, Mitchell, Haber, Alia-Klein, & Goldstein, 2018; Millan, Ong, & McNally, 2017).

Over time, users have to keep taking drugs just to feel normal. When use is stopped, in some situations, it takes years for the brain and body to re-adjust to a non-using lifestyle. Abusers lose the ability to cope and adapt to situations without depending on their substance of choice. A feedback loop is created where additional drugs or substances are used to fill the void. If we think about it, drug abuse turns our brains against us.

Chapter 6: Sleep and Substance Abuse

Sleep problems are common among substance abusing populations (Mahfoud, Talih, Streem, & Budur, 2009). Whether it is the addiction itself that produces sleep problems or sleep problems that open the door to addiction, the result is the same vicious cycle (**Figure 2.8**). Some basic knowledge of sleep serves to further understand the relationship between sleep and addiction.

Figure 2.8

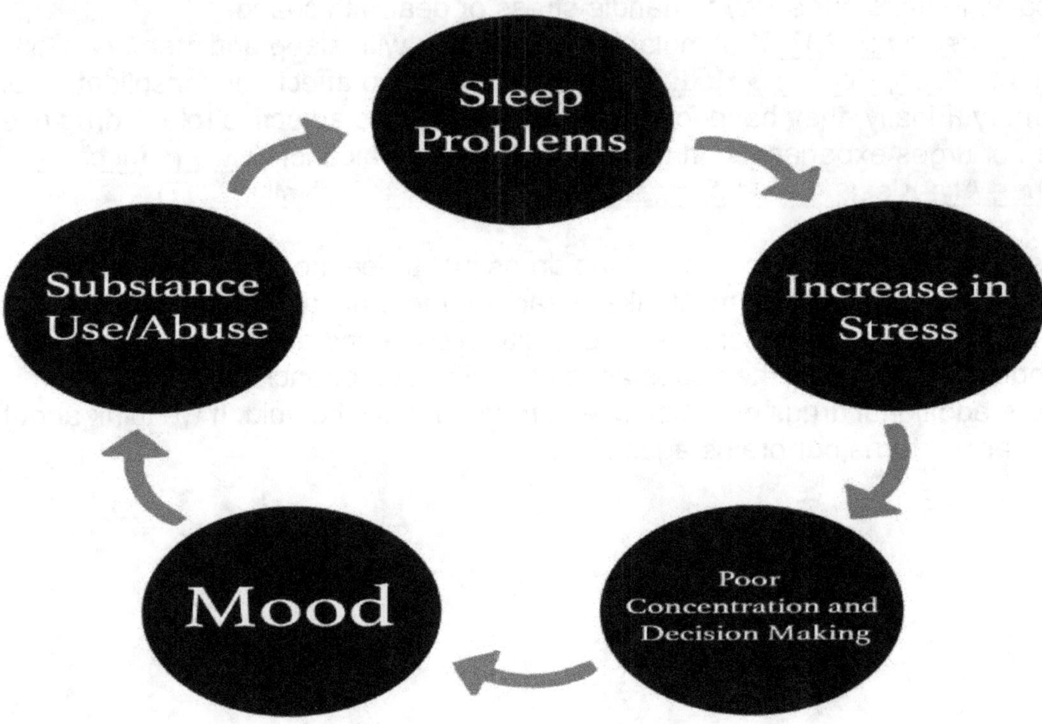

A healthy sleep cycle involves four stages. We cycle through all stages of sleep throughout the night several times. In stage 1, the brain begins its wind down process, which lasts between 5 to 10 minutes. Stage 2 lasts about 20 minutes, during which the brain activity slows down even more but with occasional spikes. This stage is usually the longest of the three and we spend approximately 50% of our sleep time in this stage. Stage 3 is a deep sleep. These are all considered non-REM sleep. REM sleep occurs 90 minutes into sleep and begins the process of memory storage and consolidation. Typically, we require 7 to 9 hours of sleep depending on our age. Adults are considered sleep deprived with less than 7 hours of sleep per night (Peters, 2017).

Essential for our survival, sleep affects every area of life. Disrupted sleep or lack of sleep impacts thinking, concentration, memory, judgment, physical dexterity, and sex drive. The health complications related to lack of sleep include obesity, heart disease, stroke, high blood pressure, and cancer. Individuals who report sleeping poorly have a higher mortality rate. Neurological disorders and increased sensitivity to pain may also afflict sleep-deprived individuals ("6 Health Problems Linked to Lack of Sleep," 2012).

Sleep plays an essential role in the brain's functioning. Researchers can actually observe decreased blood and oxygen flow in the brains of sleep-deprived individuals. As a result, sleep deprivation can create cognitive issues, such as memory loss (Park, 2014). Limited sleep also hampers decision making, which takes place in the pre-frontal cortex (Sohn, 2013). The following cognitive problems can also arise from sleep difficulties: lack of concentration, fatigue, irritability, problems attending to task, and poor sex drive. Studies have shown that sleep deprivation may also lead to depression or exacerbate symptoms of someone struggling with depression (Peri, 2014). Research further suggests a good night's sleep encourages the clearing out of waste products that build up in the brain (Sohn, 2013). Like changing the oil in our car, good sleep allows the brain to function at peak productivity.

The brain replays our experiences from the day while we sleep, although at higher speeds than the actual events (University of Bristol, 2016). During this time, called memory consolidation, the brain either stores information in the memory or disposes of it (FECYT, 2018). This process enables the brain to store relevant material and clear itself of unnecessary information. Like a computer with a capacity for storage, at some point it will slow down unless we free up space.

An alert and efficient brain is often necessary for our survival. Imagine a car coming towards you at 60 miles an hour. If you only have a few moments before it strikes you, every second you deliberate brings you closer to death. If after seeing the approaching car your brain is bogged down with superfluous data, you could experience deadly consequences. The faster we retrieve material from past events the faster we can react to a situation.

Sleep disorders range anywhere from 5 to 10 times higher in the substance abusing population (Vimont, 2013, para. 4). Substance abuse itself plays a decisive role in sleep and alters sleep patterns. Many people believe alcohol helps them sleep. This rationale does make some sense, as a couple drinks can cause a person to become drowsy. After all, alcohol is a depressant. However, alcohol consumption in fact disrupts a powerful function in our sleep cycle, the circadian rhythm (CR). CR runs in the brain's background, like a computer program, and acts as an internal clock. It also cues the brain to start your sleep/wake cycle (National Sleep Foundation, n.d.-b). This pattern creates our feelings of tiredness at night or awakeness during the day. For shift workers, CR changes and adjusts to operate effectively at the correct or productive times.

Alcohol consumption interrupts the circadian rhythm (National Sleep Foundation, n.d.-a) causing sleep disturbances. This affects the natural release of hormones that are a part of the sleep/wake cycle. As a result, an alcohol drinker might awaken in the middle of the night or earlier than one's normal rhythm would allow (News-Medical.net, 2009). The effect is an out-of-sync sleep/wake cycle that leaves one tired during the day and awake at night. The impact on our productivity and activity level can be devastating. Alcohol also blocks certain receptors in the brain affecting our capacity to remain awake ("Is Alcohol Disrupting Your Sleep?" n.d.). Frequent consumption of alcohol in excess may contribute to introducing new drugs to remain awake or assist in sleep. As our brain adapts to these substances, the consumption and frequency (and dependency) of "sleep aids" increases.

Sleep disruption occurs as a persistent problem for substance abusers. For consumers of alcohol, this may mean more frequent trips to the bathroom, disrupting needed sleep. Alcohol can further disrupt REM and cause sleep apnea (National Sleep Foundation, n.d.-a). The result will be sleep deprivation and its repercussions. Sleep deprivation generates a powerful challenge for someone who initially seeks to stop their drinking. Decision-making fatigue, memory loss, and moodiness complicate the initial stages of recovery. If someone used alcohol initially to treat a sleep problem, this problem will resurface once they end their use.

Other substances interfere with sleep. Cocaine induces sleep disturbances owing to its stimulant effects. It also impacts the circadian rhythm, REM sleep, and overall sleep time (Hill, Mendelson, & Bernstein, 1977), and disrupts the sleep/wake cycle. Cocaine users may not feel the need for sleep, especially when they are binge using. They may use more during the day (or waking hours) to compensate for fatigue. Sleep deprivation, as mentioned above, causes concentration problems, lower sex drive, and difficulty paying attention. Using cocaine to fight the side effects of these symptoms is not unusual. As counterproductive as it may seem, users take more cocaine to deal with the side effects of the initial cocaine use.

Heroin has analgesic and anxiolytic (an antianxiety agent) properties. Classified as an opiate, the high derives from the drug binding to opioid receptors in the brain, particularly in areas involving pain and pleasure. It mimics endorphins, which interact mostly with receptor cells found in parts of your brain responsible for pain and emotions. Heroin binds to these receptors and magnifies the endorphins' functions, producing the high. The opiate high itself (referred to as "on the nod") produces drowsiness or a sleepy state. The impact on sleep from heroin use includes hypersomnia, increased or intense drowsiness, bizarre or unusual dreams, unproductive sleep, an increase in depression, and a reduction in sleep hours (called morphine insomnia) ("How Heroin Affects Sleep," 2018).

Withdrawal from heroin presents its own set of challenges. These include chills, sweats, nausea, vomiting, anxiety, and agitation, all side effects that further disrupt the sleep cycle. Users might also introduce other drugs to counter the side effects of either heroin use or withdrawal.

Physicians may prescribe sleep medication and there are also numerous over-the-counter sleep medications available. Typically, sleep medication is not a problem if employed on a short-term basis to reestablish a consistent sleep/wake cycle ("Drug Treatments for Sleep Problems," 2018). Some of these medications however have addictive properties and patients can become dependent on them (Mayo Clinic Staff, 2018a). Dependence may occur in a relatively brief period of time (Informed Health Online, 2017). Each doctor prescribing the medication may have their own preference regarding how to address the dependency issue depending on how they view the problem. Over the years, there has been a significant increase in prescribing sleep medication. Between 2011 and 2016, 38 million prescriptions were written for one sleep medication alone (Ambien) (AddictionCenter, 2018).

Many individuals who use sleep aids long-term become dependent. A person often either does not realize their dependence on sleep medication or may continue to take the medication even though they may suspect they have a problem. Withdrawal symptoms can follow, depending on the medication and length of time used. The prospect of sleep deprivation may be daunting to someone thinking about halting sleep medicine. When individuals stop using sleep aids, rebound insomnia can also occur (The New York Times, 2010).

Other drugs that affect the sleep cycle include marijuana and barbiturates. Heavy marijuana use leads to a decrease in REM sleep (Jones, 2015), while stopping use (withdrawal) (Budney & Hughes, 2006) can also disrupt sleep (Babson, Sottile, & Morabito, 2017; Nicholson, Turner, Stone, & Robson, 2004; Wlassoff, 2015). Some research on marijuana has found it to be helpful, in limited quantities, as a sleep aid. Marijuana use as a sleep aid is a mixed bag. It comes with risks and it is difficult to predict its effectiveness.

Although doctors prescribe barbiturates to treat insomnia, chronic use can have the effect of further disrupting sleep. Barbiturates also decrease REM sleep (Davis, 2018) and other stages of the sleep cycle, increasing sleep time and delaying the onset of sleep (Hatfield, 2017). Increased sleep time does not mean better sleep. Quantity of sleep is different than quality of sleep.

The human body seeks homeostasis, a state of biological balance (Khan Academy, n.d.-b). The body does this by compensating for changes to our system and the environment: for instance, if we are cold, we shiver. Shivering generates heat which compensates for the cold. The opposite holds true for sweating when we are hot. Homeostasis plays a part, directly or indirectly, in addiction. Any disturbance in our system, which includes the introduction of drugs, causes our body to adapt to the substance by making more or less of a natural chemical in our body to compensate. It takes time to reverse that process.

Professionals often overlook the importance of sleep in the recovery and mental health field. Introducing any drug or alcohol has the potential to impact our sleep cycles. This applies not only to the impact of substance abuse but to those in recovery as well. Sleep concerns among those in early recovery are common (Friedmann et al., 2003; Mahfoud, Talih, Streem, & Budur, 2009) and, as we have seen, sleep deprivation significantly impacts decision making. The impact of drug use on sleep will vary from drug to drug and person to person, but since sleep is crucial to our day-to-day functioning, it needs consideration in any recovery program.

Chapter 7: Food for Thought

Diet plays a central role in substance abuse recovery, yet nutrition is often overlooked when addressing addiction. We can think of our brain and body as a car engine. If we maintain it responsibly, we can ensure it runs more efficiently. Poor maintenance causes breakdowns and poor performance. Thanks to advances in science, we understand what dietary choices are good for our health and what is unhealthy. That does not mean we apply that knowledge wisely. Fast-food consumption has increased in recent decades, particularly among children (Smith, Ng, & Popkin, 2013; St-Onge, Keller, & Heymsfield, 2003). One restaurant meal can account for more than an entire daily recommended intake for fat, salt, and calories (Scourboutakos, Semnani-Azad, & L'Abbe, 2013). In the United States alone, in 2016, an estimated nearly one-half of consumers ate out or ordered take out at least once a week. Americans spent over $200 billion dollars on fast food in 2016 (Howard, 2018). It is no surprise then that the average American's diet falls below nationally recommended dietary standards (U.S. Department of Health and Human Services and U.S. Department of Agriculture, 2015, chapter 2).

For substance abusers, problems with food are three-fold. They face nutritional challenges and problems while they use. This directly results from the substance itself or through poor self-care or diet. The second problem occurs once they begin recovering, in trying to return to a homeostatic state, our bodies will seek to compensate by developing cravings for unhealthy quick fixes (fast-foods, foods high in sugar, foods high in fat). Finally, since food impacts our mental health and outlook on life, nutritional challenges affect self-image in early recovery.

Concentration, memory, motivation, sleep, energy level, and how we feel about ourselves are all impacted by our diets (Ireland, n.d.). Substance abusers are at even greater risk of falling short of dietary needs. Addictive lifestyles often lead to poor diets, as nutritional needs are sacrificed in favor of the addiction. Priorities revolve more and more around getting or maintaining a high. Drugs can also lead to poor nutritional absorption and vitamin deficiencies.

Heavy alcohol use can lead to weight gain due to excess calories in an alcoholic beverage. Alcoholics can receive up to 50% of their calorie intake from alcohol

(National Institute on Alcohol Abuse and Alcoholism, 1993, para. 5). One glass of wine (3.2 ounces) is equal in calories to one ice cream cone. Two gin and tonics equal one chocolate pancake, while two bottles of beer have as many calories as one sirloin steak ("Alcohol and food equivalents," n.d.). Users consume more calories in a meal with alcohol, up to 20% more than without alcohol (Harbolic, n.d.). Alcohol itself possesses limited or no nutritional value. We refer to these as empty calories (Fontenot, 2011). Chronic alcohol use further damages our body's ability to absorb key nutrients, resulting in low vitamin B levels and other serious nutritional deficiencies (Perkins, 2018). Weight gain is not uncommon for alcoholics in early recovery (Castaneda, 2017). The body craves the sugar it misses from alcohol. Health risks such as diabetes and high blood pressure can also result from alcohol abuse.

Diet and nutrition are important considerations with other drugs of abuse. Most addicts, as a result of their substance abuse and lifestyle associated with it, are malnourished (Santolaria-Fernández et al., 1995). Addicts need the same calorie intake as non-addicts. However, they tend to have diets higher in sugar with less nutritional value compared to non-addicts (Morabia et al., 1989). Short-term use of heroin includes symptoms of nausea and vomiting, while longer term use leads to constipation. These side effects block the absorption of nutrients, nutritional input, and appetite of the user. Opiate addicts generally have significant nutritional deficiencies (Swanson, 2014).

Some drugs have been consumed precisely for their weight loss properties. Medical professionals used to prescribe amphetamines (speed or stimulants) to assist in weight loss. In recent years, doctors have been more wary of prescribing amphetamines because of their mixed results and high abuse potential. The effects of amphetamines include loss of appetite and an increase in energy. Users depend on the drug for sustaining energy rather than a balanced diet. When users begin to recover, their appetites return. The addict accustomed to rapid bursts of energy from the stimulant will shift to foods high in carbohydrates for quick energy (high-sugar and fatty foods). Weight gain is a common experience in early recovery for amphetamines users, as they no longer consume a drug that suppresses the appetite.

There can be significant overlap between eating disorders and substance abuse as well. Individuals with eating disorders are 5 times more likely to abuse substances, and conversely, individuals who abuse drugs or alcohol are 11 times more likely to have an eating disorder (Root et al., 2010). Both involve an obsession or preoccupation with the substance/food, secret behavior or efforts to hide the problem, an inability to stop despite negative consequences, and an escalation of addictive or unhealthy behavior, especially in stressful situations or environments. Guilt and shame also often accompany substance abuse and eating disorders.

There are several classifications of eating disorders which include:

- Anorexia nervosa: Individuals see themselves as overweight despite compelling evidence they are underweight. They will restrict the amount of food they eat, continually weigh themselves, over exercise, and purge their food through self-induced vomiting or laxatives. Furthermore, there is an intense fear of becoming overweight.
- Bulimia nervosa: This would include frequent episodes of eating or "binging" unusually large amounts of food. They then introduce behavior to compensate for the over-eating (binge-eating) through self-induced vomiting, excessive use of laxatives or diuretics, fasting, excessive exercise, or a combination of these behaviors. Unlike anorexia nervosa, people with bulimia nervosa usually maintain a relatively normal weight. Another difference between anorexia and bulimia is that there is a repetitive cycle of binging and purging with the latter.
- Binge Eating Disorder: People who have this disorder experience recurrent episodes of binge eating. Feelings of embarrassment, disgust, depression, and guilt accompany these episodes.
- Pica: Individuals who persistently eat non-nutritive substances (such as dirt) would meet the criteria for this disorder.
- Rumination Disorder: Criteria for this disorder would include repeated regurgitation of food.
- Avoidant/Restrictive Food Intake Disorder: People who struggle with this disorder have diets that do not meet appropriate nutritional needs. Nutritional deficiency and weight loss would accompany this disorder.

The relationship between eating disorders and substance abuse can be complex. Some individuals eat less to increase the effects of drinking and decrease the calories associated with drinking. This is informally called Drunkorexia. People who engage in this behavior risk malnutrition, dehydration, and long-term health problems. Some who struggle with an eating disorder, on the other hand, use substances to decrease their appetite. Stimulant-based drugs such as amphetamines, cocaine, and designer drugs are sought for their appetite suppression qualities. Although they share common characteristics, eating disorders are more likely to fall under the radar as opposed to drug or alcohol use. Consequences of eating disorders and relapses are also trickier to determine than substances.

In addressing eating disorder concerns, especially with adolescents, it is important to look for signs of a disorder. These signs would include:

- Body obsession (discussion or comments)
- Negative comments about weight

- Excessive exercise
- Unusual focus on diet programs
- Self-consciousness or avoiding eating in front of people
- Changes in appearance (loss or gain in weight)
- Hair loss or dry skin
- Extreme sensitivity to cold
- Restriction of certain foods
- Increase irritability around food
- Overconsumption of food
- Eating rituals or rules about food
- Frequent trips to the bathroom after a meal

The warning signs mentioned do not determine a diagnosis of an eating disorder but encourage further investigation. If in doubt, discuss the concerns with a doctor or other professional.

Nutrition may not be a first-tier issue in substance abuse treatment. However, those in recovery should consider how influential diet can be in recovery. Poor nutrition affects concentration, sleep, and energy levels, all of which have a direct impact on how much energy and effort a substance abuser will have to focus on their recovery. The indirect effects of nutritional imbalances (motivation, energy, sleep, moods) will hinder the recovery process and increase the struggles involved in recovery.

Chapter 8: The Mind

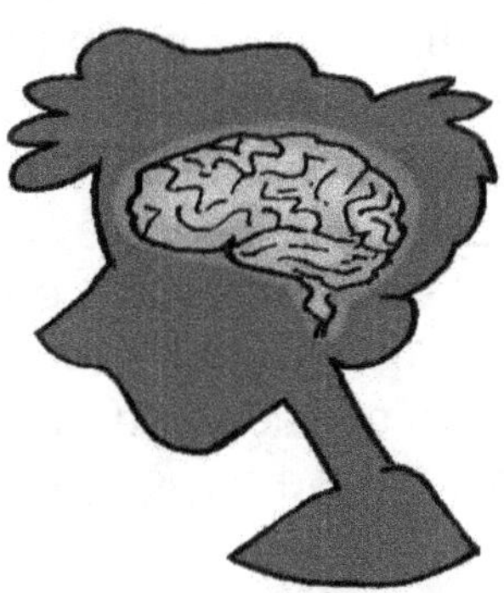

Most people view the mind and brain as the same. In the health field, the answer is less clear. For neurologists, the brain and mind are one and the same, as the brain works continuously processing surrounding stimuli and passing on information to separate parts of our body. Other scientists have argued that the mind is a separate part of our brain. For addiction treatment purposes, we consider the mind and brain separately. We look at the brain as a bodily system comprised of cells, neural pathways, tissue, and organic matter that support our body to function. The mind, meanwhile, contains our thoughts and awareness. Our knowledge, perceptions, beliefs, and attitudes are all part of our mind. If we picture a car and its operator, this provides us a further understanding of the distinction. The car (brain) has a physical structure, with tires, an engine, wheels, and other components that allow it to go from one place to another. The driver (mind) makes the decisions where to go and how to get there. The car travels (or not) based on choices made by the driver.

Previous experiences often guide our course of action (or inaction). Some decisions result from a long drawn out thought process, while many others occur on an unconscious level. When planning food for a wedding, a couple may agonize for months over *hors d'oeuvres*, the meal, and cake options, going to pre-tastings and consulting friends. Their choices will likely be affected by their experience as wedding guests themselves, recalling what did and didn't work at previous nuptials. Yet many of our more immediate food choices are more unconscious, even instinctual. Your brain may steer you to the pantry over the fridge because it remembers last time there was something tasty in there.

Perceptions play an important part in people's lives. They allow us to decide quickly. However, our perceptions are also fallible. They may not always give us the correct or most helpful information in making healthy decisions. There are numerous factors that go into our decisions and planning.

Since we can only hold on to so much information at one time (working memory), we form perceptions through our interactions with the environment. Perceptions have three stages. The first, **selection,** focuses our attention on a particular experience or part of an experience. What influences the selection is the intensity, repetition, familiarity with the stimuli, novelty, and how the stimulus presents itself. The next stage is the **organization** process. We need to organize or arrange information for it to have meaning. A common example is the illusion called Vase Face. It is a drawing (**Figure 2.9**) that when most people look at it, they will see what looks like a martini glass. However, upon closer scrutiny an individual may see figures of two heads looking at each other. If we reverse the colors (**Figure 2.9**) the people are more easily seen. This difference would be because black is a color that stands out perceptually in this example. Bright or primary colors catch our attention and we assign priority to them.

Figure 2.9

We also classify people based on the way we organize our perceptions. Short, tall, black, white, thin, heavy, young, old, Democrat or Republican. That does not mean we necessarily treat them any differently, it's just a way to assign meaning and organization. Stereotyping falls into this category. Although viewed negatively, assumptions about someone based on their outward appearance occur unconsciously as an attempt to organize experience based on previously assigned meaning. We attach a set of characteristics that help us understand what we are seeing to facilitate our actions.

After we organize our perceptions, we **interpret** them. This interpretation depends on various considerations. In **Figure 2.10**, if we often feed ducks and see that picture, most likely we will see the picture and interpret it as a duck. However, if we are playing with rabbits, we are most likely to interpret the picture to be a bunny. Context is critical to how we see things. If there is no context, it is possible we will ignore the stimulus. The video called "Test Your Awareness: Do the Test" illustrates this point. As participants in the video pass a basketball to one another, viewers are asked to count the number of times the players pass a ball between them. Most viewers do not notice a person in a bear suit walk through the video on their first viewing because it is not expected. We do not expect to see a bear and therefore do not notice him.

Figure 2.10

Another example of interpreting experience is a legend about Spanish explorer Hernan Cortes. When he sailed up the Mexican coast, it was said that the Native Americans couldn't see his ship because they never imagined such things to be real. Interpretations of events are subject to and influenced by our own bias. Social exchanges and interactions depend on our ability to interpret information from other people. We base these interpretations on previous experiences, assumptions, expectations, and attitudes. Age, life experiences, culture, and even current state of mind will be factors in interpreting stimuli. If perception is reality, decisions are based on that version of reality. The environment influences our perceptions. A cognitive bias referred to as the Halo Effect occurs when someone has a specific trait or characteristic that influences our overall judgment of that person or situation. An example would be if we see someone as good looking, we can attribute other characteristics such as intelligence to that person. If someone listens to you (good listener) and you enjoy their company (sociable) you can assign a value to them as being a great friend. This would be contrary to others' perception of him or her as a drug user or a person who influences your decision to use drugs.

Individuals from a drug using or heavy drinking family life will perceive experiences or situations differently than someone from a different background. The family culture will influence their perceptions. If they grew up in a family of heavy drinkers, they will interpret heavy drinking as normal. This differs from someone who grew up in an environment where there was no drinking. Both can observe the same drinking behavior and arrive at different conclusions about that behavior.

Even two people viewing the same event can differ in their perceptions. Studies have determined that eyewitness accounts are not entirely reliable as people can make errors in what they witness based on individual context (Arkowitz, 2010). Our emotional states influence how or if memories become stored. We store and retrieve memories in a way that makes sense to the individual both within and outside of our awareness (McLeod, 2009). For addicts, these discrepancies present themselves when there a powerful desire to use. Addicts are not able to depend on their own recall of events. This leads to misinterpretations of events and situations and leaves a notable impact on their continuing to use and on their commitment to recovery.

Drugs may alter memories more than most would suspect. This is why non-addicted people are baffled why addicts continue to use despite terrible side effects, hangovers, and so on. A recent study found that drinking alcohol can alter how memories are stored by actually changing brain pathways on a molecular level. A team of researchers found that alcohol affects a certain receptor (dopamine-2-like) responsible for the production of a protein involved in determining if a memory is good or bad. Alcohol will actually "hijack" this pathway, so a drinking experience will be remembered as a rewarding experience, and cravings will follow. The more you drink the longer it takes the pathway to return to normal (Brown University, 2018). Due to this strong reaction from the brain an addict may become convinced that using is not just okay but good. The brain (receptor) works with the mind (cognitive response, self-talk) to repeat the use despite the consequences.

Not all information is processed equally. The brain tends to perceive or notice certain details and ignore others. This is another cognitive bias called perceptual set (**Figure 2.11**). If we look at the first line of the diagram below, we see the number 13. The second line contains the same symbol but we most likely read it as the letter B. Surrounding data (numbers and letters) influences the way we look at details. Abusers may not recognize the problems accompanied with their use because they view their situation differently. Going out bowling may not be getting drunk with the boys. If they are in a bowling alley, the perceptual set is the bowling alley. This influences how participants would regard that night. Hanging out with high school friends is catching up on old times, not using cocaine.

Figure 2.11

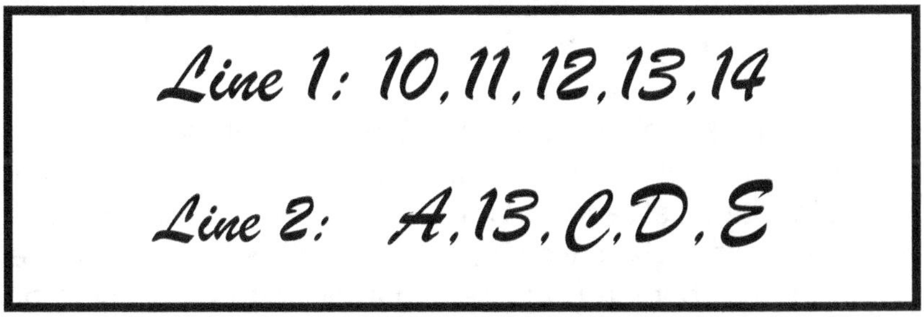

The Law of Closure principle, another perceptual quirk, occurs when our minds tend towards completing a picture. In **Figure 2.12**, there are several lines in proximity to each other. Our minds prefer to see objects in a completed fashion, so our mind places it into a form we can recognize, a square. Our minds fill in the gaps to complete our observation. If there are discrepancies in what an addict may see, he or she will complete that gap in a way that makes sense to them. Seeing the big picture is important for individuals in recovery. Closing gaps and not looking at the complete picture is detrimental to recovery. For example, regarding a situation as just "going to a wedding" would be perceptually convenient. However, if this event includes people with whom the individual used in the past, further thought needs to go into attending the event if sobriety is a goal.

Figure 2.12

Our brains can also play tricks on us when it comes to perceiving time. Looking at this from a recovery point of view, the short-term benefits of use may seem to outweigh the longer benefits of stopping. There is a point of diminishing returns in our ability to wait things out. For example, if presented with an option to receive a bonus now or wait a month for a bigger financial reward, most people would choose to wait an extra month. However, most would refuse the extra reward money if they had to wait a year (Odum, 2011, para. 14).

Numerous factors determine the interpretation of stimuli. We cannot always depend on our minds to interpret data accurately. Our minds have their own perceptual set, a tendency to notice certain incoming sensory information and ignore other data. Environmental factors, internal processes, and our brain's tendency to interpret incoming information regarding our decisions. Addicts and alcoholics will see the world through their own lens and base decisions on perceptions not reality. They cannot trust their judgment. The perceptual distortions they have formed through their use will influence decisions involving their recovery.

Chapter 9: The Turbulent Teens

Our teen years (ages 13-19) can be an amazing and memorable time. This is a point of considerable advancement, growth, foundational learning moments, and memories that will last a lifetime. As new pathways develop within the brain, new learning opportunities occur and communication within our brain travels more efficiently. Life experiences are the primary difference between an adult and 10-year-old brain and most of this substantive learning takes place during adolescence. Individuals practice the skills needed in adulthood as they attempt to fit into the grown-up world. Along with trying to fit into and navigate the adult world, they must navigate their own physiological changes. Teens also seek to manage hormones and emotions and peer relationships. We could think of the teen years as a car with high octane fuel and a big engine, but faulty brakes and poor steering (**Figure 2.13**).

Figure 2.13

Gaining a better understanding of adolescent development helps us recognize the particular challenges encountered by this age group and the roadblocks to addressing substance abuse issues. Typically, an adolescent who uses substances undergoes difficulty identifying themselves as experiencing a problem. This is in part because of developmental and physiological limitations. Consequences associated with substance abuse are also not as intense at this age as later in life. Losing a job or experiencing a family conflict because of their use may not be as catastrophic for them as for an adult. The same goes for legal, financial, and health issues (chronic health problems because of substance use rarely present at this age). For an adult, these types of problems will create conflict and potentially contemplation about substance abuse. For youth, it may not be sufficient to alter their use patterns. That does not mean that they cannot experience significant long-term substance abuse problems.

Earlier we discussed the brain. To understand teens, we need to consider the teen brain. The human brain develops from the back of our head to the front. There are three sections of the brain we will discuss. The first is the Lizard or Reptilian Brain. It controls movement and basic survival skills. It is the oldest part of our brain and develops before the other two. The next is the limbic brain. As we previously discussed, it contains many of our brain structures associated with our emotions, moods, memories, and instincts. The last part of the brain to develop is the prefrontal cortex. This is in our frontal lobe and handles decision making, planning, focusing, reasoning, and self-judgment.

All brain structures operate in sync to ensure our optimal functioning. Yet they develop at different times. Full maturation of the prefrontal cortex reaches completion around age 25, and some recent studies have put that age as high as 30 (Lebel & Beaulieu, 2011). Until then, the limbic system exerts disproportionate control over the adolescent brain. The teen prefrontal cortex can be over-matched by the limbic system and substances. Even after age 25, struggles can continue between the two systems. Teen emotions can be powerful, especially when you introduce drugs.

When we learn, we form new connections in the brain. These connections become stronger when activated. Our brain changes and alters connections in neural pathways as we garner new experiences and skills. Neuroscientists call this neuroplasticity. During adolescence, there is extensive capacity for these modifications to take place. Environmental, hereditary, personality, and experiential factors influence our brain's development. Factors that negatively influence this growth include drugs, lack of sleep, and stress (Getting Smart, 2015). We are not just talking about book knowledge, but social knowledge. Interacting with peers and navigating the social world are essential life skills that need to be practiced and learned. If acquisition of these skills is disrupted, individuals lack key competencies in adulthood.

There is another developmental milestone in the teenage brain referred to as myelination. Myelin, comprised of fatty lipids (fatty cells), plays a vital part in the transmission of messages throughout our brain. An apt comparison is well-insulated wiring. Poorly insulated wiring in a house leads to breakdowns in electronics and electrical systems within in a house. Myelin protects cells and neurons allowing for quicker and smoother communication of messages relayed within the brain and body. Myelin supports efficient transmission of messages sent back and forth. Myelination occurs throughout our lives but it is primarily during adolescence that this process takes place. The frontal lobe (the prefrontal cortex location) receives the most significant deposits of myelin. Damage to myelin, on the other hand, impacts cognitive development (Fraser-Thill, 2018).

Another physical change that occurs during this time is a process called Synaptic Pruning. We have over 100 billion neurons in our brain. These neurons make 100 trillion connections. Reduction of connections and pathways occurs as we age. This is our brain's process of finding more efficient routes to send messages and prune unneeded pathways. Imagine how we connect numerous wired electronic devices together. Behind some systems are a mess of wires. The more wires we see, the less efficiently the system will run. With wireless communications and interdependent systems now available, we have fewer wires and more effective systems. This provides for the faster and more efficient functioning of all the devices connected. The same theory applies to the brain. Less efficient and older pathways are eliminated allowing newer and more efficient pathways to take over. Stress can intensify this process and cause damage (Siegel, 2014). Adolescence is a crucial time for the restructuring of the brain and pathways close during this time because of inactivity. Neuroscientists employ the expression "use it or lose it." This refers to pathways that close or are maintained. Unused pathways are eliminated, which means a great learning opportunity may be prematurely closed.

The final adolescence brain development we will examine occurs with the white matter in our brain. White matter is the tissue of our brain and spinal cord that is comprised of myelinated nerve tissues. It occupies roughly half of our brain. It enables connections between the nerve cells and coordination with the different systems in our body. We can think of it as the subway system of our brain. During adolescence, there is a great increase in white matter (Lebel & Beaulieu, 2011). This not only helps with the transmission of signals but also is critical in the cognitive and emotional development (Barnea-Goraly, 2005). If there is interference or obstacles to white matter development at this age, this could affect learning and overall functioning of the brain. Alcohol use, marijuana use, heroin use, inhalant abuse, and methamphetamine use are all associated with impairment to the brain, particularly white matter.

Drugs introduced at this age create complex issues for teens. The teen brain is more sensitive to stress as well as drug use (Bergland, 2013). Drugs and alcohol can impact circuitry in the brain, hampering emotional and intellectual growth. This vulnerability in the adolescent brain increases the impact of drug abuse on their brain development and plasticity (Selemon, 2013). The part of the brain that says no to drugs (prefrontal cortex) is also underdeveloped at this stage of development (Cell Press, 2015). Finally, a lack of sleep can impact teens' attention spans, coping skills, healthy decision-making skills, and ability to absorb new information.

Teens are not able to recognize social cues as proficiently as adults (Yurgelun-Todd, n.d.). There have been studies suggesting that adults have considerably more activity in their prefrontal cortex (decision making part of our brain) when processing emotional outcomes than adolescents (Talukder, 2013). This means adolescents react more than think in emotional situations. There is a higher state of arousal or more activity in the amygdala of adolescents than adults, who display increased activity in the PFC. Introducing a mood-altering substance creates even more emotional intensity. Acting out behavior is amplified by the use of drugs or alcohol.

For teens, peers play an especially important role in their lives. Fellow teens are their guides and support during this transitional time. Feeling accepted into a group and a part of something is an immense need for teens. This important period of identity formation provides them a reference point in life. Reality testing and modeling provided by teens in peer groups are the best place for them to work out their uncertainties.

Friends, in some regards, become more important than family. Not only is their identity tied to peers but their self-esteem as well. Peer group values often differ from those presented at home. Kids may be a part of a peer group out of necessity or lack of options. This could be a factor if they have deficits in their own social skills. Just being in the presence of peers can modify brain waves in youth. The reward circuits in adolescent brains are activated when in the presence of peers. The parts of the brain associated with greater control and decision making are observed by researchers to be less active when in the presence of peers (Chein, Albert, O'Brien, Uckert, & Steinberg, 2010). This explains why adolescents are at greater risk of getting into traffic accidents when other youths are in the car with them (Centers for Disease Control and Prevention, 2018a). It also explains why adolescents typically commit crimes with other peers as opposed to by themselves (Albert, Chein, & Steinberg, 2013).

Along with their self-identity, teens further develop their value system as they mature. Youth decisions are complicated by increased independence and choices that come as a result of their autonomy. The values they maintain in substance abusing groups differ from the ones that are being asked of them in society. Involvement in a substance abusing group potentially compromises their ability to maintain values consistent with society. Eventually, these values become all they know.

Adolescence is also a time where mental health issues present themselves. Signs of mental health concerns become difficult to identify due to the typical turbulence of adolescence. Drug or alcohol use may either mask mental health symptoms or distract from them. This may prevent early and much-needed diagnosis and intervention. Adolescents also lose out on their ability to develop healthy coping skills to address their symptoms. Youths who suffer from mental health issues demonstrate a greater likelihood of using drugs (National Alliance on Mental Illness, n.d.). This creates a chicken or egg effect (another thought puzzle). Parents and untrained professionals often miss mental health issues because of the focus on substance use. The reverse may also hold true.

The earlier a person begins using substances, the more prone they are to form substance abuse problems. The longer one associates with peers that use substances, the more difficult it will be for them to develop peer relationships that support a drug-free lifestyle. They miss out on establishing the skills and experience to form meaningful relationships that help them navigate their social world. Confidence in changing a peer group decreases as they lose confidence in their ability to make new friends.

As much as we can educate and prepare for the challenges of teen years, it can be a trying time. As they struggle to find their place in the world, they encounter many obstacles. Introducing substances adds to the volatility, unpredictability, and impulsivity associated with this age group. It also impacts their learning to navigate in the adult world. Early substance abusers lack maturity and lag in social development. Learning delays stemming from substance use prevents teens from learning and understanding important developmental tasks. Addressing tween substance abuse is difficult but not impossible. Often, a parent's role will be to create enough speed bumps to steer them in another direction. These speed bumps will be discussed in later chapters.

Chapter 10: Seniors and Substance Abuse

A majority of older adults enjoy their golden years. Advances in medicine in the 20th-century have allowed individuals to live longer lives. Improvements in disease treatment and preventative care have led to an increase in the elderly population. Most mental health challenges that the elderly face can be easily addressed with the correct medical and psychological treatment. The elderly make up an estimated 8.5% (617 million) of the world's population. Researchers expect this number to grow to 17% (1.6 billion) by 2050 (He, Goodkind, & Kowal, 2016). By 2030, roughly 31 million Americans will be age 75 or older. There are potential problems older adults can face regarding substance abuse that are unique to this age group. We will cover those here.

A geriatrician is a physician who specializes in working with seniors. Approximately 7,000 geriatricians practice today in the United States. To meet the demand of an aging population, medical schools will need to train an additional 13,000 geriatricians just to meet the current demand, which is only rising (American Geriatrics Society, n.d.). One reason for this shortage is the additional training needed to become a geriatrician. Also, geriatricians tend to be paid less compared to other positions in the medical field. Children stay with a pediatrician until they reach 18 years of age. At that point, they will go to a primary care physician (PCP). They will transition out because they no longer need a doctor who specializes in issues specific for that age. This does not always hold true for the elderly. They may remain with their PCP even though they may require a specialist who works with their age group.

The older we become, the more health challenges we face. Our cognitive abilities decline. Attention span, memory, and the ability to carry out multiple tasks are all affected by aging (National Institute on Aging, n.d.). Along with declines in cognitive and physical abilities, the elderly usually must adjust to lower incomes. This impacts access to healthcare as well as social isolation. Friends and spouses may not be around because of death, divorce, or moves. We find an increase in the numbers of divorce elderly living alone (Mather, 2015). For seniors, technology may be difficult to navigate. As a result, it may be more difficult for them to communicate with their children. Additional developmental tasks they encounter include loss of independence, grief issues related to death of loved ones or friends, loss of financial status, limitations in their physical abilities, less active lifestyle, and a change of status with retirement.

It is therefore not a surprise that mental health issues often present themselves at this age. Researchers estimate that mental health problems affect about 1% to 5% of the general elderly population, requiring more in-home healthcare and assisted living facilities (Centers for Disease Control and Prevention, 2017a). An elderly person risks misdiagnosis or under-diagnosis being treated by someone who does not have expertise in working with this population. Often, the inability or unwillingness to recognize and discuss their mental health presents an obstacle to accurate diagnosis of mental health concerns. Also, they can have limited people in their lives to turn to for advice.

Depression and anxiety, as with other populations, are the most common mental health issues. Depression is the most common mental health disorder faced by the elderly (East, 2018). However, anxiety is a diagnosis that often falls under the radar, especially in older patients. Aged patients diagnosed with anxiety are more at risk for memory issues, dementia, and reduced quality of life. Older adults with an anxiety diagnoses will have greater challenges in managing their daily activities than those without the disorder.

Substance abuse and alcohol problems are particular risks for this age group. The elderly make up about 14% of the population but use 30% of prescription drugs (NIDA, 2018a). Sleep issues and pain management are common struggles that physicians address with medications. Doctors write nearly 17 million prescriptions for tranquilizers for older adults each year. Benzodiazepines, a tranquilizing drug, are among the more commonly misused and abused prescription medications ("Prescription Drug Abuse in the Elderly," 2017).

There is also an increase in the likelihood of mismanagement of medication if the patient is not being treated by a specialist who manages the individual's overall care. Seniors are often prescribed medications by multiple doctors who may or may not be aware of what the individual is taking. At times, seniors may not remember to report all of the medications they are taking. Older adults have slower metabolisms that make them more vulnerable to the effects of medication and alcohol. Alcohol use by the elderly patient can increase the risk of a drug overdose. Falling and injuries are commonplace for this age. Misuse of alcohol or prescription medication further increases the risk of falls and injuries.

Alcohol admissions to hospitals for the elderly are approximately 6 times higher than for other drugs (Mattson, Lipari, Hays, & Van Horn, 2017). Although this age group consumes on average less than the general population, rates have been increasing. Over a 12-year span, 2001 to 2013, drinking rates increased in this age group over 22%. There was also a 3.8% increase in high-risk drinking (Grant et al., 2017). The National Institute of Alcohol Abuse and Alcoholism recommends only one drink daily and a maximum of two on any occasion. The National Council on Alcoholism presents the following information (NIDA, n.d.-b).

- There are 2.5 million older adults with an alcohol or drug problem in the United States.
- Six to eleven percent of elderly hospital admissions result from alcohol or drug problems.
- Fourteen percent of elderly emergency room admissions, and 20% of elderly psychiatric hospital admissions, result from alcohol or drug problems.
- Widowers over the age of 75 have the highest rate of alcoholism in the United States.
- Older adult hospitalizations occur as often for alcoholic-related problems as for heart attacks.

This population, unfortunately, is often under-recognized regarding the diagnosis of substance use or alcohol problems. Symptoms associated with substance abuse are often overlooked (**Figure 2.14**).

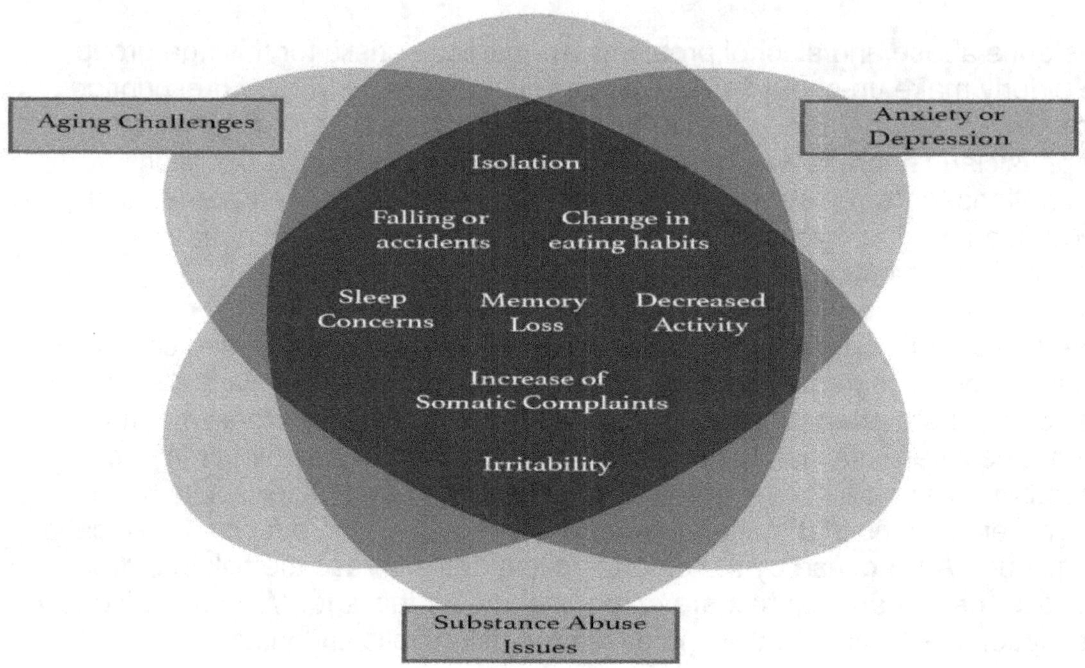

Figure 2.14

Lastly, we need to consider the impact of the medications that are prescribed for medical or psychological reasons for patients who also consume alcohol. Some health care professionals might not ask about drinking patterns in discussing medication with the elderly population, yet medications may interact dangerously with alcohol and amplify or counter the effects of the medication. This may lead to increased alcohol use, an increase of current medication, or the addition of OTC or other drugs. It can also create side effects that might require additional medication.

Statistics point to some concerns to look for regarding elderly substance abuse. Although most people slow down their use as they get older, these are areas to be mindful of regarding older adults. Percentage wise, their substance abuse problems are much lower than other populations.

Chapter 11 : Dual Diagnosis

Addiction dramatically alters the health and well-being of the substance abuser. Ironically, the complications accompanied by a user's addiction also contribute to sustained use. As symptoms (side effects of use) escalate, use typically rises. This escalation may include an increase in the substance's potency and/or frequency of consumption, creating a feedback loop. To manage the lethargy associated with coming down from a cocaine high, for example, users take more cocaine to fend off fatigue. Drinking in the morning often takes place to ward off feeling hung-over ("hair of the dog that bit you"). These attempts to avoid unpleasant side effects contribute to increased use of the drug or alcohol. Anticipation of the withdrawal effects also makes abstinence less appealing.

An actively chemically dependent person understands, to some extent, that a problem exists. Their relationship with the substance of choice likely creates conflict in every life area. However, the payoff from their use of drugs/alcohol still outweighs the drawbacks, at least in the user's perception. Using behavior usually serves a function for the substance abuser. Some alcoholics enjoy the sensation or feeling use brings (high). Others use for the social aspects and find using with friends is enjoyable for them. Still, others may partake in use because they believe it relieves stress or boredom, or to unwind after a stressful day or week. There are diverse factors that strengthen addiction as we discussed in earlier chapters.

Substance abusers may also seek their preferred drug for another reason. They use it for self-medication or to alleviate symptoms of a diagnosed or undiagnosed psychiatric condition. Professionals refer to the coexistence of mental health and substance abuse problems as dual diagnosis. An addict may not recognize that their use masks a mental health problem. Self-awareness concerning the underlying cause of their use may only surface after they stop using.

The adolescent user experiences particular risk, since the teen years tend to be when symptoms of mental health issues develop. Fifty percent of all lifetime mental health illness begins by age 14 and 75% by age 24 (National Alliance on Mental Illness, n.d.). Often young people experience difficulty understanding and explaining their emotions or what struggles they may be encountering. Multiple obstacles prevent teens from revealing their concerns including fear of being different from peers, feeling ashamed of what they are going through, or just not realizing how to resolve their feelings. Ironically, it is difficult for them to understand their struggles as being normal due to their fear of being seen as abnormal. Some studies show nearly 30% of students in 9th grade to 12th grade reported feeling hopeless or sad for an extended period during the year (Kann et al., 2014, p. 11).

Those struggling with dual diagnosis turn to drugs to either mask or help them cope with their symptoms. It is helpful to look at the symptoms of mental health problems (**Figure 2.15**) and compare them with the effects of drugs (**Figure 2.16**). We can observe how specific drugs offset symptoms. Use helps regulate the symptoms of their mental health disorder.

Figure 2.15

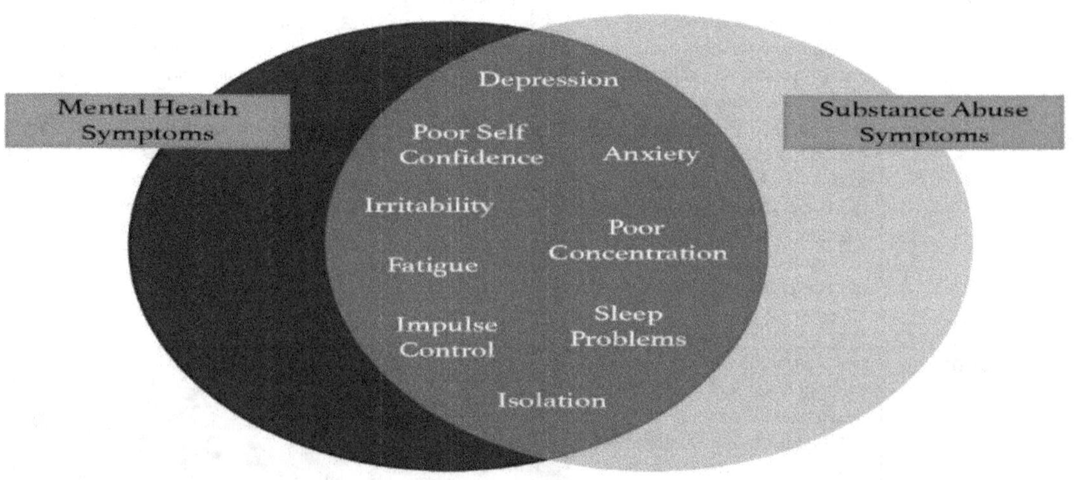

Addiction and mental health illnesses both impact the brain. Mental health issues involve changes in our brain chemistry, as does substance abuse. A person with an untreated mental health disorder experiences significantly more vulnerability to abusing alcohol and drugs. In a study conducted in 2014, over 7.9 million people were diagnosed with co-occurring disorders (Center for Behavioral Health Statistics and Quality, 2015, p. 32). In some surveys, researchers determined

Figure 2.16

Mental Health Condition	Symptoms		Mental Health Condition	Symptoms
Depression	Trouble concentrating, remembering details, and making decisions; fatigue, feeling guilt, irritability, sleep problems, change of appetite, hopelessness.		Anxiety	Panic, fear, uneasiness, sleep problems, racing thoughts, tense muscles
Panic Disorder	. Palpitations, pounding heart, or accelerated heart rate. Sweating, trembling or shaking, sensations of shortness of breath or smothering, feelings of choking, chest pain or discomfort, nausea or abdominal distress, feeling dizzy, unsteady, light-headed.		Bipolar Disorder	Includes symptoms of depression as well as: feeling very up, high, or elated, have a lot of energy, have increased activity levels, feel "jumpy" or "wired," have trouble sleeping, become more active than usual, talk really fast about a lot of different things, be agitated, irritable, or "touchy,".
Attention Deficit Hyperactivity Disorder (Hyperactive)	Fidgets with hands or feet or squirms in seat, leaves seat in classroom or in other situations in which remaining seated is expected, runs about or climbs excessively in situations in which it is inappropriate, has difficulty playing or engaging in leisure activities quietly, appears "on the go," acts as if "driven by a motor." Talks excessively. blurts out the answers before the questions have been completed, has difficulty awaiting turn, interrupts or intrudes on others.		Attention Deficit Hyperactivity Disorder (Inattention)	Fails to give close attention to details, has difficulty sustaining attention in tasks or play activities, does not seem to listen when spoken to directly, does not follow through on instructions and fails to finish schoolwork, chores, or duties in the workplace, has difficulty organizing tasks and activities, avoids, dislikes, or is reluctant to engage in tasks that require sustained mental effort, loses things necessary for tasks or activities, easily distracted by extraneous stimuli, forgetful in daily activities.
Schizophrenia	Hallucinations, delusions, thought disorders (unusual or dysfunctional ways of thinking), movement disorders (agitated body movements), reduced feelings of pleasure in everyday life, difficulty beginning and sustaining activities, reduced speaking, attention, problems with "working memory."			

that close to half of those diagnosed with a substance abuse disorder were also diagnosed with a mental health disorder (Substance Abuse and Mental Health Services Administration, 2017).

Some research lends support to the idea that substance use may cause mental health issues, rather than the other way around (Villa, n.d.). Since all mood-altering drugs affect the brain in some capacity, there is a risk of these changes becoming permanent. Ecstasy, a designer drug, damages nerve cells that contain serotonin, a vital neurotransmitter used to transmit messages and help regulate the sleep cycle. Low serotonin is, in turn, associated with depression. Other brain changes take place which can impact mental health (NIDA, 2017c). Cocaine use runs similar risks regarding changing neural pathways. Frequent cocaine use can alter pathways that respond to stress. That explains why stress can also trigger a relapse for cocaine addicts (NIDA, 2016). There is also a strong relationship between heavy cannabis drug use and increased risk for schizophrenia (Arseneault et al., 2002). Street drugs or designer drugs are furthermore risky due to the unknown and inconsistent ingredients and methods in making the drug.

Several drugs possess various and occasionally unpredictable side effects. Individuals experience the effects of drugs differently from other users when under the influence. For instance, someone may drink and become angry and aggressive, while a different person may become friendlier when drinking. The time and side effects experienced also vary for each drug and each individual. Those using designer drugs or street drugs experience even more unpredictable effects. Since there is no industry standard or guidelines regulating designer drugs, inconsistencies in potency and ingredients can vary from one batch to another.

The cycle of use continues, and drugs take a more prominent role when drug use occurs to offset the symptoms of a mental health issue. Eventually the effects of the substance wear off, creating the desire to use again as the untreated mental health symptoms will continue to be present. The user will rely on substances to cope with their mental health struggles. As they adapt to their substance of choice, various scenarios occur. Their use increases and they experience side effects from their drug of choice. This opens the door for other drugs to offset the side effects. For example, if someone is experiencing depression, they may self-medicate with cocaine. As the cocaine use continues, they may turn to alcohol to help with their feelings of agitation or jitteriness. Another problem occurs when they develop a tolerance for their drug of choice or their mental health symptoms increase. This will create a need to increase their usage of substances.

The chances of a mental health issue and substance use coexisting in harmony with an individual are not good. Substance use or abuse along with a mental illness can:

- Mask mental health symptoms and prevent accurate diagnosis
- Exacerbate existing symptoms
- Create side effects that mimic mental illness

- Increase the likelihood of self-medication which increases substance use
- Increase impulsive decisions or risk taking
- Alter brain chemistry in a long-lasting and possibly permanent way
- Increase the risk of self-harm or injury

Substance abusers often either isolate themselves or avoid people who may challenge or disapprove of their use. Guilt, shame, and embarrassment often accompany addicts and alcoholics. Mental health symptoms can intensify these feelings. Users become protective of the perceived benefits they receive from their use. They delay getting help or avoid it altogether. They tend to have limited support systems that would challenge their use. This allows the user to continue unchecked. They are reluctant to give up their use because they fear the symptoms that the use masks. It is difficult to determine in some cases where the substance abuse illness begins and mental illness ends. In section three, we will return to the problem of dial diagnosis and make suggestions on how to address this issue.

Chapter 12: Prescription and Over-the-Counter Drugs

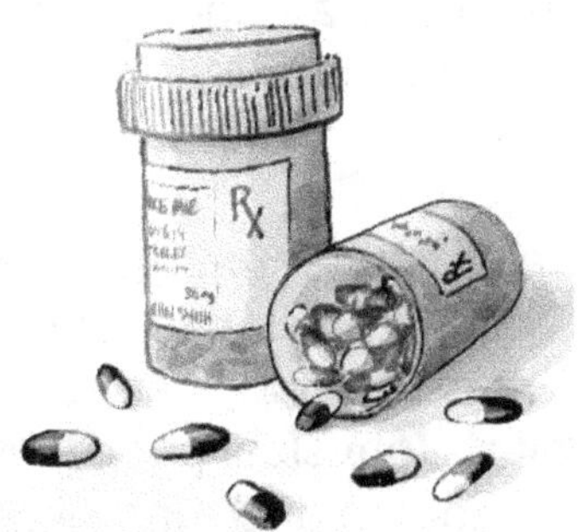

Most of our discussion has centered on the intentional misuse of substances. Now we shift to unintentional substance abuse and prescription drugs. Intentional drug abuse begins for recreational purposes such as seeking a mood-altering experience. The unintentional abuser originally took their medication for a medical reason like pain management. However, due to mismanagement of their prescriptions or over prescription, they inadvertently developed a dependency on their medication(s).

The three classes of prescription drugs typically abused are opioids, central nervous system depressants (such as tranquilizers or sedatives), and stimulants (mostly for Attention Deficit Hyperactivity Disorder). Opioids are the most frequently abused prescription drugs and as such we will focus on them here. In the United States and elsewhere, opioid abuse and addiction have become a major health epidemic. On average, 115 Americans die every day from an opioid overdose (Centers for Disease Control and Prevention, 2018). Here are some additional alarming statistics:

- From 1999 to 2012, the number of U.S. adults prescribed a medication of any kind grew from 51% to 59% (Kantor, Rehm, Haas, Chan, & Giovannucci, 2015).
- In a study completed in 2015, 20.5 million Americans reported a substance abuse disorder. In that group, over 10% (2 million) identified a prescription pain reliever as being the drug of choice.
- From 1999 to 2016, over 630,000 people died from drug overdose.
- Around 66% of the over 63,600 drug overdose deaths in 2016 involved an opioid.
- In 2016, the number of overdose deaths involving opioids (including prescription opioids and illegal opioids like heroin and illicitly manufactured fentanyl) was 5 times higher than in 1999.
- From 1999 to 2016, over 350,000 people died from an overdose involving any opioid, including prescription and illicit opioids (Centers for Disease Control and Prevention, 2018).
- In 2015, 591,000 out of 20.5 million users reported a substance use disorder involving heroin (American Society of Addiction Medicine, 2016).

- Drug overdose deaths among adolescents aged 15-19 more than doubled from 1999 to 2007 (Curtin, Tejada-Vera, & Warner, 2017).
- Death rates for drug overdoses among those aged 15-19 in 2015 were highest for opioids, specifically heroin (Curtin, Tejada-Vera, & Warner, 2017).

Opioids work by attaching to receptors in the brain. When opioids attach to the receptor site, they signal the brain to block pain and slow the respiratory system. Physicians prescribe opioids when the body cannot produce sufficient amounts of its own natural opioids to relieve physical pain. Natural opioids derived from the opium poppy plant include codeine and morphine. Semisynthetic (natural opioids created in labs) include hydrocodone and oxycodone. Man-made or synthetic opioids include heroin, fentanyl, and methadone.

Elderly adults are especially at risk for opioid addiction. As individuals age, there is a greater probability of a serious injury or illness requiring prescription medication. For people ages 50 and older, 85% receive a prescription drug within 5 years and 3 out of 4 acknowledge being prescribed an opioid medication. Those taking prescription drugs in this age group average four prescription drugs daily (American Association of Retired Persons, 2005). This population is also especially vulnerable due to other possible factors including retirement (more unstructured time, loss of status with their job), death of a loved one, isolation, placement in a nursing care facility, sleep difficulties, diminished cognitive abilities, and poor communication with their doctor. Some estimate that over 7% of people in the United States 65 years of age or older have abused prescription drugs (Kuerbis, Sacco, Blazer, & Moore, 2014).

Pharmaceutical companies contribute to substance abuse problems. They invest substantial money into the development of drugs and profit from prescriptions written by medical and mental health professionals. They also spend an exceptional amount on advertising directly to patients as well as doctors (Anderson, 2014). Their profits, by some estimates, are double that of oil companies (Anderson, 2014) and their sales revenue increased from $544 billion to $775 billion from 2006 to 2015 (United States Food & Drug Administration, 2015). Direct to consumer advertising recently intensified. Doctors have confirmed that this advertising has impacted their practices regarding prescribing medication (United States Food & Drug Administration, 2015). As a result, patients now suggest medications to their doctors, rather than the other way around.

Not all of this is legal. Drug companies can and do receive large fines from the government for misrepresenting their products in advertisements. GlaxoSmithKline was fined $3 billion in 2012 for targeting minors with antidepressant campaigns and misrepresenting drug testing results, among other violations (Thomas & Schmidt, 2012). Yet government issued fines are usually significantly less than the profits gained from the drug (Anderson, 2014). By contrast, pharmaceutical companies spend almost $60 billion a year on research and development of prescription medications (Statistica, n.d.).

Some people take prescription drugs for medical reasons. Others use them for recreational purposes. Individuals who intentionally misuse prescription medications obtain them in the following ways: from a friend or relative (50%), from one doctor (22%), bought from a friend or relative (11%), taken from a friend without asking (4%), purchased from a dealer or stranger (4%), from more than one doctor (3%), or another source (4%) (Lipari & Hughes, 2017). Med-seeking patients fake or inflate symptoms in hopes that their physician will prescribe medication. Safety protocols for writing prescriptions are constantly changing to prevent med-seekers from forging prescriptions.

Taking prescription drugs for nonmedical purposes is highest among young adults (age group 18-25) (NIDA, 2018a). Most report that they get the prescription drugs from a family member or friend (NIDA, 2018a). Early use of opioids during adolescence increases the chances of an individual developing a substance use disorder in adult life (Groenewald, Palermo, & Rabbitts, 2018). Risk taking, poor problem-solving skills, an immature prefrontal cortex, and peer pressure are all contributing factors to the use of opioids for adolescents. Another factor is shifting perspective. A study found that millennials may be less likely to take prescription opioids for pain management. However, close to one third believed it was okay to take opioids without a prescription (Newman, 2017).

Recreational opioids, heroin and synthetic street drugs, mimic the effects of prescription drugs and are made in labs. Since there is no industry standard or regulation for street drugs there is no way of knowing what comprises the drug. Most heroin users begin with heroin following prescription drug misuse. They turn to heroin because it is less expensive and simpler to obtain (Cicero, Ellis, Surratt, & Kurtz, 2014). Fentanyl use is also popular among opioid users and has recently been mixed with heroin to increase its effects. Researchers originally developed fentanyl as an anesthetic for surgery. It is estimated it to be 100 times more powerful than morphine. It requires only small amounts to produce a high. Dealers also pass it off as other drugs, such as oxycodone, as fentanyl is often less expensive.

Prescription drugs are only part of the problem. Over the counter (OTC) medication usage has intensified in recent years. The average U.S. household spending on OTCs in 2015 was $338 (Consumer Healthcare Products Association, n.d.). Individuals have access to an extraordinary variety of choices for OTCs. Awareness of these options has expanded with commercials. Some of them or combinations of them can be potentially addictive or toxic. Cough suppressants for example have become popular drugs used for recreational purposes and as a result now have greater security measures when purchased.

When abused, they can produce an effect that ranges from stimulation to hallucination. OTCs may also enhance the effects of recreational drugs. Their convenience, affordability, and availability make OTC meds more prone to being abused. The user in most instances will not have a professional administering the medication, leaving them unaccountable and perhaps undetected to significant others. The signs of abuse include overusing OTCs, using longer than recommended on the label, and combining OTC drugs or prescription drugs to create highs.

Physicians play a role in the current prescription medication abuse epidemic. Doctors who address patients from a purely pharmacological and reactive approach are quick to prescribe medication for the reduction of symptoms. Although information and safety protocols for prescribing addictive medications have improved, physicians and patients continue to make choices that put patients at risk for prescription abuse. For some problems, lifestyle can transform circumstances, as with depression or sleeping problems. Medication treatment alone provides a quick fix that may mask the cause of the problem (life choices, events, lifestyle of a patient). If side effects occur from medication, doctors may introduce another medication to counter those effects.

Prescription drug abuse has increased over the years, with more medications to choose from and more drugs being prescribed. Physicians will have to play a major role in preventing or intervening in prescription drug abuse. Coordination of care by doctors or professionals must be a priority. Without asking the right questions, patients can be put at risk for substance abuse issues. Jim would be a good example of this. Jim is a 54-year-old self-employed businessman. Five years ago, his doctor prescribed him Ambien, a sleep medication. Jim had been experiencing difficulties in getting to sleep due to an increased workload. The doctor prescribed 5 mg (the minimum dosage) to help him stay asleep through the night. He found it helpful and used the recommended dosage. His work situation settled down, but he nevertheless still had trouble going to sleep. He continued taking the Ambien and became dependent on it to sleep. The doctor eventually doubled the medication dosage, yet he continued to have sleeping difficulties. Jim began to drink to aid him with his sleep. He would have a couple of shots before bed. Although some mornings he had trouble getting up, he found this routine effective to help him sleep. The only problem he had was waking up in the morning. He has recently been oversleeping and was late to work several times. One morning, he fell asleep at the wheel and had an accident. He attributed it to the sleep medication and decreased his dosage. His sleep difficulties worsened. His sleep had deteriorated beyond what he had ever experienced before. One night, after he tried stopping his medication altogether, Jim experienced intense anxiety, agitation, and tremors. The emergency doctors diagnosed him with a substance abuse disorder. He had become addicted to his medication and was experiencing withdrawal symptoms.

Chapter 13: Families

Chemical dependency not only affects all areas of an addict's life, it affects everyone who is a part of their lives. Their family in particular is most vulnerable to addiction's impact. After all, family relationships often play a huge part in our lives and families are a source of enormous emotional investment. We count on them for learning, growth, support, connectivity, direction, and emotional and physical security. Most families provide comfort and support to one another. Obviously, there are exceptions. Some individuals come from unhealthy and dysfunctional families. Those types of homes create struggles that extend into other relationships long after someone has left home. We will discuss the effects of substance abuse on families (and the effects of families on substance abuse) in this chapter.

Every family has its own organization and structure. The way they get things done and function. Family members develop their own styles of responding and reacting with one another and with the outside world. These patterns between family members provide each family system a sense of balance. These expectations (spoken or unspoken) include the expression of feelings (or not), managing conflict (or avoiding), how they communicate issues outside the family system, and assignment of responsibilities of family members, whether consciously and unconsciously. They assign roles to ensure that system runs as smoothly and efficiently as possible. Some roles may be minor while others will be more vital. If a family member requires additional attention or is not filling his or her role, this affects other members and the family system. Addiction operates as a destructive force in families. This impact can have a generational effect.

A change in any part of the family system leads to changes in all other parts of the system. Envision a mobile hanging over a crib in a child's room. All the parts are connected and influenced by the other parts. When one part moves, the other parts move in response to it. For families, when one family member abuses substances this influences the attitudes and behaviors of other family members. It shapes behavior in the family (mobile).

Substance abuse touches many lives. We have included information and statistics to show its impact on families.

- Twelve percent of American children live with one parent who abuses alcohol or drugs (Child Welfare Information Gateway, 2014).
- Over 30% of children in foster homes were removed from their homes because of drug or alcohol abuse by a parent (Child Welfare Information Gateway, 2014, p. 2).
- Two-thirds of child abuse cases involve chemical dependency in some form (Child Welfare Information Gateway, 2014).
- Among children 17 or younger, 12.3% lived with a parent who had a substance abuse disorder (Lipari & Van Horn, 2017).
- Children growing up with a parent who abuses substances are at greater risk of developing substance abuse problems themselves. They also have higher rates of mental health and behavioral problems (Lipari & Van Horn, 2017).
- Children with a parent who abuses substances are at greater risk for neglect (Lipari & Van Horn, 2017).

There are other factors to consider that can be difficult to track statistically. Families are what children rely on for reference points growing up. They are a safety net for children and a home base from which to navigate the adult world. Growing up in a substance-abusing family disrupts the child's sense of right or wrong and alters their perspective of what is and isn't normal. Substance abusing families often exhibit the following traits:

- Secrecy. The abuser wants to keep using while experiencing minimal conflicts or confrontations. Their families learn not to discuss use to avoid outside threats to the user's substance use (for example, inviting friends to the house).
- Denial. This creates confusion and doubts for the rest of the family about their own perceptions. If they see substance abuse as a problem yet are told it is not, they grow up doubting their ability to perceive problems and trust their own judgment.
- Betrayal. Promises to end substance use create mistrust. This also carries over into future relationships.
- Helplessness and/or over control. Children feel powerless in getting a parent to stop their use. This may affect their future relationships and lead to overcompensating by trying to (over) control adult relationships.
- Fear/worry. Family arguments or substance use behaviors create fear or worry about future episodes.
- Upheaval. Instability, arguments, and unpredictability typically present themselves in substance abusing families.

When substance abuse takes over an abuser's life, it undermines their roles in the family. Other family members must pick up the slack in responsibilities. This causes confusion in roles. Children may have to take on greater responsibility if a parent is faltering in their caregiver role. This can lead to confused boundary issues as children take on responsibilities of impaired parents. Also, children learn to hide signs of substance abuse from the outside world. They discourage friendships not only to protect the family system but also because they must pick up responsibilities the abuser neglects.

Spouses face their own challenges. They will likely feel conflicted about the concessions made to the substances. Factors such as a lack of financial resources, wanting to protect their children, a lack of support systems, low confidence, and uncertainty that they could live on their own will often keep them in a substance-abusing relationship. If they grew up in a family that abused substances, they may view their current experiences as normal.

Parents are faced with distinct dilemmas when their child is the one abusing substances. Parents often do not know where to start to address the problem and are fearful of taking the wrong approach. As a result, they are often divided regarding how to address the problem. They can have limited knowledge and resources to address the issue, and shame, guilt and embarrassment may further limit parents' responses to their child's use. Parents can perceive that they have limited power to intervene with the use. A teen may intimidate a parent when confronted, which can be especially dangerous if their child becomes aggressive or is under the influence. One of the tactics substance abusers of any age may use is emotional blackmail. If the substance using child threatens suicide, a parent may delay or avoid interventions or treatment for fear of such threats. Yet parents are understandably reluctant to force the child to leave home. Unable to imagine their child (even an adult child) living on the street, they allow the use to continue.

Substance abuse affects other family members including siblings. Most family resources are devoted to the chemically dependent person, leaving siblings to feel lost or disconnected, resentful or angry. He or she becomes invisible, making great efforts not to create any more stress on the family system. All family members take on new roles to keep the system afloat. These roles often carry over into adult relationships.

A family experiencing chemical dependency will isolate themselves not only from the outside world but from their extended family. Shame and guilt drives family members to keep secrets. Even though siblings and parents can be supportive most of the time, they will not understand their child's struggles unless they experience it for themselves. Extended family members often have difficulty supporting the teen and the family. Impatience and lack of understanding are stumbling blocks.

Often the change required for family members to act is a lengthy process. One or two members of the family may be reluctant to address substance abuse which slows down or interferes with addressing the problem. This is an area to which we could devote a whole book (or series). Yet the lasting impact on families is significant. Even after an addict's recovery, families require a long time to recover from the impact of their use.

Chapter 14: Summing Up

In the 1980s, First Lady Nancy Reagan launched a national campaign imploring children to "Just Say No" to illegal drugs. How successful this was is difficult to say. Simple and catchy, Mrs. Reagan did create a prominent slogan and heightened awareness of drug abuse. Yet we in the treatment field also recognize that just saying no is not that simple. People do not intentionally put themselves through the devastation of addiction. This section has shown just how difficult it can be to just say no to drugs and alcohol once down the road of addiction. We have seen how addiction can take many forms, and that addiction can be tricky to define. Perspectives vary among societies, nations, neighborhoods, families, and individuals. This subjectivity in defining what a substance abuse problem looks like makes it difficult to address addiction. Also, since drugs and alcohol addiction overtake one's life, users themselves are not reliable resources in defining abuse. They cannot always trust themselves or their brain to give them accurate information regarding their use.

What initially draws someone to drugs is just one part of the equation. There is no one cause of addiction. Genetics, environment, family, life circumstances, and individual personalities affect chemical dependence. Some individuals can use substances recreationally and not develop problems. Others may use, and have a problem with using, but stay under the radar. Their use is not a recognizable concern to outsiders (tree falling in the forest).

Sometimes a person just wakes up in the morning and realizes they have a problem. They experience enough negative events to determine using is no longer worth it for them. These negative events may be internal (hung-over, feeling guilty about use, seeing friends having problems with their use) or external. Some do not need prompting by family, employers, the legal system, or others to tell them they have a problem. They come to this realization on their own.

For others, it's less simple. For example, someone reprimanded at work for having alcohol on his breath may begin to see his drinking as problematic. However, a passage of time may diminish that viewpoint. Several months later they may view their drinking as less problematic. The impact of the event lessens over time and remaining sober may be challenging enough for them to change how they perceive their drinking, rather than give it up all together. A life event (marriage, having a child, new job) can also help shed light on a problem. Demands placed on individuals experiencing major life changes may be too difficult to balance along with their substance abuse.

Diagnosing a substance abuse problem is just as complicated for professionals. If a harmful relationship has formed with the abuser and his or her drug of choice, there will be a reluctance to give up the substance. The pleasure of use and obstacles they encounter in quitting create circumstances that will often make them resistant to change. The fear of losing their substance of choice prevents them from being open and honest about their using history. Addicts often see the interviewer as a threat to something meaningful for them (relationship with their substance of choice). The timing of the evaluation is a factor. If enough time has passed, negative events could lose the intensity they had when they first occurred. Motivation and perspective can change with time and distance. This could also apply to family members who are taking part in a diagnostic interview.

There are several standardized assessments that aid in diagnosing a substance abuse problem. Those will have limits. Most of them will still depend on the openness of the interviewee. Even if there is an acknowledgment that a problem exists, it does not then mean that a person will want to do anything about it. Or they can accept the loses associated with their continued use. An example is an individual who has several arrests for driving under the influence and a wife who is confronting him about his excessive drinking. He may give up his driving license so he can continue to drink. He may even allow his marriage to end and live a solitary lifestyle rather than change his drinking habits.

Substance abusers need to have a number of pieces fall into place to address their issues. Once a problem is identified and a person resolves to stop their use, this will require an abundance of time, effort, and patience. Even if there is a desire to stop, resources may not be available to assist them. A 2013 study by the Substance Abuse and Mental Health Services Administration found that close to 90% of individuals may not receive the services they need for substance abuse treatment (2014). Transportation, availability, and affordability are all deterrents.

This is not a hopeless picture. People recover from addiction. However, there are numerous factors that need to be considered for someone to be pointed in a direction of recovery. Once all of the pieces are in place, the work towards recovery begins. We have talked about trees in the forest, beetles in boxes, dying donkeys, and spiders in urinals. Our discussion now turns to a color blind neuroscientist named Mary.

SECTION 3

Chapter 15: Color Blind Scientists

Australian philosopher Frank Johnson offers the following thought puzzle. Mary is a neurophysiologist scientist who studies the human nervous system. Her area of expertise is the study of color vision, although she herself has never been allowed to see color. She is asked to conduct a study on how the human eye perceives and reacts to color. Her study is conducted in a black and white room and her observations are made with the aid of a black and white monitor. Mary can study, learn, and observe on a physical level how the human eye processes color. All the biological reactions and interactions in the human body can be observed, monitored, and recorded. However, her knowledge is limited to black and white observations. Can she really understand the process of the human eye seeing color without the ability to see color herself? Once she leaves the black and white room, will her observations be different? (Nida-Rümelin, 2009).

In posing this problem, Frank Jackson challenged a belief that knowledge only comes through physical experience. Mary can know all the physical facts there are to know about color, but will that knowledge prepare her for the experience of actually seeing color, of being awestruck by autumn foliage, or a radiant sunset, or cherry blossoms in bloom? The same argument could be made about music, could one truly know music without ever hearing it? Jackson's point was that nonphysical properties and knowledge exists beyond material existence and must be discovered through conscious experiences.

Those outside the life of an addict will see the situation in black and white. They question why substance abusers keep making the same choices. Don't they see how destructive those choices are? Family members are often most frustrated by an addict's defense of their habit. Minimization, denial, avoidance, and anger are among the first responses from an addict who doesn't want to give up something important to them (their addiction). This denial may also frustrate professionals trying to get through to the abuser. But those who have never experienced addiction can't really know just how consuming addiction can be, and how hard the choices and challengers are. Addicts, meanwhile, will see their world in color. They know that choices are not that simple. Addiction can be mentally and physically all consuming.

If someone is feeling anxious, they will usually share that information with their doctor or therapist. This will assist the doctor to help address their symptoms. If they are experiencing severe stomachaches, they will share that information with a doctor to ease their discomfort. Addicts, on the other hand, will do everything possible to avoid scrutiny. The previous chapters have focused on the reasons why the resistance can be so strong to giving up something that is so destructive. Addiction takes over lives. The relapse rate for drugs and alcohol abuse is high. How high is not entirely clear. Some studies show it is comparable to other illness (40 to 60%) such as diabetes (30 to 50%), hypertension (50 to 70%), or asthma (50 to 70%) (NIDA, 2018b). Other studies estimate that for those struggling with alcohol, close to 90% will relapse within 4 years (Mosel, 2017). For drugs, the percentages can range from 40% (hallucinogens) to 88% (heroin) ("Relapsing back to sobriety," 2014).

Now that we have seen how powerful addiction can be, we can begin to understand the lengths to which addicts may go to deceive those around them. This includes people who can help. They do this to continue their use.

The remaining chapters will lay out what a person needs to do to recover from their addiction. Just as there are many theories on how someone becomes addicted, there are many opinions on the best treatment approach. We know that no single treatment approach works best. Throughout our counseling careers, we have seen treatment professionals or support groups try to get addicts and alcoholics to fit into the therapist's goals, not what fits for the person. This creates a one-size-fits-all approach. It does not include individual personalities or situations. A one-dimensional treatment approach in many cases will be unhelpful for those struggling with addiction. Addressing only one area of recovery or simply stopping often will not be enough. Thankfully, the substance abuse treatment field has evolved and expanded to offer not just many different models and settings but also more complete and lasting recovery plans.

Before discussing the treatment of substance abuse, it is important to keep certain points in mind. A person deciding to change their substance using patterns, whether through moderation or abstinence, will first need to establish clear goals. Cutting back, slowing down, and other such statements are too vague to be real goals. Notions are not measurable and do not lend themselves to accountability. If you are drinking a pint of whiskey daily, cutting back could just mean drinking a three-fourths pint 1 day a week, and drinking the same 6 days a week. The vaguer the statement, the less committed one is to a goal. Goals, by contrast, are measurable and can create clear guidelines for accountability. The more accountability an addict has, the greater the likelihood of success. Accountability can mean to yourself (as an addict) or to others.

Individuals stop using in all sizes, shapes, and forms. It is more important to commit to the journey of recovery. How an addict will stay sober depends on many factors. These would include: the drug of choice, motivation of the user, duration of use, support systems in place, individual personalities and disposition, environment, other mental health challenges, and resources available. There are many ways a person can get from point A (using) to point B (recovery). It is impossible to know which course of treatment will be the most effective for the chemically dependent person. This is especially true for someone who makes their first attempt to stop their use.

The journey of recovery can involve many roads. An individual treatment approach is important in recovery. One size does not fit all. There are different settings that could accomplish the goal of abstinence (or moderation). We will discuss those in subsequent chapters. If someone chooses a treatment setting to stop their use, it is important to evaluate the effectiveness of that choice. For example, if someone quits on their own, with no help, they can decide on seeking professional help if they relapse. Conversely, someone may be successful in stopping their use by seeking individual counseling once a week after failing at sobriety in a more intensive setting. The journey could start in any setting. The decision should involve family, individual, and professional input.

There are many ways that someone can enter recovery. It is not unusual for someone to enter treatment through someone else's decision, whether that of a spouse, a parent, an employer, or the courts. Involuntary (mandated) treatment has equally favorable success rates as voluntary (Kelly, Finney, and Moos, 2005). We will discuss this in greater detail later in the book.

Addiction affects numerous areas of someone's life. Deciding to stop using often is only the beginning of the journey. It makes sense that the recovering addict will need to address more than one challenge (life area) in recovery. As a result, the initial stopping of use may be difficult. A term used in the recovery field is S.O.B.E.R., or **S**onna **o**f a **B**it** **E**verything is **R**eal. Someone's situation may seem initially worse than when they were using. Learning to live without substances will require adjustments. Recovery does not just involve stopping the drug of choice.

For those abstaining, a clear goal of abstinence must be established. There should be no exceptions. This is a pass or fail goal. In recovery, there is a saying: "One drink is too many and a dozen not enough." There are individuals that decide to just stop using and do not need any additional support or treatment. They just decide to stop. This is referred to as spontaneous remission or natural recovery.

There is not a lot of data on spontaneous remission or natural recovery. It was simply something that was not given much consideration. Individuals who did stop on their own were referred to as "dry drunks" (having the same behaviors and attitudes associated with drinking, just without the drinking) or seen as someone who would inevitably return to use. There are complications when we try to measure long term success for spontaneous remission or natural recovery. Harm reduction (cutting back to safer levels or moderating use) would need to be included in those figures. If you decide to moderate or control your use, this approach will be discussed in Chapter 20.

The possibility of coexisting disorders should be considered, as substances could have masked serious mental health issues. Stopping the drug of choice can bring the discovery of a dual diagnosis. As with other medical conditions, a relapse can also happen, even for those committed to abstinence. There is a difference between wanting to stop and being able to stop. Relapse does not mean the end of the world. For many, it is not a straight path to recovery and may involve several detours or missteps.

Long term use of a mood-altering substance, regardless of what it is, will involve withdrawal. This withdrawal can present itself from mild symptoms to severe. For marijuana, it could mean sleep difficulties. Cocaine withdrawals can include anxiety and/or depression. For alcohol and heroin, withdrawal symptoms could even be fatal. It is important to assess risk factors involved in stopping. Consult a medical doctor to assist with or monitor the withdrawal.

Once someone has committed to stopping their use, their journey begins. There are different paths to stop abusive patterns of substance use. Regardless of how you plan to stop using, the road to recovery involves addressing how substance use impacts many aspects of our lives. We now turn our attention to recovery and rebuilding these same life areas, which brings up the question of fixing wooden ships.

Chapter 16: Repair or Replace: Types of Treatment

The ship of Theseus is a thought puzzle presented by Plutarch in *Life of Theseus*. Theseus, a mythical King of Athens, had fought many naval battles. To honor him, the people of Athens dedicated his ship as a memorial by preserving it in their port. This ship stayed there for hundreds of years. Over time, parts of the ship rotted away. To preserve the ship, they replaced the rotted planks with new planks made of the same material. The question becomes: over time, with the replacing of numerous planks, is it still the same ship? At what point is the ship a different ship entirely?

In recovery, addicts face their own ship of Theseus question. The damage by substance abuse can be substantial. Repair or replacement (finding another job, new friends, new activities) will be a part of their recovery. The amount of repair and replacement will depend on the impact of their use and length of time using. An addict's brain, body, and lifestyle will have adapted to their use, even come to depend on it. Adjustments will have to be made to compensate for the drug's absence. Before addressing specific areas in recovery, a good place to start is to review the treatment options available. Availability and types of programs can vary from state to state and between insurance plans. The least restrictive settings are encouraged and often mandated by insurance.

Individuals can and do quit with no professional or support group help (Roan, 2009). Addiction is unique. Some addicts decide enough is enough and quit. Just as treatment comes in all sizes, shapes, and forms, so does addiction and the addict. It is important to steer away from only one approach to addiction. For many, a more individualized approach is beneficial, while others succeed in support groups.

If there is concern about medical complications because of withdrawal of a substance, then detoxification (detox) would be necessary. Doctors supervise withdrawal and medically wean patients off their drug of choice, minimizing the discomfort they experience. Participants would need to complete this before starting actual treatment. This usually lasts two to four days, depending on the level of withdrawal someone is experiencing.

Day programs offer all-day treatment, usually in a hospital setting. Participants go home at night. These can last three to six weeks. The programs are similar to short-term residential facilities except that the participant is allowed to go home at night. An Intensive Outpatient Program (IOP) is another part-time option. In most cases, it can last three to seven weeks and sessions are held in the evening hours and total 12 hours a week. These programs usually limit individual counseling in favor of group counseling. They do assign most participants a case manager to help with treatment planning, assessment, and management.

There are also short-term residential and inpatient programs run by professionals. The overnight stay usually lasts three to four weeks with numerous groups run throughout the day. The amount and type of groups vary with each facility. These settings offer individual counseling but focus on group counseling. They all should include aftercare in their program.

Residential or long-term treatment can last anywhere from 6 to 12 months. Participants are required to stay overnight in a nonhospital setting. While in treatment, therapy also includes other components that support recovery such as diet, employment, and other life areas impacted by substance abuse. This setting is also referred to as a therapeutic community. When substance abusers, families, and professionals are discussing treatment options it is important to make sure all parties are on the same page. Ensure that everyone's definition and understanding of what each treatment program offers is consistent.

A half-way house is one long-term facility for addicts and alcoholics with a length of stay of up to one to three years. These are also referred to as residential settings or transitional living. These facilities offer a transition from a treatment setting back into the community. Recovering individuals (paraprofessionals) run the programs and groups and residents have the support of, and accountability to, the rest of the recovering community (fellow residents). There is typically not as much treatment or structure offered as in other placements. There are curfews and rules that govern the facility that support sober living.

It is important that in all treatment approaches there should be aftercare or a plan for follow-up treatment. A program should discuss discharge planning and transition from care at the end of their program. For the more intensive and longer-term treatments, a step down in treatment should be offered. This involves a transition from a more intensive treatment setting to a less intensive one. A reentry into a less intensive level of care can be challenging for the recovering addict, especially if they have been in a closed community. They will need additional support to help with temptations and stressors of the home environment.

Support groups are an excellent resource and are offered at no cost within the community. Recovering addicts typically facilitate these groups. Group times, focus, and locations will vary. There are also groups online. Most treatment programs will offer these groups as part of their program, either on-site or elsewhere. Some facilities rely heavily on support groups in their programming. Someone seeing an individual therapist may also attend a support group. Other therapists may not include this in their treatment approach. We will cover the wide variety of support groups available in the next chapter.

Individual counseling is more in-depth and focused on individual needs and concerns. In an outpatient counseling setting, therapists meet with their clients (patients) one to two times a week in a private or community mental health/substance abuse center. Sessions usually last 50 minutes to one hour. This could include couples or family counseling. Ideally, two different therapists, one for the family and one the individual, would conduct the sessions.

Program costs vary with each treatment and type of program. Some programming costs over $1,000 a day, or more. Insurance generally offers partial to full coverage. This again varies with each insurance plan. There are government programs that can cover participation. We include a comparative summary of these many treatment (**Figure 3.1**).

Figure 3.1

Type of Facility/Treatment	Length of Stay	Criteria for Admission/Comments
Halfway House	This could vary from house to house. Usually longer-term stay, 6 months to over a year	Drug or alcohol free upon admission. Each facility can have different admissions criteria. This is a live-in facility run by recovering addicts/alcoholics. Goal is reentry into society
Long-term Residential	6 to 12 months	This is rarely a first-tier treatment setting option. Criteria for entering usually require previous treatment experiences and a severe addiction. Ancillary treatments, such as mediation, exercise, nutrition, as well as medical consultations, are usually offered. These are usually self-funded or through insurance. Some states may offer programs that offer financial assistance.
Short-term Residential	3 to 4 weeks	Length of stay varies but is usually around 3 to 4 weeks. This is usually not a first-tier treatment setting either. Placement in this setting would depend on severity of addiction and previous treatment experiences.
Partial Hospitalization	14 to 21 days	Participants meet 5 days a week. Programs last all day. Once they have completed the programming in the daytime, they return home at night.
Intensive Out-Patient	3 to 6 weeks, 10 to 16 hours a week	This programming would take place in the evenings most of the time. It is designed for individuals who may require more than an individual approach can offer but not as intensive as those previously mentioned. In some cases, individuals may start out in an intensive outpatient setting if they have been unsuccessful at remaining sober through individual counseling or their addiction is severe or life threatening enough to warrant intensive out-patient care.
Individual counseling on outpatient basis	1 to 2 times a week (possibly more). Sessions are 45 minutes to 1 hour. Open ended.	This type of therapy should be the starting point in most cases. Exceptions include severe addiction, a difficult home environment, previous attempts at quitting, drug of choice, and motivation. Individual counseling could also be offered as an aftercare component. Family or couples counseling is often necessary to support the client and their loved ones in developing and maintaining a sober lifestyle.
Detox	1 to 5 days	This would be offered to individuals where there is a concern about medical repercussions if they stopped using. A sudden stopping of certain drugs could be extremely uncomfortable and in some cases life threatening. Once this is completed, it is recommended that the individual participate in the above-mentioned programs. It is not recommended as a treatment alone.
Support groups	As often as needed	These groups are offered in the community. Frequency and length are an individual choice. They can be offered as a component of or to supplement the previously mentioned programs. There are no costs to these, and they are run by paraprofessionals.

The length of treatment (how long it lasts on not the frequency) is just as important in recovery as the level of care. Longer treatment has a better success rate than short term (Hser et al., 2001). The data on the success rates for specific levels of care is not consistent, making it difficult to draw conclusions on which setting is more successful (Miller & Hester, 1986). Specific populations seem to benefit from more intensive treatment settings. For instance, chronic heroin abusers who have had a long history of use and relapse often require a longer-term setting. A teenager who smokes marijuana daily would benefit more from outpatient counseling, both for the individual and family.

The National Institute on Alcohol Abuse and Alcoholism conducted a study in 1989 to determine what types of treatment are most effective for alcoholics. They found that no single treatment setting or approach was statistically more effective than another. Cognitive-Behavioral Therapy, Motivational Enhancement Therapy, and Twelve-Step were all found to have comparable results (Project MATCH, 1993). When choosing a treatment plan, it is important to keep in mind the individual's needs and the resources of the client. Individualized treatment approaches and a deep understanding of how addiction impacts you and your family lead to more effective treatment outcomes.

There are many programs that advertise success rates. These statistics can be misleading. If participants are surveyed immediately after completing a program, positive results are likely to be high. Yet a more meaningful and indicative statistic for recovery would track participants' long-term recovery (five years or more). For example, if someone is in a 30-day program and they complete it, the program could interpret success based only on those 30 days, not length of subsequent sobriety. Return to use does not necessarily show a failure of the program or treatment approach. As we will discuss, clients' setting of treatment goals is key for defining recovery. A reduction in use or in risky behavior associated with use can be an indicator of success. Research also supports that treatment is more effective if it addresses multiple needs (NIDA, 2018b). Failure to screen for other mental health concerns, underqualified staff, rigid treatment approaches (not individualized), lack of a family component, and poor aftercare planning contribute to poor success in some treatment settings.

In the substance abuse community, the term "Hitting Bottom" refers to the lowest point someone can reach in their addiction. The user experiences enough serious consequences of their use that they finally acknowledge their problem and become motivated to get help. In the early days of substance abuse treatment, there was a belief that unless someone had already hit rock bottom, they were not ready for treatment. There are several problems with this approach. Mandated treatments can be enormously beneficial. The road to recovery does not necessarily follow a self-realization or epiphany moment that might accompany hitting bottom. Hitting bottom is also a subjective term. Early intervention can create a better likelihood of success in reducing substance use, in a sense raising someone's lowest point (U.S. Department of Health and Human Services, Office of the Surgeon General, 2016).

In the treatment field, professionals are encouraged to start "where the client is at," not where you want him or her to be. This means there are numerous factors to consider when deciding which treatment should be pursued. Length of use, previous treatment experiences, what substance is being used, support systems (or lack thereof), and what impact the use has had on their life.

Chapter 17: Types of Support Groups

There are several advantages to taking part in a support group. Not everyone needs or wants to attend a support group of course. However, they can offer validation that the struggles you face are not unique. Knowing there are others facing the same hurdles can be reassuring. For the addict, they can feel connected to the group, a comrade-in-arms mentality toward recovery. Information gleaned from members in the group can also give you direction on helpful resources in the sober community. Suggestions on coping skills are also another benefit. Having a group of individuals brainstorming their ideas for addressing issues is often more productive than thinking it through individually. Addicts and alcoholics in many cases isolate themselves in their attempts to hide the severity of their problem. For many, they are more open to receiving feedback from peers as opposed to from authority figures or professionals. It is comforting for addicts and alcoholics to know there are other people out there who have faced or are facing the same struggles, and can furthermore offer suggestions and support. This can help with feelings of isolation many addicts go through in early recovery. Lastly, groups can offer more accountability to recovery.

There are many support groups available. Accessibility of resources is easier than ever before thanks to the internet. The two most popular groups in the United States are Alcoholics Anonymous and Smart Recovery, but many additional options will be covered here as well.

Alcoholics Anonymous (AA) is the oldest support group and the most available, with meetings held globally. In some cities, someone could attend meetings several times a day. They also offer online groups. Famous for its 12-step program, participants progressively work through each step, which involves its own task and challenge. The first step asks participants to acknowledge their powerlessness over alcohol and recognize that their lives are out of control because of drinking. The steps work progressively from there. AA has a spiritual and Christian worldview and calls for a surrender to God or a higher power. There are numerous support groups that have evolved from AA, which include

Marijuana Anonymous, Cocaine Anonymous, Family Anonymous, and Narcotics Anonymous.

The advantage of AA is the availability. AA meetings are easily accessible and convenient, and they enthusiastically welcome newcomers. They also encourage members to reach out to each other in times of need. Support, in most cases, is unconditional. Members can pursue many sobriety resources and activities through AA. Participants are encouraged to get a sponsor. This person acts as a mentor to guide them through the program.

A potential disadvantage is their religious component, which is not a good fit for non-religious individuals. AA asks newcomers to turn their will and lives over to a higher power as part of the 12-step program. A higher power refers to something the alcoholic can see as a power greater than him/her self. Some groups will emphasize this more than others. Participants will also find little flexibility in individualizing the program to fit their unique challenges in recovery. Finally, AA does not have a stated end or completion time for the group. Members are strongly encouraged to continue participation indefinitely.

Smart Recovery is an abstinence-based program that distances itself from the AA approach. A relatively new program compared to AA, they steer away from labeling someone an addict or alcoholic. They also avoid the AA approach that people are powerless over their addiction and focus on the present rather than the past. Smart Recovery is cognitively behavioral based (focusing on thoughts, attitudes, behaviors, and beliefs) and focuses on interactive strategies and approaches to assist in sobriety. They tailor their approach to specific challenges addicts face and address specific thoughts and behaviors that would challenge abstinence. Their approach offers tools and techniques to address the challenges of recovery and includes problem-solving, motivational, and behavioral techniques. Meeting facilitators are recovering volunteers who have completed mandatory training to conduct the meetings.

Smart Recovery does not address the spiritual component of recovery and is more scientifically based. Most of them are time limited. This means that they are not usually looked at as ongoing and continuous. Attendees can attend for a lifetime if they choose, however the usual attendance in these groups is for weeks or months. One drawback is that Smart Recovery is not as widely available in communities and institutions as AA. They are growing and becoming accepted in many of the same institutions as AA.

Women for Sobriety (WFS) is a program that believes that there are specific challenges for women in recovery. Like Smart Recovery, WFS moves away from the concept of powerlessness and more to self-empowerment. Formed in 1976, they follow a 13-step program and offer a variety of different recovery tools to target issues such as self-worth, self-value, and guilt and shame. Their approach is cognitive behavioral, and they work on self-esteem, spirituality, and healthy lifestyle. They offer online and in-person meetings.

Secular Organization for Sobriety (SOS), founded in 1984, offers online and in-person meetings. They base their program on developing strategies to acknowledge, accept, and prioritize their sobriety. SOS encourages taking responsibility for sobriety and excludes the spiritual component.

LifeRing Secular Recovery offers support in strengthening the Sober Self and weakening the Addict Self. There is more focus on the here and now as opposed to the past. The program encourages participants to design their own programs and path in recovery. LifeRing offers online and in-person group meetings.

Recovery International (RI) is a cognitive-based, peer-to-peer support group. It addresses both mental health and addiction issues. Started in 1937, it offers techniques for coping with nervous reactions and feelings that accompany them.

Celebrate Recovery is a Christ-centered 12-step program started in 1991. It focuses on the 12 steps of AA and supports the steps with biblical references. They center their program on the Eight Beatitudes, blessings recounted by Jesus in the Sermon on the Mount in the Gospel of Matthew.

Moderation Management is a harm reduction program. They set goals to moderate drinking, rather than abstain. They pursue moderate, responsible drinking and provide tools to support that lifestyle.

These groups are not the only recovery groups available. They are, at this writing, the most well-known groups. The growth of technology has allowed us to reach areas we never have in the past. This is a great advantage for those in recovery. Almost all of these groups allow online meetings.

Styles of groups can vary even within the same organization offering the group. Moderators and support group facilitators can have varying focuses and styles. Group leaders and attendees can create their own unique presentation in a group. Group dynamics, the timing, and topics can make a group different from one meeting to the next. If you are open to support groups, we would recommend giving a group several tries before decide on how well it fits for you. A change of locations (facilitators and group members) can make a significant difference in the dynamics of a group. AA and NA meetings can be especially different as they offer more varieties of meetings than other support groups. Some meetings focus on specific steps while others focus more on speakers, or the traditions of AA.

Support groups are not for everyone. There are several studies that show people can stop using on their own without support groups (Bai, 2011; Finney, Hahn, & Moos, 1996). However, support, connection, validation, and accountability are helpful starts. This can be particularly useful in early recovery. Potential participants should research which group best fits their needs. If spirituality and religion are important, AA and Celebrate Recovery would most likely be a better fit. For a direct, problem-solving approach, Smart Recovery, Secular Organization for Sobriety, and LifeRing could be a better fit. Women for Sobriety could be helpful for a woman in recovery addressing self-worth issues. If online groups are not for you, then location and availability would be a deciding factor.

Support groups do have mixed results. It is difficult to track long term outcomes as members come and go. Longitudinal studies are also difficult to manage due to the anonymity of the groups. There are studies that stress the importance of establishing a sober support group in recovery (Laudet, Savage, and Mahmood, 2007; Tracy & Wallace, 2016). Another study shows evidence for reduced relapse rates and improved social supports from peer-led support groups (Mental Health America, 2018).

Substance abusers have often driven away their sober support systems. They may have made conscious and unconscious efforts to separate themselves from their friends and family. In support groups, they will usually find a network of individuals who will be more forgiving and have less of a history with the user. The support group tends to be more willing to accept the recovering user. The costs, accessibility, and availability are additional advantages. Lastly, guilt and shame are emotions abusers struggle with, especially in early recovery. In support group settings, it can be easier to talk and address these feelings knowing others share their struggles.

Figure 3.2

Chapter 18: Motivation, Setting a Goal

Many users are understandably ambivalent about giving up their use. Substances can bring temporary relief of negative feelings, create a feeling of social connectivity, provide relief from boredom, or offer other perceived benefits. As previously discussed, using is sometimes self-medication for an underlying mental health issue. Yet as consequences pile up, it becomes more difficult to avoid reality.

Most people are aware of their self-talk or internal dialogue. We all have our own inner voice. Addicts and alcoholics struggle with that voice as they try to maintain control of their drinking. It urges them to keep using and downplays the consequences associated with use. This relationship becomes a dance with both sides fighting to lead (**Figure 3.3**). The dance comprises internal bargaining (with themselves), excuses, and rationalizations. Some come to terms with the fact that they are no longer leading. They realize that the perceived benefits of using are no longer worth the consequences. Those individuals leave the dance floor and end their relationship with substances.

Figure 3.3

Motivation to stop may wax and wane for substance abusers. They might increasingly minimize or deny their use and the impact it has on their life. If they are forced into therapy by a spouse, they will try to throw the spotlight back on their spouse. Accurate substance abuse histories can be very difficult to obtain, even for the seasoned substance abuse counselor. It takes great effort and patience to collect data from reluctant patients. The abuser avoids specifics for fear that complete disclosure would box them into a corner. They meet firm commitments to stop using with ambiguity and loopholes (**Figure 3.4**).

Figure 3.4

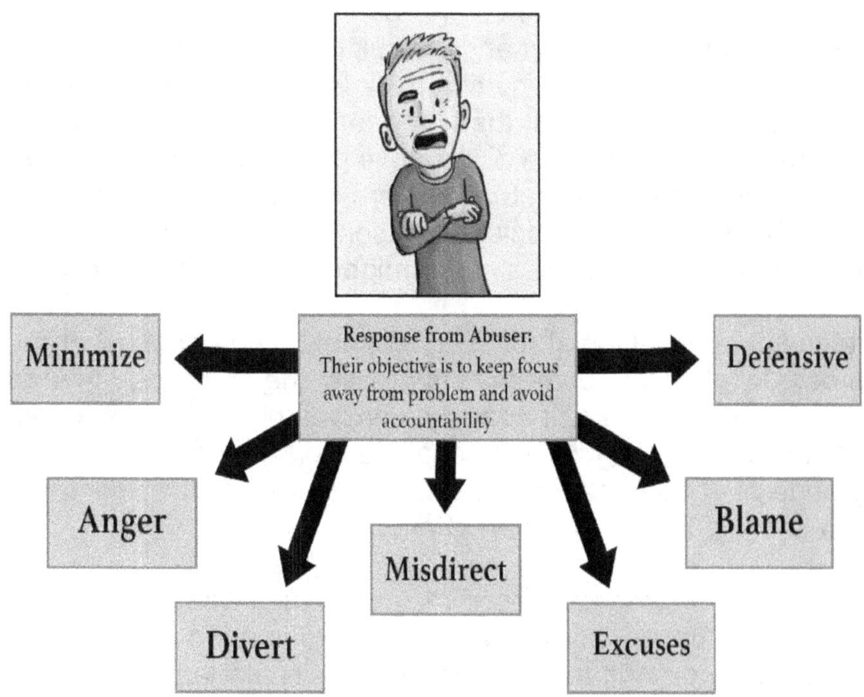

An abuser can also become very persuasive not only to significant others but to professionals as well. The vaguer they are about their use, the harder it is to hold them accountable. For example:

Wife: "Your drinking is a problem. I want you to stop."
Husband: "Ok, I will cut back."

Or

Therapist: "How often do you drink?"
Client (abuser): "I drink socially, not as much as some of my friends."

Or

Supervisor: "I have noticed a drop in your performance lately. You look hung-over. You smell of alcohol. You need help."
Employee (abuser): "I need more sleep. My drinking is not a problem. I have slowed down lately."

The key words in the above scenarios are "cut back," "not as much," and "slowed down." These are subjective terms and difficult to quantify. For example, if they are drinking a case of beer a day, cutting back is anything below that amount, and 22 cans of beer a day is fewer than 24 beers. "Drinking socially" is also difficult to define, as it is relative. A 6'5" man is usually considered very tall, however, if he hung out with basketball players, he would likely be slightly below average in height. If someone's social circle consists of heavy users, then consuming anything less than one's peers might seem normal or even moderate.

The importance of goal setting in recovery cannot be emphasized enough for all family members involved in treatment. Otherwise, the addict and their family may have different goals. Therefore, if a family member thinks their loved one has committed to abstaining, they will expect abstention. All participants will view the drinking episode as a failed attempt at sobriety. However, the user may be committed to drinking less rather than attempting to stop.

In our previous chapters, we discussed the challenges with defining substance abuse. Timing, life situation, age, and other factors need to be considered. Relapse is a similarly difficult term to define. What is a relapse? Does it matter if the person who has allegedly relapsed sees himself or herself as relapsing? This leads us to another thought puzzle.

Is water wet? At first this seems like a common-sense question. Water is wet, of course. If we feel moisture on something, it is by definition wet. Right? However, there is another side to this question. Wet is a sensation and water itself does not create that sensation. Snow and ice do not create the same wet sensation the liquid form does. Therefore, we could describe water in other states as dry.

This thought puzzle helps us think about relapse. There is not an easy answer. Can we consider reductions in the frequency and intensity of using a successful recovery? Addicts can stop their use, but if they return to using again, without experiencing the same consequences, can we still consider that a relapse? If someone who drank whiskey and became a furious drunk, then switched to drinking beer and no longer became angry when drinking, is that a relapse? It is important to understand the reason why someone returned to use. The focus of discussion or treatment approach can be significantly different based on the reason for relapse. **Figure 3.5**

Figure 3.5

Using Episode	
A using episode (either drug or alcohol) is defined as either a relapse or return to use. It is possible that at some point the user may move from one label to another, it is not always static. What helps distinguish the difference is prior to the using episode, how would they categorize themselves (relapse or return to use), and how they view the using episode after the fact. It is common for a person to start building up to a change in commitment about being abstinent. For example, a week prior to use they may be committed to avoiding use. However, through a series of events, they change their commitment and use. The areas listed below help distinguish whether a person relapsed or just decided to return to drug and alcohol use.	
RELAPSE	**DECISION TO USE**
Thoughts: "I don't want to use," "I want to stop," "my use is a problem," "I feel bad about using." **Behaviors**: Making an active commitment to avoid use, conscious of using situations. **Motivation**: Does not want to use. **Attitude after use:** "I was making an effort to stop and messed up," "I did not anticipate problems." **Emotions after use:** Feel guilty.	**Thoughts**: "Using is no problem," "I want to cut back but not stop," "it is okay to use every now and then," "my use is not a problem." **Behaviors:** No changes from when first using, actions geared more toward hiding use then stopping use. **Motivation**: Low. **Attitude after use:** "I got caught," "no big deal." **Emotions after use**: Irritated that being questioned about use. Awkward that they were caught, defensive.
When a using episode occurs, it is important to evaluate where you see yourself. If you view yourself presently as seeing the episode as a **relapse**, efforts would need to be focused on relapse prevention. If you see yourself in the **decision to use** column, focus your efforts on reexamining the costs and benefits to use, including what brought you into therapy in the first place.	

Motivation to change substance abusing patterns can be broken into stages of change. Each level involves a different level of commitment from the abuser and different roles a therapist would play depending on the stage of change. Prochaska, Norcross, and DiClemente, a team of Psychology Professors, present six key stages of change in their 1994 book *Changing for Good*:

1. Not seeing yourself as having a problem (Precontemplation)
2. Seeing a possible problem (Contemplation)
3. Identifying a problem and preparing to do something about it (Preparation)
4. Taking action to overcome a behavior (Action)
5. Maintaining behaviors and self-control to sustain changes (Maintenance)
6. Leaving the problem altogether (Termination)

These are important stages to understand both for the professional and family members. For the professional, interventions geared toward one stage would be ineffective if a client is at a different stage. For instance, a therapist can offer suggestions on how to attend a sober support groups (Action stage). However, for someone who does not see themselves as having a problem (Precontemplation), this would miss the mark. Understanding these stages can be helpful for families when identifying what change they hope to see happen when a loved one enters counseling. These stages are further broken down in figure 3.9(Chapter 19)

This does not mean that mandated therapy will never work. Our next chapter discusses the pros and cons of mandated counseling. However, it is important to understand the potential mismatch in goals and expectations of all parties involved.

For those ready to act to stop their use, setting goals is essential in recovery. Visualizing a goal, and sharing it with others, will increase chances for success. A clear goal is especially important to overcome the struggle to remain sober. In early recovery, individuals often talk themselves back into using. Their ambivalence could slowly build up as they face the challenges of stopping their use. It could start with making "just-this-once" exceptions to their commitment to stay abstinent. An example would be someone who believes that there is an occasion that lends itself to a onetime exception to their goal of stopping their drinking or drug use. These exceptions become the rule and often lead them right back to where they started.

Effective goal setting includes:

- Identify your substance use as a problem. This will give you a focus. This moves you away from making excuses and deflecting the issue. Now you see your use as a problem and are committing to doing something about it.

- Accountability for your addiction.
- Building back trust in relationships.
- Taking charge of your life.
- Finding a tool to counter the using voice.

If abstinence is the goal, that decision leads to other goals. For example, let's say someone sets a goal of abstinence. That person hopefully realizes that he or she will have difficulty being around the same peer group and stopping use. Now they see a new goal of replacing a using peer group with a sober one.

Other goals that develop for a commitment to abstinence include addressing mental health issues that substances may mask. Shifting focus from substances to a non-using lifestyle may include a plan for improving exercise, diet, and even new career goals. Often addicts and alcoholics do not realize how consuming their addiction was and what new doors open for them once they commit to sobriety. In previous chapters, we have presented the challenges to recovery and specific areas that are impacted by addictions. Addressing these areas can involve their own goals. We have included a goal setting worksheet for readers to use in their recovery in our section 3 chapter (Motivation and Setting a Goal).

When setting goals:

- Make them specific (this leads to more accountability).
- Include steps to obtain the goal. Just stating that you want to stop using may not be enough. Lay out a plan to achieve the goal to make success more likely.
- Include others in your goal. Additional support can be helpful.
- Recognize the challenges that will present themselves in early recovery. If you must give up friends, include developing new friends in your goals.
- Goals should be reliant on your behavior alone and not dependent on others.
- Include short-term steps. Since abstinence is a lifetime pursuit, an end date to your goal is difficult to establish. Shorter term goals can help with motivation. Recovery is a process and not an event.
- Evaluate the goals as you progress in your recovery. Changes should only be made if they support the main goal. For example, starting off with abstinence, and then changing a goal to moderation, is not advised.
- Writing down your goals can help you with being accountable to your recovery.
- Set a time to reevaluate your goals WHEN you set your goals, not after. Changes to your initial goal should be discussed with significant others and other members of your support network.

Lifelong goals are more difficult to keep and require long-term motivation. In AA, they mark sober anniversary dates with coins and recognition of the event. Unfortunately, despite our best efforts, people are not always successful in their attempts. Recovery is not always a direct route (**Figure 3.6**). If you do have a setback, keep in mind:

- **Stay positive.** Setbacks happen.
- **Don't give up.** It is not unusual for people to have setbacks. In recovery, what becomes problematic is when individuals slip and just give up on recovery. Or if they beat themselves up creating more despair and losing motivation.
- **Be honest and open to others about your slip.** If you keep it a secret it can create a sense of getting away with something, and feed into previous behaviors of hiding use. It will also impact trust with others.
- **Reevaluate your plan.** Determine what went wrong. Relapses do not happen spontaneously. Either an over or underestimation of part(s) of your plan contributed to the setback. If your plan involved controlling your use, it may be time to consider plan B, abstinence.
- **Understand your support systems.** A difficult part of recovery is making the lifestyle changes to sustain goals. This could include new peer groups and relationships. If you are doing a recovery plan without professional help or support, the addition of one or both will be helpful.

Figure 3.6

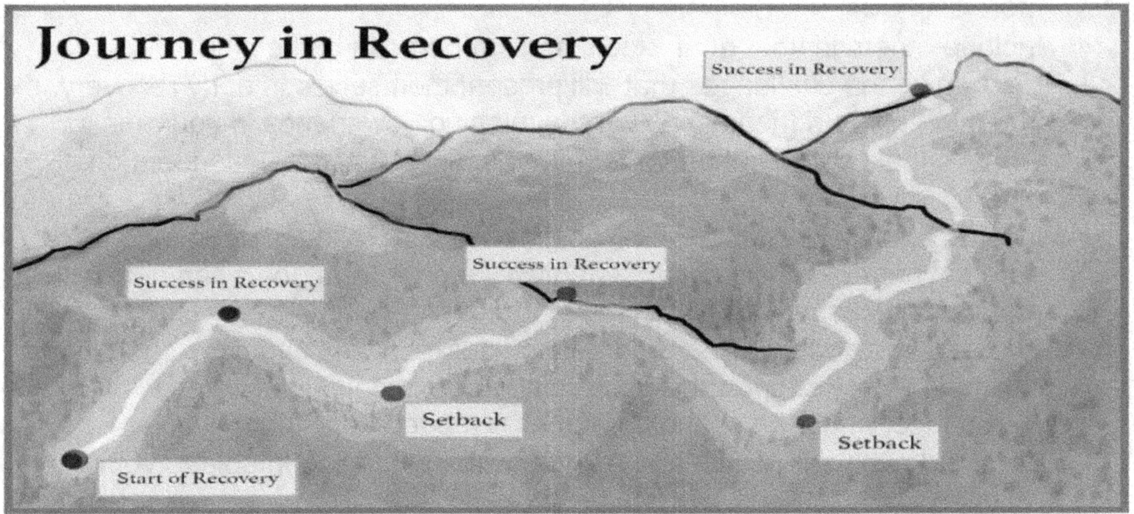

We already discussed how addicts struggle with a harmful inner voice. There are different names associated with this voice: Stinking Thinking, Addictive Voice, Unhelpful Voice, Beast, and Faulty Thinking to name a few. For those in recovery, this voice could be especially strong. The goal of the addict's inner voice is to get the person to return to using. We will name it M.A.S.T., or **M**anipulative **A**ddictive **S**elf **T**alk. MAST will bargain, barter, and beg its way into getting someone to return to their addiction. (**Figure 3.7**)

Figure 3.7

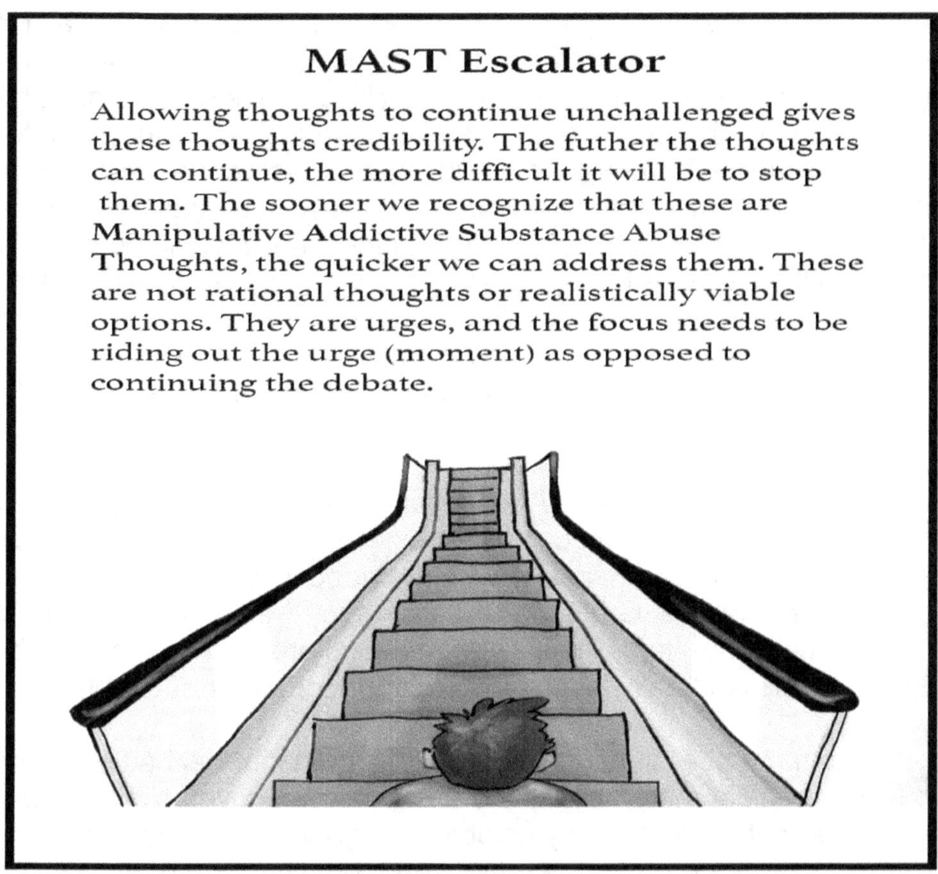

MAST can present itself in unusual ways. Some people have an internal dialogue going before they use. Self-critical thinking impacts self-confidence in recovery and leads to lack of motivation, lack of confidence, and pessimism in one's ability to remain abstinent. This self-deprecating dialogue can also present itself externally. Others will see this as being negative and may avoid you. This is a setup for relapse as it creates a self-fulfilling prophecy. Therapists also refer to this as cognitive distortion or thinking errors.

Journaling your thoughts can help with clarity and direction (covered in another section). Identifying harmful thoughts before they take over is the first step to overcoming them. There is an expression in the mental health field, "You name it, you tame it." The sooner you recognize your thoughts as self-defeating the sooner you can challenge or adjust your thoughts. This allows you the ability to recognize and challenge thoughts as thoughts rather than reality.

It is important to note that the sooner you can recognize and dismiss thoughts as MAST, the less inner turmoil you will feel. For instance, consider Ralph. Ralph is struggling with cocaine addiction. Most of the time he used, it would be at a local bar with his friends. After starting at the bar, he would go on several day long cocaine binges. Then, after several weeks of abstaining from use (and avoiding the bar), he ran into one of these friends while filling up his car at a gas station. The friend invited him for a drink at the bar, which in the past usually led to cocaine use. Ralph initially thought it would be okay, as he would order a non-alcoholic drink. He was sober for a few weeks so why not hang out with his friends? As he drove, his thoughts turned to "a few drinks would be okay." The closer he got to the bar the more convincing MAST became. A few blocks from the bar he recognized how deep he was into MAST. He was able to label it and recognize it as an urge to use and not as a realistic option. He focused on tools he had learned to address the urge rather than debate himself if going to the bar was okay.

There are other ways to address MAST. Meditation, mindfulness, yoga, and exercise are also a few tools you can use to counter MAST. Surround yourself with positive people who can help and who are good influences. Negativity feeds on not only itself but others. Gratitude can also help. We can achieve this by volunteering or helping others. Positive affirmations are also beneficial. There are many apps that will send daily inspirations to your computer or telephone.

It's important to remember that addicts are fighting an internal battle. At times, a return to using is easier than facing the challenges of recovery. That is why it is important to start out in recovery by establishing goals. Setbacks can present themselves and it is important to be patient and forgiving. Recognize and ultimately progress toward your goals.

The reasons why someone uses drugs/alcohol and/or develops a substance abuse problem is unknown. Genetics, individual personality, environment, and life experiences all influence the mental health and/or substance abuse problems. There is not always going to be one constant factor that will cause these problems to happen. It is most likely a combination of factors. It will be helpful to see the relationship with drug and/or alcohol use and mental health symptoms and how they impact the brain. Let's look at mental health concerns first.

The effects of each drug are different. The length of time and side effects experienced are unique for each drug. If the user is involved in use to offset the symptoms of a mental health issue, eventually the effects of the drug wear off. This will create the desire to use again. As this cycle of use continues, the drugs take a more prominent role. The side effects experienced from the drug itself could potentially either encourage more use to avoid the side effects they are experiencing, or the addition of a new drug to try to balance out effects. For example, if someone is experiencing depression, they may self-medicate with cocaine. As the cocaine use continues, they could turn to alcohol to help with their feelings of agitation or jitteriness they are experiencing.

Science is still working on the exact causes of mental health issues. As many strides as we have undergone in the medical field, we are still working on effective approaches to mental health struggles. The difficulties lie with the uniqueness of individuals. Although we share the same brain chemistry, there are varied factors and circumstances that will create a mental health struggle. Mental health struggles do involve changes in our brain chemistry. Substance use does as well. Individuals struggling with mental health issues are more vulnerable to abusing alcohol/drugs. Addiction and mental health illnesses both impact on our brain.

Chapter 19: Mandated vs. Voluntary Therapy

Therapy can help us navigate important life changes. It can help us make improvements to our lives and mental health. For example, therapy helps some people make decisions such as whether to stay at a job or end a relationship. It can also help us work through a tough time, deal with a mental health challenge, or simply offer support and validation. The therapist and client are usually on the same page regarding treatment goals. A client seeking therapy is motivated, and the therapist and client work collaboratively to address the presenting problem. Full disclosure about life events is forthcoming.

Not all clients are in therapy by choice, however. For one reason or another, people enter therapy because of external motivators rather than the belief that change needs to happen. These clients are mandated participants. This group includes:

- Court ordered clients (a judge orders mental health or substance abuse treatment)
- Adolescents (parents are concerned about a child's drug use, failing grades, harmful behaviors, or attitude)
- Spouses (husband or wife requests therapy as an attempt to repair relationship, even if other spouse sees no concerns in the relationship)
- Employees (a failed drug screen or concerning behavior causes the employer to require counseling)

In these cases, there is typically a disconnect between how the patient sees their use and how their spouse/parent/employer view the problem. As a result, the therapist will have a challenging job of effectively engaging the client and determining treatment goals. They will have to balance matching the needs of the client, at that time, with the external forces pressing for change. There are going to be limitations as to what can be achieved under these circumstances. There are therapeutic techniques that can address client ambivalence. Those techniques will be limited if the therapist is only given one perspective or does not have enough information. Also, both therapist and families need to understand which stage the addict/alcoholic is in. It is important to gear discussions and interventions to the user's stage of motivation. (**Figure 3.9**).

Figure 3.9

Stage of Change	Client Motivation	Therapist Intervention
Precontemplation	Individual does not see a problem. No intention of stopping.	Create conflicts or discrepancies in the way an alcoholic views the problem. Education about the issue or challenge they are facing. Explain risks and consequences.
Contemplation	Realizes there may be a problem but is not motivated to change.	Identify costs and behaviors associated with use. Identify and acknowledge barriers to change.
Preparation	Identifies that there is a problem. Prepares to take action. Commits to change.	Identify goals. Write them down. Help identify a course of action.
Action	Actively working on their problem.	Reward success. Encouragement. Support.
Maintenance	Change is being maintained. New behaviors replace old.	Develop strategies to sustain change. Continue to develop coping strategies.
Relapse (Not everyone will experience a relapse.)	Falls back into previous patterns of behavior.	Identify triggers associated with relapse. Develop a recovery plan.
Individuals may go in and out of these stages. If they relapse, they ideally learn from this experience. This learning experience can prevent a future relapse or shorten the relapse.		

Source: Prochaska & DiClemente, 1983; Prochaska, DiClemente, & Norcross, 1992

Participation in therapy does not guarantee change. Therapists struggle with family members who mandate treatment and expect immediate results. Family members (or other external motivators such as the courts or an employer) need to be involved, not only in the initial process to make sure the presenting problem is clearly defined, but periodically going forward (or regularly in some cases) to gauge progress. It is also helpful for those encouraging counseling to present consequences for the behavior to encourage accountability and change. For instance, a substance-abusing teen may not see the need to stop abusing drugs. They may be more motivated to change if there are consequences, such as losing car privileges or being grounded. A resistant spouse may see a need to change when faced with imminent divorce. Someone mandated by the courts will be motivated to avoid jail, or an employee will be motivated to keep their job. The therapist will of course attempt to convey the importance of therapy and how the client may benefit from counseling, but ultimately it is up to the client to communicate openly and honestly with the therapist.

Commitment to recovery can be difficult to gauge, even for trained professionals. A person may commit to recovery but be on the fence about stopping their use of substances. An addict may verbally present a positive picture of progress to those around him, yet still be using. Lies, broken promises, and failed attempts are common. Commitment to recovery can also wane.

For the professional, it is important to determine where their client is regarding his or her commitment to stopping use. Introducing tools and feedback at the wrong stage can be counterproductive in therapy. As we previously discussed, the six stages of change may not be a straight-forward path. For example, if someone is ambivalent in stopping their use (Contemplation), suggestions such as giving up friends who use and attending Alcoholics Anonymous would not only fall on deaf ears but would probably drive someone away from counseling. Interventions and interviewing techniques are best geared toward where the client is "at" in terms of their stage of change.

Families can benefit from this approach as well. Discussions centered on how to stop can be futile if the client does not want to change. The correct treatment setting, or approach has to match up with where a person stands in their commitment to stopping their use.

These are some points to consider for the person or place mandating therapy:

- Make your concerns clear for the therapist and client. Without your input, the client is going to state the problem differently than you see it.
- State the behaviors you want addressed clearly and focus on objective, not subjective, information. For example, expecting teenagers to understand what you mean by wanting "better behavior" is dependent on your observations and interpretations. If you ask them not to call you names, be home on time, and do chores, then they have clear behavioral expectations and goals to be met.
- Remember, initial goals will be different. The client is less likely to want change than you do. The therapist is going to need your assistance in making sure accurate information is provided.
- It is also important to understand that whatever consequences you agree on must be followed through by you. Inconsistency or lack of follow-through can affect the client's motivation and sabotage treatment.
- Therapists have limitations about what they can disclose. They are bound by confidentiality laws that prohibit them from disclosing what specifically is said in counseling. Progress or even goals cannot be shared outside the session without the client's permission. Do not expect progress reports about how well therapy is going.
- Consider counseling for yourself. Often these situations can be very stressful for family members and having your own support system can be helpful.
- Mandated therapy usually has a limited shelf life. Unless there are mutually agreed upon goals, this means at some point it can be

unproductive to continue. Therapy will need to end. Either a client's lack of participation makes further sessions unnecessary, or perhaps the client has changed for the better and counseling has been productive.

Mutually agreed upon goals between the people mandating counseling and the person seeking counseling do not necessarily have to start out the same. Therapists strive to work at a comfortable starting point for the client. They focus on behavioral changes that may eventually get everyone to the same goals. For example, a husband whose wife is unhappy with his drinking may not see his drinking as a problem. However, a therapist will help identify patterns that point to problem drinking. If his goal is to not have his wife so angry with him, eventually he can be helped to see a pattern of misuse. Presenting discrepancies in how he sees his problems can be enough to get him to invest in abstaining.

The person mandating therapy is looking for behaviors and values to change through therapy. In some instances, you can only address the behavior, but not the underlying values. For example, a wife attends counseling because her husband is concerned about her drinking. She may stop drinking not because she believes her drinking or behaviors were concerning (value), but because she does not want her husband divorcing her. Her behavior changed but not her values regarding the drinking.

The client should take into consideration:

- Misrepresenting information to your therapist will not help you. The decision to change is entirely up to you. It is important to understand that avoiding or hiding information does not mean the problem or the events that led to counseling will go away.
- It is not about being right or wrong but what is expected of you. For instance, we can argue about if marijuana use is harmful or not. However, the argument is irrelevant if your next drug screen comes up positive and you are terminated from your job.
- Your sincerity about change will be determined in time. If you are not sincere, it will become evident to all parties and you will eventually experience the consequences of your actions.
- There is a reason you were asked to attend counseling. This could be an appropriate time for you to do your own self-evaluation.
- Therapy can help you to prepare for the consequences if you choose not to change. This could be an opportunity to evaluate life decisions and direction in life. It can also assist you with moving forward with the consequences of your decision (seeking a new job, experiencing a divorce, moving out of your parent's home if of legal age).

Everyone has choices in life. Not everyone has numerous choices or great choices, but there are still choices nonetheless. Decisions will need to be made by family members or employers in the case of a refusal or inability to change. Both the mandated client and the one encouraging therapy need to consider their "end of the line" point. Therapy is not a miracle cure. Wonderful benefits can happen through therapy but there are many factors to consider when thinking about your expectations. The least therapy could offer is the opportunity for change. A door is opened, and in the best circumstances, the mandated client walks through it. Goals are established and met.

Let's look at Wendy. Wendy is a local sales rep for a manufacturing company. She has been with her company for several years and has a solid work history. She was in good standing with the company and enjoyed her work. Her job did not require overnight travel but during the day it was common for her to meet and dine with clients. One day Wendy was asked to meet with Human Resources and her supervisor. Management was concerned over a report that Wendy was noticeably intoxicated during a meeting she had with one of her customers. Even more concerning was that fact that she drove under the influence back and forth from the meeting. Wendy acknowledged she drank but she did not believe she was drunk. The company's policy required her to be evaluated by the Employee Assistance Program. Wendy acknowledged that she drank daily and had one or two drinks during the day to ease her stress. She also recalled that some of her family members were concerned about her drinking. Wendy felt that her drinking was not a problem and that she did not need to drink. After meeting with the evaluator, he recommended 10 additional sessions to educate her about the problems associated with drinking and further assess her relationship with alcohol. As a condition of her employment, she reluctantly agreed to continue with sessions with the Employee Assistance Program (EAP) therapist.

During her sessions, she was asked to stop drinking as long as she was in the EAP. The total time with the EAP was 15 months as sessions were spread out. During this time Wendy struggled with stopping and recognized how much a part of her life drinking had become. She learned that drinking did not need to be an important part of her life and a return to drinking, even if moderating her drinking was possible, was not worth the risks. She decided to continue to remain abstinent after the EAP sessions were over. Wendy learned new coping skills and created an alcohol-free lifestyle.

We could also see the limitations of mandated counseling without some accountability built into it. Rick would be a good example. Rick, a 32 year old, also did not enter counseling on his own. Rick's family strongly encouraged him to seek counseling. He presented that his wife was concerned about his drinking. Rick chose an agency near his home and explained to his counselor that he was getting into arguments with his wife and felt she was picking on him. He acknowledged that his wife brought up concerns about his drinking but that is "par for the course as she complains about everything." Rick stated that his wife was controlling, never satisfied, and verbally abusive to him. She made things up just to complain. Forcing him to go to therapy was another sign that she was a "nut job." He told the counselor that his wife refused to go to counseling with him because he is the problem. Rick stated that he drinks, but only has a few drinks and did not see his drinking as the issue. Rick and the therapist spend the next several sessions discussing his wife, how he could cope with such as a stressful home environment, and strategies to address her "control issues."

After several weeks of going to counseling by himself, Rick and his wife Beth greeted Rick's therapist in the waiting room. She attended the session, much to Rick's dismay, to see how and what he was doing in counseling. During their session, she presented the counselor information that conflicted with Rick's presentation. She discussed numerous situations where Rick's drinking was problematic. He had legal problems because of his drinking. He was fired because of his alcohol use and was drinking every night until he passed out. Rick tried defending himself saying he only had three to four drinks a night. His wife presented those drinks were in 10-ounce containers and were vodka. Furthermore, the container was over three-quarters filled with alcohol. His three to four drinks a night was approximately 20 ounces of alcohol. This was the equivalent of thirteen shots per night. Beth also informed the counselor that Rick told her that the therapist agreed his wife was overbearing and controlling. This meeting provided Beth and his therapist new information about Rick's commitment to stop drinking. Periodically, Beth would attend sessions with Rick to ensure accurate reporting. Rick was compliant with stopping his drinking. And Beth understood that his motivation lay solely on her dissatisfaction and possible divorce if he continued to drink. Eventually, Rick came to an understanding that his drinking was not only destructive to his marriage but other life areas as well. He also realized it was all or nothing for him. If he drank some, he would drink a lot, often not stopping until he was passed out.

Chapter 20: Harm Reduction

Most recovery programs focus on abstinence. Yet substance abuse counseling has come a long way since its inception. Harm reduction is one approach to substance abuse that seeks to diminish the dangers involved in using. The concept of harm reduction includes needle exchange programs for heroin users, supervised locations where users can shoot heroin (lowering their risk for overdosing), controlled drinking, switching from hard liquor to beer, and additional measures that try to lower risks associated with continued drug or alcohol use.

For recreational drugs, this may mean a medication-assisted regimen. We will discuss this in greater detail in Chapter 22. Risks of overdose are too great to suggest simply moderating drug use. We recommend professional guidance for those deciding on this route. There is always an inherent risk with taking mood altering substances without supervision. The inconsistent makeup of street drugs provides a greater risk of overdosing. These drugs are not regulated and what you get with street drugs is not always guaranteed (actual dosage, inclusion of other drugs to increase the high, etc.).

For drinking, harm reduction is synonymous with moderation or controlled drinking. The most well-known support group for this approach is Moderation Management (MM). They offer an alternative to abstinence and believe that problem drinkers should have a choice in how they approach their problem. For MM, moderation is not necessarily the final goal, and their own estimate is that 30% of their members go on abstinence-based programs ("What is Moderation Management?" n.d.). However, they believe that moderation is an achievable goal for many problem drinkers.

Controlled drinking is not an option agreed upon by all professionals. It continues to find its place in the treatment field. Clinically, this can be a tougher road to pursue than abstaining. For example, picture riding a bicycle down a hill. As you start down the hill, the bicycle, its speed, and the rider must all be managed at once to achieve the safest descent. Physics will make the bike go faster and faster. The rider must simultaneously manage his speed going down the hill (or controlling his use) and prepare for a safe stop as the bike hurdles toward the bottom (the urge to continue drinking). Because the bike is already in motion when it is time to stop, it will be hard to stop. Great effort and skill are needed to stop drinking when you are already in motion.

Drinkers also need to recognize what makes up a drink. A standard drink is any drink that contains about 0.6 ounces of pure alcohol (**Figure 3.10**). If the drink is 8 ounces of rum and 4 ounces of cola that is approximately five standard drinks. Individuals with alcohol problems who limit their drinking to a couple drinks a night might convince themselves that they are only having two drinks. When we do substance abuse evaluations, we try to gather information on how much individuals are drinking. The amounts usually change when we start pursuing how much hard liquor is in "a drink." Once we get into alcohol content and how much is in the drink, the actual number of drinks increases. Users do this consciously or subconsciously to try to protect their drinking as they know that full disclosure threatens their relationship with alcohol.

Figure 3.10

Standard Drink

| 5% Alcohol Content | 7% Alcohol Content | 12% Alcohol Content | 40%+ Alcohol Content |

For beer, the approximate number of drinks (SD) in

12 oz = 1 SD
16 oz = 1.3 SD

For malt liquor, the approximate number of standard drinks in

12 oz = 1.5 SD
16 oz = 2 SD

For table wine, the approximate number of standard drinks in

5 oz = 1 SD

For 80-proof spirits, the approximate number of standard drinks in

1.5 oz (shot) = 1 SD

A standard drink in the United States is any drink that contains about 14 grams of pure alcohol (about 0.6 fluid ounces or 1.2 tablespoons)

Most of our clients who try controlled drinking eventually choose abstinence. If you go down this path, we recommend the following:

- Establish a clear goal of how much and how often you will drink. This includes specific amounts.
- Keep track of this goal in a convenient location. Research phone apps with reminders that can help you monitor your use.
- This goal should involve keeping track of daily and weekly totals. It is important to determine how risky your drinking patterns were before moderation.
- Assess which situations can lead to going beyond your limit. This would include people, places, events, and moods.
- Pace yourself and plan out an evening of drinking. This could include drinking nonalcoholic beverages in between drinks.
- Exceptions become the rule. Stick to a goal. Any deviation of that goal (no matter how slight) is considered falling short of the goal. Holidays, birthdays, and other special occasions will come and go. Allowing yourself to exceed the limit will only give you permission for other special occasions.
- Eating before drinking can help slow down the absorption of alcohol into the system. If you drink on an empty stomach and

become intoxicated or tipsy before reaching your limit, this state of mind increases the likelihood of exceeding your limit.

- Moderation Management recommends a month of complete abstinence before starting the moderation plan.
- If you are not able to adhere to these goals, consider plan B (abstinence). Moderation is only a suggested course of action if there are not high risks involved with drinking. If there are health concerns or safety issues (drinking and driving, operating machinery) or dangerous interactions with prescription medication, then abstinence is the recommended course of action.

"If I only knew yesterday what I know today, I would have played different lottery ticket numbers." Most people would like to have the ability to see into the future. Unfortunately, we cannot predict results of events or situations in our lives. We need to experientially go through processes to better understand our choices. For some, moderation may work. For others, it can be a steppingstone to committing to abstaining. Our next section will focus on making an abstinence plan, but first let us consider what makes up Heaps of Sand.

Chapter 21: Deciding What to Do

Our next thought puzzle brings us to the Sorites Paradox, which references the Greek word for heap. We start out with a heap of sand. If we remove one grain of sand, is it still a heap? The answer would be yes. The removal of one grain will not change the characteristics of the heap. Most would still see it as a heap. If we remove two or three more grains, will the heap no longer be a heap? At some point, we will have removed enough grains for most people to no longer see the sand as a heap. Heap is an imprecise description and will appear different from one observer to another. If we see a larger pile of sand or we had seen this heap of sand diminish since its inception, our views may be different.

The same thoughts present themselves with substance abuse. When have enough issues presented themselves to become a recognizable problem? Professionals use several screening tools to help assess drug and alcohol problems including AUDIT, CRAFFT, CAGE, BSTAD, Addiction Severity Index (ASI), Substance Involvement (SI), and Drug Alcohol Screening Test (DAST). Professionals administer and interpret these tests.

Self-administered tests are abundant on the internet. An interactive test administered by the National Institute of Drug Abuse covers both drug and alcohol use (NIDA, n.d.-a). These tests can provide you with more insight into your problem. The following are also considerations to examine in determining if you have a substance abuse problem (either alcohol or drugs):

- Have you wanted to cut down on your use but not been successful?
- When you have stopped using/drinking, have you experienced trouble sleeping, shakiness, nausea, racing heart, seizures, or sensing things that were not there (symptoms of withdrawal)?

- Have you used/drank in dangerous situations? Put yourself or others at risk?
- Have you had memory loss in the last six months because of your use/drinking?
- Do you continue to drink/use even after it creates problems with your family or friends?
- Have you ever hidden your use from others?
- Has your use interfered with social, family, school, or employment?
- Have you experienced legal trouble because of use?
- Have you lied about using? This would include under-reporting how much you are using or used.
- Have you given up activities because of your use? Or, do you plan your activities around your use?
- Have you experienced health concerns because of your use? Or been told by a medical professional you should stop?
- Do you spend a lot of time thinking about when you can next use/drink?

A yes to any of these questions would indicate a concern. We have discussed in previous chapters how substances take over someone's entire life. The next step, if you are still on the fence, is to complete a cost-benefit analysis regarding your decision to stop using (**Figure 3.11**).

Figure 3.11

Cost Benefit Worksheet			
This worksheet will help you understand what you enjoy about your use and the costs of continuing it. When completing this worksheet, weigh the benefits and costs of your use on a 1 to 3 scale with the highest value as 3 and lowest as 1. This is not a ranking system. The worksheet could include several 1's, 2's, or 3's.			
Benefits	**Value 1-3**	**Cost**	**Value 1-3**

If you decide that you have a problem and controlled use is not an option, the next logical step would be stopping your substance abuse. If that decision is made, you can keep the cost benefit worksheet as a guide. This could help address future struggles and challenges. If you move forward and commit to abstinence, this allows you to stay focused on what you need to do rather than revisiting and deliberating that decision. It is not unusual in early recovery to struggle with sobriety. This struggle leads to ambivalence. Having this worksheet available will help with motivation and focus. Also, we stress the importance in making sure there will be medical issues (physical reactions or detox from substances) that present themselves. If in doubt, we strongly suggest you contact a physician. This is particularly important when withdrawal issues are a concern. The Change Plan Worksheet (**Figure 3.12**) is a helpful next step. This solidifies the direction and lays out a plan.

Figure 3.12

Change Plan

I have decided it is in my best interest to make a change in my life. I commit to the following behavioral change (if there is more than one change you are seeking; we advise you to include it on a separate Change Plan):

The reason I want to make the change is:

____

____

I identify the following obstacles in implementing my change plan (include people, places, things and if it applies, past events/situations that interfered with achieving change):
1. ____
2. ____
3. ____

The steps I plan to take to achieve change include:

1. ____
2. ____
3. ____

The behaviors that will support this change include:

1. ____
2. ____
3. ____

The following people will help support my goals:

1. ____
2. ____
3. ____

These are indications that I know my plan is working:

1. ____
2. ____
3. ____

It is important to understand what function your use offered you. The next worksheet, Functional Analysis Worksheet (**Figure 3.13**) will help identify areas to address once you stop using. Using drugs or alcohol offered some benefit. You will need to fill gaps in once you stop. These gaps could be minor adjustments or significant lifestyle changes.

(Figure 3.13)

Functional Analysis of Use	
People I used with	
Places I used	
Events I used at	
Moods I was in **before** I used	Sad, happy, angry, bored, stressed, anxious, annoyed, playful, worried, confident, confused, lonely, _____, _____,
Moods I was in **after** I used	Sad, happy, angry, bored, stressed, anxious, annoyed, playful, worried, confident, confused, lonely, _____,

After completing this worksheet, you can work on a Goal Sheet (**Figure 3.14**). This is helpful in not only organizing your goals but assigning tasks to complete those goals. It also works as a road map to recovery. There are additional tools that can aid in this journey. This would include the Urge Card (**Figure 3.15**) and Trigger Worksheet (**Figure 3.16**). As previously mentioned, the quicker we recognize urges for what they are (MAST trying to convince you to return to use) the sooner you can tap into your toolbox.

Considering each of the following life areas below, list the current state of your life and the life you would wish for yourself. It is important that you be as specific as possible. The more measurable the goals, the more likely we can achieve them. An important starting point is understanding what you would like changed.

Life Areas
- Physical: health, wellness
- Emotional: self-image, attitudes, behaviors
- Recreational: social
- Family: spouse, children, parents, siblings
- Employment
- Spiritual: religion, spirituality

Figure 3.14

The Goal Tree includes the following worksheet to be completed in order.
When you are completing this section, do not just right the opposite in each column. Try to be specific and picture the way you want things. State it in a positive way.

Presently, this is where things are:	This is the way I would like things to be:

In the columns below list what your life would be like if your situation did not change. In the second column, indicate what change would mean for you.

What will my life look like if it stays the way it is?	What will my life look like if I change?

Once you complete the portions above, pick a goal you would want to work on first. Once you set a goal, list the steps to complete the goal. It is common for new goals to develop in starting the goal tree. For instance, getting to the gym could create another challenge regarding scheduling time. It is important not to stray too of course.

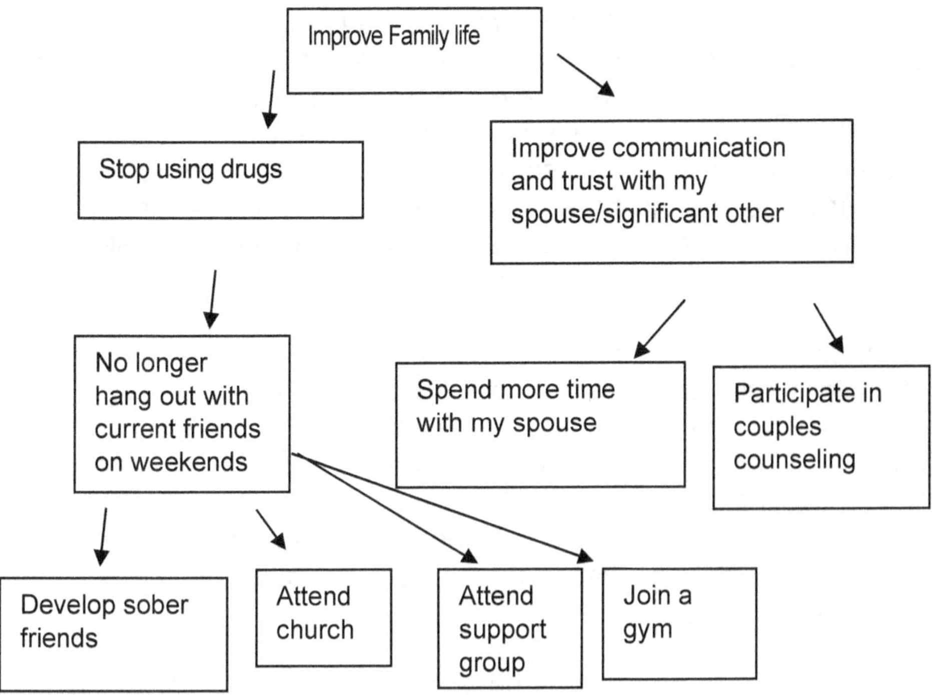

 Next, choose tasks that will help you achieve your goal. Make sure they are measurable and achievable.

Task	Date to be done

Energy is best spent dealing with the urge rather than debating your choice to stop. Imagine if a 4-year-old asked a parent if they could have a big piece of chocolate cake right before dinner. Most parents (we would hope) would say no. For the less assertive parent, they may try to give reasons to explain the decision. Cake will ruin your appetite, it is unhealthy, not a good diet choice, etc. The longer this discussion continues, the longer the child will focus on getting that piece of cake. There is no information out there that would get the child to see the merit in not having that piece of cake before dinner. 4-year-olds want what they want, and logic does not have a place in this discussion. Also, if the dialogue continues, the child may believe the parent can be convinced. However, if the parent states a firm no, and there is not a dialogue, the child can focus his or her energy on something else.

The same applies to the substance abuser. If we recognize the moment as an urge, then we can work on riding out the urge. It is not productive to debate and revisit a decision you have already made (abstinence). This is what keeps the cycle of addiction going. Addicts and alcoholics keep repeating the same behavior and hoping for different results. The sooner someone can make the shift and focus on dealing with the urge rather than debating their use the better.

At some point, a person pursuing abstinence will find him or herself in a situation where others are using or drinking. The person may indirectly feel urges or feel pressured to join in. Self-talk under these circumstances should be direct, concise, and clear. Avoid the need to come up with different reasons not to partake in using. You do not need to convince others of your position. You are not asking them to explain why they are using or drinking or to defend themselves about their choices. All you need to do is inform them of your decision not to use. They could ask you why you are deciding not to use in a dozen different ways. Do not feel the need to come up with different reasons for making your choice. All they must do is honor, not agree with, your decision. If they persist, change the topic or walk away. This is not an argument you need to win.

125

Figure 3.15

Trigger Worksheet	
Internal triggers are emotions or feelings that can create urges to use drugs or alcohol. They could be positive emotions or negative ones.	
External triggers are people, places, events, things, or situations that can create an urge to use. Most of the time they are predictable.	
Date of Trigger	
Situation	
Internal or external trigger	
Thoughts associated with trigger	
How strong was the thought (1 being least strong and 10 most strong)?	
How long did it last?	
How did it end?	
What can I do to address this trigger, make it less intense, or avoid it all together in the future?	

Figure 3.16

<table>
<tr><td>

Guide to Handling Urges to Use

Feeling the urge to use\drink is common among those in recovery, especially during the initial stages. Urges can be set off internally or externally. There are some triggers that we can predict, others seem to come out of nowhere. Other urges can be the result of self-talk. "I know this will be too difficult to do without using," "There is no way I can stop myself from drinking when I go there." As time passes, provided you do not give in to the urge and use, they will go away. The further along you are in your recovery, the more skillful you will be in not only predicting triggers but managing them when they present themselves.

- Predict and plan for elevated risk situations.
- Plan strategies to address urges. This includes transportation (having no ride home from party) and supportive people who you surround yourself with.
- Recognize how your own self-talk contributes to your struggle. Challenge these thoughts.
- Ride the wave. Remember the urge will be short-lived. It will pass.
- Solicit help. If you are experiencing an urge, reach out to someone who can talk you off the ledge.
- Download an app for your cell phone. This can help ground you in sober thoughts.
- Remind yourself of the costs of giving in to the urge.
- Leave the situation. The longer you stay in the moment (urge) the more likely you will give in to it.

</td></tr>
</table>

Figure 3.17

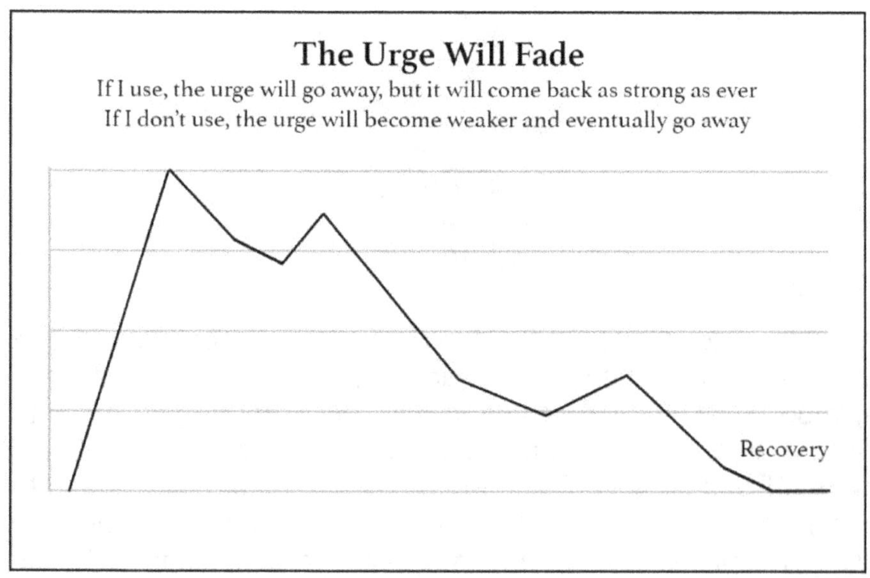

We cannot always predict when a trigger may present itself. Our brains as well as situations lend themselves to some unpredictability. In recovery, it is important to stay in black and white thinking. A well laid out recovery plan can help you stay on that path. When urges present themselves, develop a strategy to address them. We already discussed problems that substance abuse either masks or creates, from poor nutrition to sleep deprivation. We will address each of these areas in turn and offer tools for a healthier lifestyle.

Chapter 22: Medication Assisted Treatment (MAT)

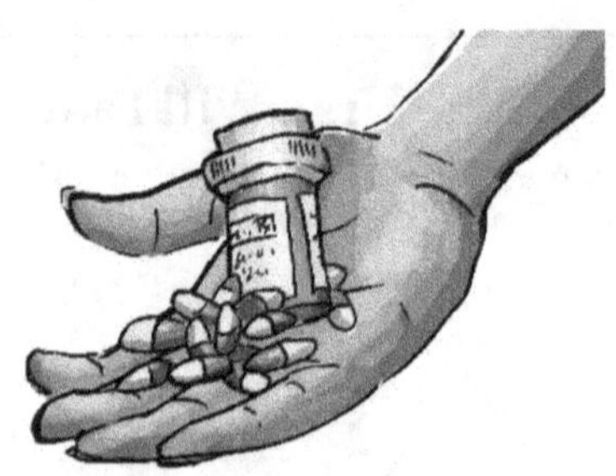

Prior to the mid-to-late 1990's, the recovery field generally frowned on the use of any type of medication to aid with abuse treatment. Many looked at medication skeptically, even though pharmaceutical aids have been used to treat substance abuse for over 100 years. Sigmund Freud, in the 1880s, touted the benefits of cocaine to treat alcoholism and morphine addiction. There have been medical advancements since then, and in recent years Medication Assisted Treatment (MAT) for substance abuse has met greater acceptance. A doctor is required to administer these medications, although this can vary from state to state. With some medications, a special additional license in addiction is needed.

Most studies support the effectiveness of MAT, showing that it can lead to longer stays in treatment, fewer high-risk HIV behaviors, reduced criminal behavior, and longer duration of abstinence (Bruce, 2010; Fullerton et al., 2014). There is a greater likelihood of success for MAT participants if they have a stable job and good support systems. In **figure 3.18** we have listed the different medications available (at this writing) that can assist individuals struggling with addiction.

Often when following a detox or maintenance regimen for addiction, no additional counseling or support is offered. This is one of the current shortcomings in the addiction field. There is limited effectiveness in MAT without adjunct services. We therefore strongly recommend behavioral counseling in addition to this treatment approach, especially in the beginning stages of recovery.

If you pursue this route, it is important that you and your doctor discuss specific treatment goals. Timelines may be difficult to establish as individual reactions, motivation, and challenges in recovery are difficult to predict at the onset of therapy. Therefore, tapering off drugs using MAT can take a substantial amount of time. It is important that you and the psychiatrist prescribing the medication have an open dialogue. Discuss with him or her how long you would be on the medication. The time on the medications could range from weeks to years to sometimes indefinite use.

Figure 3.18

Medication	Uses	Effects	Treatment Goal
Buprenorphine (Subutex) Probuphine	Opioid withdrawal, cravings	Minimizes the effects of the high and helps suppress the cravings. There is potential for misuse.	Maintenance, Abstinence, Withdrawal
Naltrexone (Vivitrol)	Opioid withdrawal, cravings	Opioid antagonist. Minimal side effects compared to heroin.	Maintenance, Abstinence, Withdrawal
Suboxone or Zubsolv	Opioid withdrawal, cravings	Combination of Naltrexone & Buprenorphine. Can reduce withdrawal and cravings. Blocks the effect of the high.	Withdrawal and cravings. Zusolv is a tablet while Subix Maintenance, Abstinence
Methadone	Opioid withdrawal, cravings	Methadone is used to decrease the side effects of opioid withdrawal. Used since 1965. Acts as a mild sedative. High abuse potential.	Maintenance, Abstinence, Withdrawal
Narcan (naloxone)	Opioid overdose	Used to treat heroin overdoses. Blocks the effects of opioids and reverses an overdose.	Survival

It is difficult to categorize the treatment goal of opioid addiction medications. The goals of the addict and the doctor administering are not always the same. Some addicts may stay on it for years as a maintenance program while others use it as a steppingstone to get off all medications. Administration and convenience of taking these medications vary. Most require daily dosages and, depending on the patient and setting, can be taken at home.

Besides MAT, a doctor may prescribe psychotropic medications (prescription drugs for mental health). Symptoms of mental health issues are often masked by substance abuse. Also called dual diagnosis, we will discuss the coexistence of mental health disorders and addiction more thoroughly in the next chapter. Patients should consider the use of psychotropic medication if they were experiencing mental health issues prior to the abuse of the substance. This should also be considered if mental health symptoms continue to present themselves when drug use is stopped. In our experience, it is best to treat the addiction and mental health disorder at the same time. Using psychotropic drugs and illicit drugs at the same time is counterproductive and dangerous.

Pain management can be problematic in recovery. Since pain can be subjective, it can be difficult to assess. For example, doctors ask individuals struggling with pain to rate their pain on a 1 to 10 scale, with 10 being the highest. The numeric value the patient presents is based on their own subjective pain thresholds as well as motivation to receive the medication. Pain management drugs are highly addictive and should be used cautiously. Also, if a pain management doctor is not addressing the patient holistically, and just focusing on the pain, patients may not develop healthy coping strategies to address their pain. This can lead to a dependence on medication and inadequate coping skills.

While not applicable to everyone, we recommend exploring non-pharmaceutical approaches to pain management. This includes diet, exercise, meditation, mindfulness, and relaxation techniques, to name a few. If someone is experiencing chronic pain and a substance disorder, it would also be helpful to explore the additional possible diagnosis of depression or anxiety. The chances of mental health issues being present with someone with chronic pain and addiction is increased.

Most highly abused medications are for pain management, and as such these should be used only with great caution to address chronic health issues in addicts. These would include Vicodin, OxyContin, Demerol, Percocet, Fentanyl, Codeine, and Darvocet. Doctors, meanwhile, prescribe Ritalin (an amphetamine) and Adderall for Attention Deficit Hyperactivity Disorder, another group of prescription medication that are often abused. Most doctors are cautious in prescribing these for someone who struggles with substance abuse. Taking some of these medications can mimic the feelings from when they were using. This opens the door for a relapse.

Benzodiazepines, which include anti-anxiety medications such as Xanax, Valium, and Klonopin, also have a high abuse potential. This does not mean that they should not be prescribed. For someone who has had or is having concerns with substance abuse, however, prescribing these medications should be done with caution and monitoring. As we have discussed before, a good portion of people have problems with substance abuse through the unintentional misuse of their medications.

Note that there is a difference between psychiatrists and therapists. Psychiatrists are doctors who prescribe medication and may see the patient once every few weeks or months. In substance abuse treatment, this length of time is an eternity. A lot could happen in a few weeks and the additional support will be helpful. Therapists, meanwhile, will see their patients more frequently and for longer times. If you are seeing a psychiatrist who can see you frequently, then this should not be an issue. In Illinois (where we practice), most psychiatrists are focused exclusively on medication management.

Prescribing medications can significantly aid recovery in substance abusers. Yet they can also be counterproductive without close medical care and coordination between care providers. Finally, any MAT plan should include a major counseling or therapy component.

Chapter 23, Dual Diagnosis

There is a strong relationship between mental health problems and substance abuse. For people with both a mental health condition and a substance abuse problem, it can be difficult to identify which came first. Either condition can mask or exacerbate the symptoms of the other. Typically, both exist simultaneously and feed off each other. We call this co-occurring conditions, comorbidity or dual diagnosis.

Substance usage can create symptoms of a mental health problem, such as:

- Anxiety
- Depression
- Sleep problems
- Psychosis
- Bipolar Disorder
- Neurocognitive disorders
- Obsessive Compulsion Disorder
- Attention Deficit Hyperactivity Disorder

Symptoms can present themselves at any stage: during urges to use, while a person is feeling the effects of the drug, or after use. The likelihood of these symptoms will depend on the drug taken, the potency of the drug, length of time taking the drug, and individual makeup of the user. We know that the substance use is causing the mental health symptoms when the effects of the drugs subside and the mental health problems are no longer present.

If substance use itself is creating the problem, the focus of treatment is developing a sobriety plan. This plan would include addressing emotions common in early recovery. Anxiety in early recovery is normal and understandable. Worrying about the challenges in recovery is not only typical but a positive sign. Concern about relapsing shows that abstinence is important. Feeling sad in early recovery is also common. A relationship with drugs/alcohol is ending. Substance use served a real purpose, however damaging it may have been. The sense of loss can extend to the loss of a lifestyle revolving around using. There is likely to be some sadness when adjusting to a new lifestyle.

If substance use is in fact masking the symptoms of a mental health disorder, on the other hand, we would need to take a different treatment direction. The decision to use drugs to mask mental health problems is not always a conscious one. The chemically dependent person is not always aware of any underlying mental health condition when using. If there is any awareness, it may be the case that a user can underestimate the scope and intensity of their mental health problems. Some make a conscious decision to self-medicate to counter the effects. Using substances may serve a purpose in addressing symptoms, but they are two different problems existing in the same person. For example, drinking before social events can ease anxiety about being in an uncomfortable situation (social anxiety). This creates a negative feedback loop. When the effects of the drug wear off, the symptoms return, often with greater intensity.

Addressing dual diagnosis early in treatment will offer a greater chance of success. In the past, professionals would start with halting the substance use and then addressing the mental health issues second. Current research supports addressing both the addiction and mental health issues at the same time. Stopping the negative feedback loop would include professional interventions for both at the same time.

One of the more difficult aspects in addressing the dual diagnosis patient is getting dual diagnosis patients to buy into recovery. They are being asked to give up something (substances) that has provided relief for symptoms of their mental health problem. When dual diagnosis patients initially stop using, they are faced with not just giving up an addictive drug but also having to cope with their mental health symptoms and managing treatment. Depending on when the substances were introduced, the user could have limited experience in learning to address mental health symptoms on their own, without the substances, a potentially scary and overwhelming task. Educating addicts and preparing them for the initial challenges they will face is helpful. It is also important to understand that psychotropic medication is not as an exact science as we would hope for. It may take up to several weeks for the medication to reach a therapeutic level. There is also often a lot of trial and error regarding medication and dosage as different people react differently to psychotropic medication.

Professionals facing a possible dual diagnosis will address the problem causing the most concern first. If a patient's mental health symptoms draw most of the attention, then substance abuse might exist under the radar. For example, someone may display psychotic tendencies which can obscure their substance abuse. Our immediate concern and focus is drawn to the more obvious and troubling symptoms. The same can be said about substance abuse. Mental health symptoms such as anxiety and depression (or other mental health issues) in a substance abuser may be less obvious. The active drug use would be the immediate focus.

Professionals should screen abusers for the possibility of coexisting problems. Undiagnosed co-occurring conditions not only minimize the likelihood of successful treatment but can be dangerous. Stopping substance abuse without addressing the underlying mental health issue will likely allow symptoms to return, possibly more intensely. The substance abuser will also not have the coping skills to address the surfacing symptoms and their alcohol/drug abuse. If depression and suicidal thoughts are present, stopping can increase the risks of a suicide attempt. Substance abuse served a purpose, it helped them cope (not productively) with their struggles with mental health symptoms and taking it away will create a return of these symptoms, often at a greater intensity. Users also often lose their natural ability to cope with daily life struggles. To determine if a dual diagnosis problem exists, the first step is seeking out a professional experienced in working with dual diagnosis. A comprehensive exam could include psychological testing, screening for cognitive impairments, a diagnostic interview and/or a complete medical workup. If someone has identified a substance problem, screening for a co-occurring disorder(s) would include:

- Feelings of helplessness/hopelessness
- Loss of interest in daily activities
- Unrealistic, grandiose beliefs
- Starving or binge eating and purging
- Evidence of self-injury
- Rapid speech and racing thoughts
- Impaired judgment and impulsivity
- Excessive tension and worry
- Feeling restless or jumpy
- Irritability or feeling on edge
- Racing heart or shortness of breath
- Appetite or weight changes
- Sleep issues
- Changes in levels of energy
- Strong feelings of worthlessness or guilt
- Concentration problems
- Anger, rage, and reckless behavior
- Feelings of euphoria or extreme irritability

Other considerations include:

- If these symptoms either predated the use or appear to be present when not under the influence or withdrawing from the substance.
- If there is a previous history of mental health symptoms or family history.
- If after the substance use has stopped, these feelings are still present after a reasonable amount of time, or if they have intensified.
- If there are episodes of concern that did not involve substance use.

The longer the dual diagnosis continues, the more complicated the recovery can be. As time goes along; the abuser will lose the ability to use their own coping skills. The cycle of substance abuse and self-medication continues. The longer this goes on the greater the likelihood of consequences piling up. There are a disproportionate number of individuals in jail who have substance abuse, mental health, or both disorders present (Peters, Wexler, & Lurigio, 2015).

During the detoxification of drugs, medical monitoring of symptoms is important. During this time, when drugs are leaving the body's system, there is a greater risk for mental health symptoms to increase. When medication is prescribed for mental health symptoms as part of a treatment plan both the doctor and patient should give consideration to the medication prescribed. We have previously discussed potential problems with prescription medication(s) and abuse.

Some mental health issues require psychotropic medication. The medication prescribed should also be considered as some medications have a high abuse potential, while others do not. We suggest close monitoring of certain medications. Benzodiazepines (Xanax, Ativan, Klonopin, Valium, and Restoril) should be taken on a short-term basis because of their high abuse potential. Individuals can also experience withdrawal if they abruptly stop using them.

For dual diagnosis patients, we recommend the following guidelines:

- Medication with a high abuse potential should be avoided or strictly monitored.
- Coordination of care should be closely established between all physicians and therapists involved with the patient.
- Patients should not take any medication that's not prescribed to them.
- Don't change any medication dosages without first talking with your physician.
- Exceptions to medication dosages should be discussed in advance and planned. These exceptions can suddenly slide into former patterns of abuse.
- Develop a plan of action for all substances and medications, regardless of history. The use of any mood-altering substance, even if it was not their original drug of choice, is risky for dual diagnosis patients. It is common for individuals abusing one drug to turn to another as a replacement.

- Involve a therapist well versed in addiction to help manage all care and coordinate with physicians.
- Consider additional support with family members. They could help with monitoring medication and administration.
- Set clear and measurable goals.
- Seek out dual diagnosis websites (www.dualdiagnosis.com) and support groups (NAMI).

We recommended in our previous section on medications that individuals should see a doctor/psychiatrist who specializes in addiction. Furthermore, we also strongly recommended that you also meet with a therapist regularly if medication is prescribed. These meetings would take the place in addition to your psychiatric appointments. Therapists can meet with you for longer, more frequently, and more in-depth time than a psychiatrist or doctor can, as a rule. Typically, doctors are focused on medication management and not able to address day to day concerns or issues as intensely as a therapist. All parties involved can decide the frequency of sessions. Family involvement should also be a part of the treatment plan.

Additional support includes counseling centers, professional groups, or community organizations for those addressing dual diagnosis. Depending on the severity of the symptoms, residential facilities (half-way houses) can be a treatment option. There are several organizations that offer more information, education, and support groups for co-occurring problems. These support groups may not be available in all areas, but at least offer education and resources. We have included a few for reference. At the time of this publication, we cannot guarantee they are still operating or to what degree. If the links no longer exist, we encourage you to do your own research in finding these types of resources.

Double Trouble In Recovery (more information at www.bhevolution.org/public/doubletroubleinrecovery.page)
C. O. Mental Health Empowerment Project
271 Central Ave, Albany New York 12209
(518) 434-1393

<u>Dual Recovery Anonymous</u> (www.draonline.org)
"Dual Diagnosis Anonymous is a program of simplicity based on a version of the 12 Steps of Recovery and the additional 5 Steps of DDA. Regular attendance at these meetings and the application of these steps provide us with spiritual support needed for Dual Diagnosis recovery."

<u>Mental Health Alliance</u> (www.mentalhealthamerica.net/find-support-groups)
"Mental Health America (MHA), founded in 1909, is the nation's leading community-based nonprofit dedicated to addressing the needs of those living with mental illness and to promoting the overall mental health of all Americans. Their programs and initiatives fulfill the mission of promoting mental health, preventing mental disorders and achieving victory over mental illness through advocacy, education, research, and services."

<u>SAMSHA</u> (www.findtreatment.samhsa.gov)
"This government organization offers a Behavioral Health Treatment Services Locator, a confidential and anonymous source of information for persons seeking treatment facilities in the United States or U.S. Territories for substance abuse/addiction and/or mental health problems."

<u>NAMI</u> (www.nami.org)
"NAMI, the National Alliance on Mental Illness, is the nation's largest grassroots mental health organization dedicated to building better lives for the millions of Americans affected by mental illness. They offer education, advocacy, and programs assisting people with mental illness."

Chapter 24: The Triggered Brain

The design of our brain contributes to the challenges of addiction. The brain's reward pathways associate pleasurable experiences with good and healthy ones, and our ability to remember experiences enables us to repeat them. It is these pathways that get turned against us during addiction. Most observers would recognize the self-destructive behavior in the poor choices addicts and alcoholics make, but addicts' and alcoholics' brains are telling them something different.

Rewards (or perceptions of rewards) shape our behaviors and perceptions. Substances intensify this reaction more than any natural event. Dopamine, a neurotransmitter released in the brain which helps control our reward system, plays an integral role in this reaction. Once we experience intense pleasure, we commit it to our memory. This increases the likelihood we will repeat this behavior. In fact, the mere anticipation of the pleasurable experience (substance use) will start the dopamine firing process (**Figure 3.19**). Once the reward (the high produced from the substance) takes place it reinforces the experience for the next time. This is how addiction becomes an addiction. The function, effects, and speed of delivery can significantly solidify this experience.

It becomes such a powerful association that addicts, and alcoholics make choices counterintuitive to their survival. They do things that run counter to their own built-in survival mechanism. The decision-making part of our brain, the prefrontal cortex (PFC), loses out to the limbic system, the pleasure-seeking region of our brain. Our limbic system reacts instinctively and does not always allow us to think of consequences. It bypasses logic and goes right to pleasure or survival. Given the right circumstances, when faced with a decision to improve your life in the long run (not using drugs) the PFC will lose out to intense short-term rewards (using drugs).

Not only does the PFC lose this battle, but future battle outlooks do not look good. The limbic system will also make associations or pairings with other parts of the environment. The pairing does not always involve a direct connection to substance use. Just an association with using can set off a dopamine firing process. Examples of this include bars, friends with whom one used to used, certain moods, and even paraphernalia. Exposure can create a dopamine firing which further overvalues and reinforces the reward value. It doubles down on the experience.

Figure 3.19

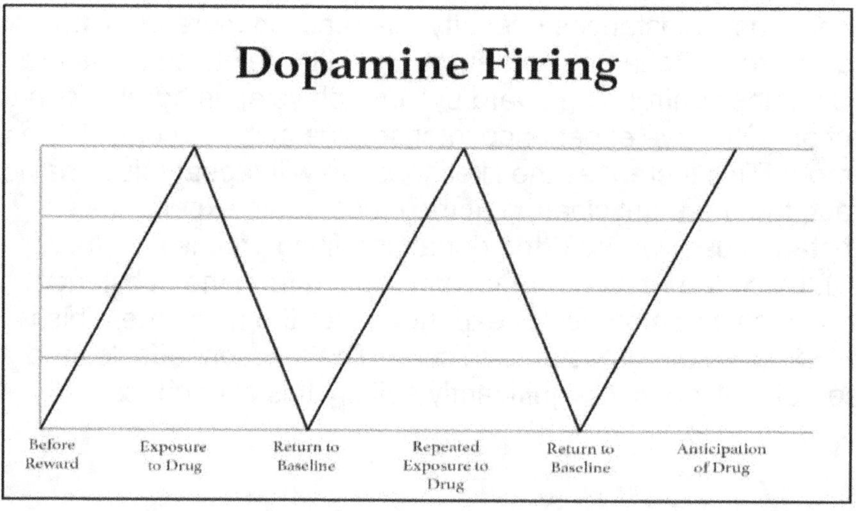

The challenge for addicts is applying the brakes to a system that is designed to bypass logic. Our overall wellbeing takes a back seat to a using experience. Pleasure and short-term gratification lead to future harmful consequences. It is not a fair fight. The longer this cycle continues, the more solidified it becomes. The limbic system uses a much simpler decision-making process than the PFC.

Fortunately, there is a way to lessen the impact and defend yourself from this pathway. The key is not putting yourself in a position where reason and logic (PFC) compete with immediate gratification (limbic system). Several behaviors will be helpful with managing this reaction.

- Create as much of a stress-free environment as possible. Stressful situations lead us to either not responding well or making poor decisions.
- Use tools and strategies that can aid in addressing stresses and urges (covered in mindfulness and progressive relaxation section in our Chapter on Inner Thoughts).
- Develop healthy habits and routines. Substance-free routines, once established, allow predictability and planning. This helps prevent being overrun by the limbic system.
- Create new substance-free experiences for yourself. This helps to avoid boredom. Stimulation is important in recovery.
- Involve others. Support is important, especially in early recovery.
- Develop a strong network of non-using friends.

Decreasing stress in our environment should be a priority in recovery. First, the less stress we are under, the better decisions we make (Wemm & Wulfert, 2017). Stress also increases the probability of relapse (Sinha et al., 2011). To create a less stressful environment, individuals will have to make difficult choices. Friendships, activities, and even career choices are major factors in early recovery. Going out with the same friends as you did before could prove too challenging for your recovery. Sporting events, weddings, or holidays are triggers for some people. Understanding and preparing for triggers will increase chances of success. The terms craving and urges are interchangeable. A trigger is something that ignites these feelings. A trigger could be momentary, like a spark, and may pass shortly. Urges and cravings usually start from a trigger and build up to something more intense. Individuals may not know of a trigger until they ignite it from something, we are not always consciously aware of some triggers (i.e. the ways something smells, the crinkle of something, a song, a poster, etc.).

The longer someone remains in a trigger moment, the greater the chance for relapse. There are some situations we cannot avoid. However, it is important to plan and prepare for them whenever possible. Individuals have had to make career changes to protect their sobriety. Businesspeople who travel may find themselves frequently away from their support system. Some are surrounded by individuals who drink or use drugs in the workplace. In some sales jobs, a part of the unspoken job description is courting customers around drinking activities.

It is not always going to be possible to predict triggers (see Kevin's story below). They can come out of nowhere. For those situations, individuals still work to minimize the risks of a relapse. It will be important to move yourself out of the moment, call a support person, and focus on some coping statements and strategies.

Using our PFC abilities when they are not being tested by reward-based limbic urges increases the chances for success. In order to develop new habit loops, we need to rehearse new skills when our PFC is available to learn. This happens best when we are not under stress. The more time you think about your trigger the stronger the sensation becomes. The key is not staying on that thought too long. There are several strategies to ride out urges. We have previously included one method of riding out an urge (in **Figure 3.17**). The most successful is to plan and structure your time in healthy and productive ways. We want to create as few situations as possible to activate our limbic system responses. Lifestyle changes will be helpful. Incorporating a schedule and developing routines will be key. Sleep and diet will be discussed next in greater detail as both play an integral role in recovery.

Kevin is 40 years old and recovering from cocaine and alcohol addiction. He had been struggling with cocaine addiction for several years. His drinking problems were present before he used cocaine. A recent cocaine binge convinced him he needed to stop both his cocaine and alcohol use. He believed that if he continued to use, he would eventually lose his family, including his wife. Kevin was motivated and committed to 6 weeks of abstinence. He gave up his using friends, found constructive recreational pursuits, and spent more time with his family. He met with me for several weeks to work on his recovery plan.

One day, Kevin called me to see if I had some availability to see him on the same day. Fortunately, I had a cancellation and was able to see him. When he came to session, he was stressed out. He discussed how situations kept presenting themselves that challenged his commitment to abstaining. He informed me that he was able to deal with most of his challenges but felt that he was being tested. In addition to noticing more alcohol commercials, an old using buddy had called him to talk. He also was filling up his gas tank and when he was walking to pay for his gas, he noticed a plastic bag on the ground by another car's door. He realized it likely contained cocaine.

Kevin took the right course of action. He kept walking and took his time leaving the gas station (allowing the person who dropped the bag to retrieve it). Furthermore, by scheduling a time with me, he was able to recognize the buildup of the urges. Although he was not able to predict the sudden appearance of cocaine, he dealt with it well. He also had a contingency plan in place if he was not able to see me. He discussed this incident with his wife. Kevin was very aware of his state of mind and was able to deal with this sudden situation. In fact, he was able to joke about this and referred to this as a "test from above."

Chapter 25: Sleep

Sleep is essential for our overall mental health and wellbeing. Sleep deficits affect our decision-making abilities, moods, motivation, and concentration. Substance abuse hinders sleep, either because a person who is abusing substances can develop sleep problems, or because sleep problems opened the door for substance abuse. This is another chicken and egg dilemma. Regardless, if you have both substance abuse and sleep problems, both need to be addressed. If you neglect one, you neglect both.

Studies show that those suffering from alcoholism are more likely to have a sleep problem (Crum, Ford, Storr, & Chan, 2004). We also know that sleep difficulties can lead to alcohol problems (Crum, Storr, Chan, & Ford, 2004). Illicit drugs furthermore create sleep disturbances and contribute to substance abuse (Mahfoud, Talih, Streem, & Budur, 2009). Illicit drugs, such as heroin, may create feelings of drowsiness but negatively affect the sleep cycle. Cocaine, stimulants, and designer drugs are stimulants and will decrease the ability to sleep. In adolescents, studies have also supported a strong relationship between sleep problems and an increased risk of substance abuse problems (Wong, Robertson, & Dyson, 2015). Also, children who have sleep challenges are more likely to experience substance abuse issues later in life (Ranaivo, 2010). Finally, the risk for a psychiatric disorder increases with sleep problems and insomnia (Ford & Kamerow, 1989).

Sleep problems include: insomnia (difficulties getting to or staying asleep), sleep apnea (shallow breathing when asleep), restless leg syndrome (irresistible urge to move your legs at night), hypersomnia (daytime sleepiness), parasomnia (nightmares or night terrors), medication-induced sleep disorder, and narcolepsy. The majority of sleep problems in substance abusers are either insomnia, hypersomnia, or a medication-induced disorder. Warning signs for a sleep disorder include:

- Difficulty going to sleep at night
- Awakening earlier than you planned or wanted to
- Awakening in the middle of the night
- Irritability
- Looking or feeling tired during the day
- Difficulties managing emotions
- Urge to nap during the day or napping during the day
- Difficulties in concentrating
- Falling asleep or feeling sleepy while driving
- Slow reaction time
- Increased use of caffeine to stay awake

Medications can assist with sleep problems. The more commonly used sleep medications are called Z-drugs. These include Zolpidem, Zaleplon, Zopiclone, and eszopiclone. However, caution should be taken as these medications can lead to the same sleep-substance abuse cycle. In **Figure 3.20**, you will find a list of sleep medications. Any sleep medication must be monitored by a doctor well versed in addiction.

Figure 3.20   Drug Classification/Abuse Chart

Classification of medication	Types of medication	Effects	Abuse potential
Benzodiazepines	Ativan, Quazepam, Estazolam, Restoril, Dalmane, Klonopin, Librium, Halcion	Binds to the receptors of GABA neurotransmitter promoting sleepiness.	High. Should only be used short term. Can cause withdrawal reactions if stopped suddenly.
Tricyclic antidepressants	Silenor, Zonalon, and Prudoxin	Blocks histamine receptors.	High
Orexin Receptor Antagonists	Suvorexant, Belsomra	Targets the action of Orexin (wake neurotransmitters).	Lower
Hypnotic	Sonata, Zaleplon Ambien\Zolpidem (Z drugs), Zaleplon Lunesta, Eszopiclone	Causes release of GABA in the brain. Decreases excitability of many brain cells.	Midrange
Melatonin Receptor Agonists	Ramelteon, Valdoxan, Melitor, Tasimelton	Works similarly to melatonin, a natural substance in the brain that is needed for sleep.	None

Let your physician know about the coexisting problem of sleep and substance abuse, otherwise the treatment may be, at best, ineffective, and at worse, a fatal combination. If you are considering the use of sleep medication, it is important to understand the overdose potential if you are continuing the use of substances. Mixing alcohol or certain substances with medication can significantly affect the potency. These interactions can also increase the risk of overdose.

Over-the-counter medications should be taken with caution too. The same abuse potential exists with medications such as cough syrup (sometimes used to aid in sleep), cold meds (containing dyphenhydramine or dextromethorphan), and medications specifically designed to aid in sleep (Restoril, Sonata, and Ambien to name a few) (NIDA, 2018c; Sansgiry, Bhansali, Bapat, & Xu, 2017). These should be only taken over a brief period. If your sleep problem lasts longer than 10 days, consult your doctor. Signs that someone is abusing over-the-counter medication would include:

- Experiencing memory loss.
- Increasing dosage of medication, or taking more than indicated.
- Taking the medication for longer than 10 days.
- Using the medication with other medications without a doctor's or pharmacist's advice.
- Preoccupation with taking the medication.
- Hiding use.
- Doctor shopping, or going to different doctors and not disclosing medications you are using.
- Taking someone else's prescription.
- Using illicit drugs or alcohol along with medication.

Medication should not be the first line of defense when addressing sleep concerns. This is especially true for chemically dependent people. Non-pharmacological approaches include relaxation techniques, which are especially helpful before going to bed. These can include imagery, progressive relaxation, mindfulness, hypnosis, and biofeedback, to name a few. We will discuss mindfulness and progressive relaxation in further detail in a later chapter. Here are further resources for relaxation techniques:

Biofeedback: The Association for Applied Psychophysiology and Biofeedback (AAPB)
Hypnosis: American Association of Professional Hypnotherapists, Hypnosis Motivation Institute
Progressive Relaxation: National Center for Complementary and Integrative Health

There are other helpful lifestyle adjustments that can help with sleep difficulties, including:

- Create a regular bedtime hour. When you vary bedtimes, this can disrupt the sleep cycle.

- Evaluate your diet. Spicy foods, chocolate, caffeine, foods high in fat, and onions can disrupt your sleep. Eating heavy meals before bedtime or skipping a meal (going to bed hungry) can also be problematic. Cigarettes and nicotine are something you should avoid.
- Limit liquid intake before bedtime. However, herbal (non-caffeinated) tea such as chamomile or warm milk before bedtime (in moderation) can be beneficial.
- Exercise is good for overall health and sleep. However, avoid doing it too close to bedtime as the increase in adrenaline may disrupt your sleep cycle.
- Only go to bed when you are sleepy. If you wake up in the middle of the night and cannot go back to sleep, leave the room. The more you fight it (sleep difficulties) the greater the chance you will have sleep disruption. If you are spending over 15 minutes trying to go to sleep, go to another room. This could offer a break from your struggle as fighting it becomes counterproductive.
- Keep a sleep journal (**Figure 3.21**). This could help determine patterns and aid in developing strategies.
- Look for wind down activities before going to bed. Television, bill paying, intense discussions, and other activities can affect sleep.
- Try to only use your bed for sleeping. Other activities (television watching, reading in bed) can hamper sleep. If you find yourself worrying at night, assign a time to work these challenges out before bedtime.
- Set your alarm to wake up at a consistent time. Even on weekends. Sleeping in may feel good but is not good for sleep hygiene.
- Avoid or limit naps during the day. Anything over 20 minutes may throw off your schedule. Do not take naps too close to bedtime.
- Make sure your sleep environment is conducive to sleep. Sound machines or fans can help muffle distracting sounds that may interfere with sleep. Make sure your room temperature is adequate. Cool sleep environments are best, but some individuals prefer otherwise. If lighting is an issue, invest in a sleep shade.
- Use an essential oil diffuser with lavender.

Figure 3.21

<table>
<tr><td colspan="7" align="center"><h1>Sleep Journal</h1></td></tr>
<tr><td>Day of week

(Date)</td><td>Activities before bedtime</td><td>Last meal (include time)</td><td>Time to sleep</td><td>Any awakenings (if so for how long?)</td><td>Nap time (if any)</td><td>Stress level during the day, 1 to 10 (highest)</td></tr>
<tr><td>Sunday</td><td></td><td></td><td></td><td></td><td></td><td></td></tr>
<tr><td>Monday</td><td></td><td></td><td></td><td></td><td></td><td></td></tr>
<tr><td>Tuesday</td><td></td><td></td><td></td><td></td><td></td><td></td></tr>
<tr><td>Wednesday</td><td></td><td></td><td></td><td></td><td></td><td></td></tr>
<tr><td>Thursday</td><td></td><td></td><td></td><td></td><td></td><td></td></tr>
<tr><td>Friday</td><td></td><td></td><td></td><td></td><td></td><td></td></tr>
<tr><td>Saturday</td><td></td><td></td><td></td><td></td><td></td><td></td></tr>
</table>

It is important to know and expect that in the initial stages of recovery there will be degrees of sleep disturbances. The brain and body need time to recover from the ordeal of substance abuse. This could take weeks and even months. The key is trying to stay on top of sleep problems. Preparing and educating yourself is essential to making changes. Approaching this proactively and educating yourself are key factors in recovery.

Chapter 26: Diet

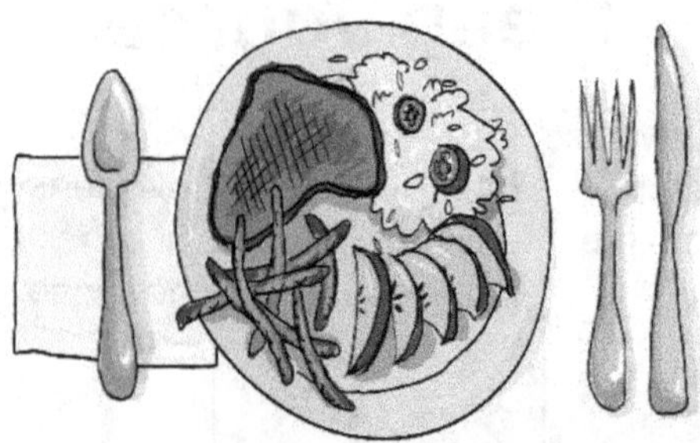

Healthy eating, in most cases, is not a priority for substance abusers. Yet all recovering addicts should give diet real consideration. A thoughtful approach to this area can head off discouraging effects of stopping substance usage. Stopping substance abuse can open the door to other concerns. These concerns predated, were exacerbated by, or were created by substance abuse. It will take time for your body to adjust to a substance-free life. This not only includes the reaction your body will have once you stop using but lifestyle patterns associated with your use.

Food can become an addiction in itself. We refer this to as an eating disorder. Research supports a strong likelihood of someone having both diagnoses (cross addiction). The challenges of substance abuse do not always lead to an eating disorder. Dietary needs nevertheless take a back seat to addiction. Each substance can bring on different dietary problems.

For example, amphetamines create a decrease in appetite, while alcohol will increase empty calorie intake. In heroin use, vomiting and nausea that accompany use can decrease appetite. In early recovery for alcohol abuse, the body seeks sugar it used to receive from alcohol. Weight gain in early recovery from alcohol abuse is common. Regardless of the drug of choice, the escalation of drug or alcohol use will affect your metabolism which further impacts weight gain or loss. It is also not unusual for weight gain to be a side effect of prescription drugs (Booth, 2015). Discuss any concerns with your doctor as there may be medications that would create less chance of weight gain.

Considerations need to be given to the primary and secondary dietary impact of substance abuse ("Malnutrition," 2010). Primary impact would be where the addiction is so pronounced that the addict's food intake and nutrition suffers. Malnutrition would be a result. Inadequate food intake results in a lack of energy ("Malnutrition," 2010). The addict/alcoholic then turns to quick fixes (more drugs, high energy foods, or coffee) to sustain their energy. Secondary malnutrition presents itself when dietary intake may be enough but is not properly absorbed by the body. This is especially true for the alcoholic. This presents challenges down the road including digestive, metabolic, and oral problems (Salz, 2014).

It is important to know of diet issues related to substance abuse, but tackling them right away might not be productive. Diets themselves create stress and diving into a major diet plan may lead to setbacks. If you feel you are in a good position to focus more on diet, test out what works best for you and your lifestyle. If you tried a diet before, evaluate what you liked, didn't like, and how effective it was for you. If you solicit the help of a doctor, we strongly suggest that you stay away from medications to assist in weight loss. This includes over-the-counter aids. There are risks of developing an addiction to the medications and results are typically not long lasting. Lifestyle changes are much more effective than going the medication route (Mayo Clinic Staff, 2018b).

We have included popular diets to consider. There are many diets to choose from. We encourage further research to determine which would work best for you.

Mayo Clinic Diet
This is the Mayo Clinic's take on how to make healthy eating a lifelong habit. This plan earned especially high ratings from experts for its nutritional value, safety, and as a tool against diabetes. They also found it moderately effective for weight loss.

Jenny Craig
This diet follows the theory that our metabolism is not in a constant state. It has a predictable curve, increasing in the morning, peaking during midday, and tapering off at night. They base their meal plan on this curve and offer, at additional costs, prepackaged meals. They also offer support groups in this program.

South Beach

The South Beach Diet allows certain foods in a controlled fashion. It comprises two phases. Phase 1 emphasizes chicken, beef, turkey, fish, and shellfish. Phase 2 introduces other foods in controlled portions. Participants eat six times a day using their prepackaged meals.

Zone Diet

The theory behind the Zone Diet are the numbers: 40-30-30. Zone dieters balance their meals and snacks so that their calories come from 40% carbohydrates, 30% protein, and 30% percent "friendly" fats.

Ketogenic Diet

The ketogenic diet is a low carb, moderate protein, and high-fat diet that puts the body into a metabolic state known as ketosis. When your body is in a state of ketosis, the liver produced ketones which become the main energy source for the body. They also refer to the ketogenic diet to as the keto (key-toe) diet, low-carb diet, and low carb high fat (LCHF).

Paleo Diet

Paleo is a diet that involves consuming unprocessed foods. These foods are whole, organic, and resemble what they look like in their natural form. The Paleo Diet, in theory, mirrors the diet previously consumed by hunter-gatherer ancestors. The main objective of the Paleo Diet is to improve the health of people by keeping them free of health disorders such as diabetes, heart disease, and obesity by cutting out processed foods. According to Authority Nutrition, the Paleo Diet leads to significant weight loss without counting calories. People using this approach eat either a high-carb diet alongside plant products or a low-carb diet with lots of animal foods. Tubers, fish, salt, healthy fats, fruits, and eggs are examples of foods to eat when following the Paleo diet.

Weight Watchers

This program includes regular meetings, self-help type learning sessions, group support, and a points system. The WW dieter aims for a target weight or a body mass index (BMI) between 20 and 25, considered the ideal range.

<u>Atkins Diet</u>
Limits carbohydrates so the body burns fat, including body fat, for energy. Atkins also offers their own food program. Many items are available in grocery stores.

<u>Mediterranean Diet</u>
The Mediterranean diet is based primarily on the eating habits of southern European countries, with an emphasis on plant foods, olive oil, fish, poultry, beans, and grains. There is not a single diet or website for this diet, but the concept draws together the common food types and healthy habits from the traditions of several regions.

There are other considerations when one thinks of a diet plan. If you feel additional support will be helpful in pursuing a diet, a program that has its own support group or network would be helpful, such as Weight Watchers or Jenny Craig. Also, consider your lifestyle and your ability to have access to your food. If you travel often, do not have a refrigerator to store food, or are on a limited budget, these are considerations in choosing a healthy lifestyle plan. If there are any health concerns that predated the substance use or followed the abuse, it is then suggested you consult a doctor to make sure the diet you choose is safe. You should include physical activity in your plan. We will cover exercise in the next chapter.

Food plays an important part in our lives. Preparing for some dietary adjustments can aid in recovery. Energy levels, moods, confidence, and motivation are influenced by diet. Maintaining a realistic diet with healthy expectations can also aid in the feeling of being in control. Weight gain in early recovery can create a negative feedback loop. Changes may not happen overnight but creating an awareness of potential challenges in this area can help stave off discouraging weight gain and aid in your recovery. A healthy lifestyle is a step in the right direction. Developing a routine for a diet plan can be helpful. Water intake is also important for diet. They recommend that you drink one half your body weight in water in ounces a day. If you weigh 120 pounds, you should be drinking 60 ounces of water.

It is important to consider your relationship with food. If you feel that a possibility exists of an eating disorder, we recommend that you get evaluated by a medical or mental health professional. Someone who specializes in addiction only would not have the area of expertise needed to address the issues associated with an eating disorder. This can be a serious and life-threatening diagnosis that might require hospitalization. Professionals also advise a nutritionist to be a part of the treatment planning. In some circumstances, doctors may prescribe medication, but medication alone will not address the challenges of this disorder. If someone is struggling with both addictions, we strongly suggest a setting that specializes in both. Support groups and additional information can be found at:

- The National Association of Anorexia Nervosa and Associated Disorders, Inc. (ANAD) is a non-profit (501c3) organization working in the areas of support, awareness, advocacy, referral, education, and prevention.
- Bulimia.com provides information and treatment options for individuals suffering from bulimia nervosa and co-occurring eating disorders, or substance use disorders. They provide support groups, treatment centers, and professionals who specialize in eating disorders.
- Eating Disorder Hope offers education, support, and resources for those struggling with eating disorders. They include a resource page for support groups within this site.
- The National Eating Disorders Association (NEDA) provides information and resources for those struggling with an eating disorder.
- Overeaters Anonymous (OA) is a support group that uses the 12 step philosophy of Alcoholics Anonymous.

Obviously, we all need food to sustain ourselves. We cannot eliminate food. In most cases, a complete stoppage of substance use is easier to measure than defining an unhealthy relationship with food. Professionals recommend a food plan to follow in most cases.

Undertaking a strict diet routine while addressing early recovery issues is a challenging task. It is understandable if your first impression is not a positive one. However, this need not be a huge undertaking. Even subtle changes can help. Being mindful of making healthy dietary choices can make a difference. We refer to this as the **Don't Eat As Much Stuff (DEAMS)** diet. (DEATS is not an actual diet, but a suggested approach to maintaining a healthy lifestyle). Making simple choices daily can point you in a positive direction, such as only having one slice of bread on a sandwich instead of two. Better yet, have a lettuce wrap for your sandwich instead of a bun. Order a medium drink instead of a large shake, or vegetables instead of fries. Subtle changes can lead to big results over time. There are many healthy choices that can benefit you and help create a healthy lifestyle. Seeking out a professional, such as a Dietician or Nutritionist, are also options.

Chapter 27: Exercise

Just as diet can aid in recovery, exercise is also important. Addicts and alcoholics experience significant lifestyle changes as they become altered by substances. Their relationship with their substance of choice has a ripple effect of unhealthy consequences for their mental and physical wellbeing. To lead a healthier lifestyle and reclaim your life, incorporating exercise is an important piece of the puzzle.

Exercise provides many direct and indirect benefits to someone recovering from substance abuse. When our bodies are under stress, a part of our brain called the hypothalamus releases chemicals called endorphins. These chemicals activate opioid receptors in our brain that help ease discomfort. They work as natural painkillers and play a key role in our natural reward system. When we exercise, we stress our bodies (in this case stress is good), which causes the release of these helpful chemicals. The result is a feeling of pleasure, sometimes euphoria. A regular exercise routine can offer many benefits. Although the feelings (release of endorphins) you may experience will not be as intense as artificial ones (substances), they can do a lot to boost your mood and feelings of wellbeing. This is a start to putting yourself back in the driver's seat.

Aside from the endorphin release, additional benefits of exercise include:

- Reduction of stress
- Improved sleep
- Increase in confidence
- Routine and structure
- Improved mental and physical health
- A healthier lifestyle
- Increased motivation
- Improved goal setting
- A healthier weight
- Greater clarity and focus
- A sense of accomplishment
- Better mood
- Increased energy
- Connecting with other people (depending on exercise chosen)
- More efficient memory (Patten et al., 2013)

Aside from all the above benefits, there are other advantages specific to recovery. The University of Colorado performed a study in which they found that regular aerobic exercise can help protect the brain against damage to white matter due to long-term alcohol abuse ("Aerobic exercise may protect cognitive abilities of heavy drinkers," 2013). Exercise can also help improve the plasticity in the hippocampus, improving learning and memory tasks (Patten et al., 2013) and can also reduce symptoms of alcohol withdrawal (Logan, Seggio, Robinson, Richard, & Rosenwasser, 2010). Another study, in a rat model, further supported the benefits of exercise in early recovery and the potential to reduce the chances of relapse (Beiter, Peterson, Abel, & Lynch, 2016).

How much exercise you need depends on your goals. Some exercise is better than no exercise. Usually, at minimum, we need 150 minutes a week (moderate heart rate), ideally broken up several times a week. If you are exercising at a more vigorous rate, then 75 minutes a week, broken up to several times a week, may suffice (Laskowski, 2018).

Take an honest appraisal of your lifestyle when deciding on an exercise program, including your individual personality and resources. Although gym memberships are not as costly as they once were, not everyone has access to a gym. If you have a gym conveniently located by you, make sure it fits your needs, especially at the time you will be going. A gym's environment can change in a short time. In the same workout area, you could see senior citizens working out and in 2 hours, young bodybuilders. If you enjoy competitive sports, a gym with a basketball, volleyball, or racquetball court could provide a social and physical outlet for you. Some gyms are chains with many locations. If you travel, this can also be a consideration. Doing exercise at home or outside is also an option. For some individuals, this may not work because of distractions and motivation. They should also take the type of exercise into consideration. Choosing the type of exercise should be the first step. Identifying what you hope to gain from exercising is important to establishing goals. The different exercise groups include:

- Aerobic/Endurance: Increases your breathing and heart rate.
- Strength training: Strengthens your muscles.
- Flexibility: Stretches your muscles to help you stay limber. Increases range of motion.
- Balance: Helps prevent falls and promotes stability.

Your workout should include a combination of these types of exercises. Each has their own benefits. If you are new to exercise, you should not only research beforehand but also have supervision when starting your routine, such as a personal trainer or a trusted friend.

Here are suggestions of exercise with no gym required:

- Brisk walking
- Cycling
- Swimming
- Jogging or running
- Playing tennis
- Dancing
- Rollerblading at a fast pace
- Ice skating

- Playing a competitive sport such as basketball, football, or soccer
- Skipping with a rope
- Walking up and down stairs
- Yoga
- Hiking

Here are our recommendations for a productive routine:

- **Set realistic goals**. Overdoing it can lead to injuries and burnout.
- **Keep an exercise journal**. This can help in reaching goals and monitoring your progress.
- **Do what works.** Identify what type of workout environment suits your personality, such as size of the gym classes (if any), offered hours, or working out at home.
- **Consider a personal trainer or reliable workout partner**. Having someone else you are accountable to can help you be consistent.
- **Set your own goals.** Monitor your own progress and do not gauge your workouts based on what you are observing from others.
- **Be patient**. It is important to keep in mind that the substance abuse has taken its toll on your body. It may take a longer time to recover from exercise. Take it slow and steady.
- **Reinforce good habits.** Reward yourself for achieving consistency and taking part in a routine. Massages, new workout clothes, or new gym shoes are a few suggestions.
- **Find a good balance between sticking to a routine and allowing variation**. It's counterproductive to feel like your routine is mundane or monotonous.
- **Start small.** Even going to a gym and walking around the track could be a good start.
- **Being a part of a group is important.** There is a website called Meetup where you can find group activities in your area at minimal or no charge.

When taking part in an exercise program, be careful not to overdo it. Some individuals are wired to overdo pursuits. Substance abusers are at risk for turning from one compulsive act (substance abuse) to another (extreme exercise). Signs you are over-exercising include:

- Experiencing an uncontrollable desire to exercise.
- Continuing to exercise despite injuries.
- Reducing activities in your life to focus on your exercise.
- Feeling like you must keep pushing yourself to meet unrealistic goals.
- Getting angry when not able to complete a workout.
- Spending a great deal of time working out.
- Thinking and talking only about workouts.
- Feeling guilty and\or depressed if you do not achieve your workout goals.
- Frequently setting time limits to your workout then breaking those limits.
- Workout time negatively impacting relationships.

It is important to keep in mind that some elements of the above-mentioned signs are healthy. Just be aware that addicts often have a difficult time finding the right balance. The obsessive traits that showed during addiction often play out in other life areas. Therefore, it is important to monitor your involvement in an exercise routine and be sure to incorporate it into your life in a balanced and healthy manner.

Chapter 28: Inner Thoughts

Talking to ourselves is nothing new. Soviet psychologist Dr. Lev Vygotsky referenced "inner speech" in 1934. He referred to it as Private Speech and believed it plays a large part in the development of critical thinking. In the 1980s, Dr. Shad Helmstetter launched a pioneering series of lectures and books on what he called motivational "self-talk." Sports psychologists have since embraced this concept. The importance of self-talk has also found its way into stress management (Girodo & Roehl, 1978).

In the mental health field, we refer to our internal dialogue as our inner voice. Sometimes it's a supportive and productive voice and other times it can be an inner critic. When we have a negative or self-defeating internal dialogue, mental health professionals refer to it as cognitive distortions or thinking errors. In the recovery field, some call it "Stinking Thinking," or MAST (**M**anipulative **A**ddictive **S**elf **T**alk) depending on which model you follow. We will use Stinking Thinking and MAST interchangeably.

Our internal dialogue is not only important for our sobriety but also our mental health. Studies support the positive role self-talk can play in our lives (Kross et al., 2014) and how it can be helpful for self-motivation (Senay, Albarracín, & Noguchi, 2010). Numerous motivational and public speakers discuss forms of positive self-talk.

Self-talk presents itself in numerous ways. When we are trying to figure something out, or are upset or working through an emotion, we have a private conversation in our heads sometimes in response to our own thoughts. This internal dialogue is self-talk. Most of the time, we do not share our thoughts with others until we are confident in what conclusions we have reached and how they will be received. The thoughts could be positive, negative, or neutral. They strongly influence how we think about ourselves, life, and specific situations. For example, if you miss a turn at an intersection, the self-talk could sound like this: "What an idiot I am," "That was stupid of me." If faced with a challenging situation, one might psyche themselves up by thinking "I got this." We create our own thought bubbles to help interpret situations. It is our way of processing and understanding situations.

For an addict, both your brain and body work against staying sober. Our minds can work against us, and we cannot always trust this inner dialogue. In the addiction field, negative self-talk is known as Stinking Thinking (ST). This term, especially used in Alcoholics Anonymous, is important in maintaining sobriety. It's also important to be aware that the internal discussions alcoholics have with themselves could open the way to relapsing. ST thoughts want to give us permission to return to harmful behaviors. There is a part of individuals in recovery that understands a certain behavior most likely would lead to a relapse. However, their self-talk could convince them the behavior is okay. An example is someone thinking it was okay to hang out at a bar with drinking buddies and that this would not be a threat to their sobriety. Logically, they realize that it is not a good idea, but the drinking thoughts tell them differently. **Figure 3.22** illustrates how this unfolds.

Figure 3.22

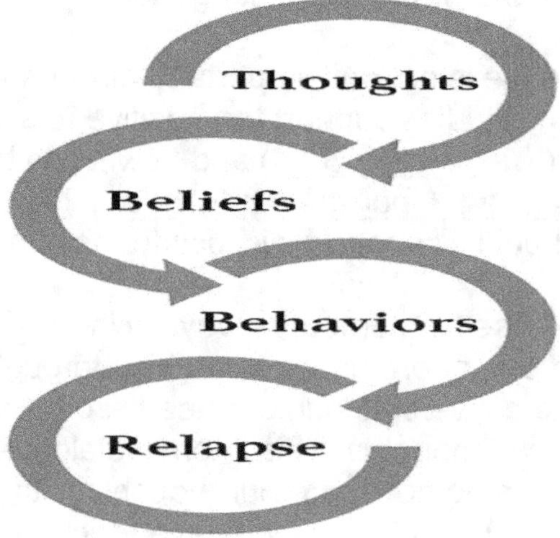

Stinking Thinking (also called MAST, or **M**anipulative **A**ddictive **S**elf Talk, Refer to **Figure 3.7**) can present itself differently. In mental health, it's also referred to as cognitive distortions. **Figure 3.24** illustrates some cognitive distortions people can have. In **Figure 3.27**, we show how it can present itself in recovery. It's important to understand how convincing these thoughts are.

Figure 3.24

Addictive Thinking

It is common for those in early recovery to struggle with thoughts that would point them in a direction to return to using/drinking. We have included some examples below.

1. Just a little bit won't hurt
2. I should be able to drink/use every now and then
3. Life stinks. Drinking makes it better
4. This is a special occasion
5. I need something to relax after today
6. I am bored
7. I deserve to be able to use, I earned it
8. You can handle it this time
9. I am not addicted, I just love to party
10. It's too hard
11. Just one bag and then I'll stop
12. I don't need to quit...I'm not addicted
13. There's nothing wrong with feeling good
14. You stayed sober for a week...good for you...reward yourself!
15. This is just too painful...I need to get numb
16. I will quit later when things are easier and there isn't so much stress in my life
17. I don't have to really quit, maybe cut down a little
18. If I quit, all the fun will be gone from my life
19. Just for old time's sake
20. I've got it under control, it's ok to have "one"
21. It's a special occasion...one won't hurt...

It is important to distinguish the difference between an Addictive Thought and a realistic one. The longer we allow these thoughts and dialogue to continue, the stronger the thoughts will become. Take some time to think of how your Addictive Thoughts sound. Write down some opposing thoughts (why you should not give in to these thoughts). The sooner you recognize the Addictive Voice and shut down the conversation, the greater the likelihood you will continue the path of recovery.

In recovery, especially in early recovery, there will be times when urges present themselves. As recovery becomes more challenging, dialogues become stronger. Addicts may deviate from the behaviors that supported their abstinence. They make concessions, shortcuts, and exceptions which compromise their recovery. This type of thinking leads to an eventual relapse if not kept in check. The longer these thoughts continue the more difficult they will be and the more likely you will give in to them.

A helpful tool to address MAST is journaling, (**Figure 3.25**) which allows you to be accountable to your thoughts. Writing them down can give you a fresh perspective to see faulty thoughts as they present themselves and to help you gain better self-awareness. Journaling also allows you to recognize patterns in your thinking and behavior and help you stay ahead of your triggers.

Figure 3.25

Journaling

Writing down your thoughts is helpful in many ways. First, journaling gives you an opportunity to reflect on a situation or encounter that you had during the day. By documenting this, you will be able to look back on it with more of a rational view. Once we are further removed from a situation, we can critique it in a more objective light. Another advantage we have is that we are able to detect patterns in our moments of discomfort. We could determine if people, places, times, or situations have an impact on how we feel.

Once we can detect patterns, this would enable us to better prepare for them. Journaling will also allow us to observe how our thoughts affect our feelings. Research supports the fact that our impressions have a great influence on our emotions. We could identify these thoughts and begin to alter our perspective on the situation. The events in our lives may not change, but our perspectives can.

Lastly, by Journaling, we will be able to see the changes we have made in our lives. We will be able to recognize that the changes that we have experienced were not coincidental. These changes happen through an active process. This will be helpful to have these changes documented to enable us to continue to progress and have these changes documented in case other situations arise in the future.

Areas to cover * The day's events

* Moments of distress. Include who you were with, when it happens, and what you were thinking.

* How long the moment of discomfort continued.

Once you identify your faulty thinking, you need to correct the problem. Identifying these thoughts is important but presenting an alternative thought is equally important. You can list these either in your journal or on a separate worksheet. **Figure 3.26** presents the ABC's of coping with challenging thoughts. The ABC Theory of Emotional Disturbance graphic is an example of how a person initially views a situation affects our mood or feelings. In this worksheet, a person gets in a fight with his romantic partner (**A**ctivating event). Most people, understandably, would be upset. However, his **belief** (**B**) about the argument, how he thought about it, created more intense feelings (**C**) and a potential return to drinking. Once he **d**isputed (**D**) his belief and looked at the situation from another perspective (rational), he had a different **e**ffect or attitude (**E**). Again, it is important not only to recognize these thoughts occur, but to actively replace them with healthier responses.

Figure 3.26

A-B-C Theory of Emotional Disturbance

"Men are disturbed not by things, but the view which they take of them."
-1st Century A.D., Epictetus

It is not the event but our interpretation of the event that causes our emotional reaction

A. **Activating Event**
A man gets into a heated argument with his romantic partner.

B. **Belief about or interpretation of the experience.**
"I thought when I stopped drinking things would get better."
"I stopped drinking and we are still fighting."
"Why bother to stop drinking if she is gonna yell at me anyway?"'
"Would wouldn't want a drink when they get yelled at all the time?"

C. **Upsetting emotional consequence/behavior.**
Anger/resentment. Hopelessness. Lack of commitment to stopping drinking. Urge or
decision to drink.

D. **Disputing of irrational thought.**
"Couples get in fights. It does not mean she does not want to see me stop drinking."
"If I drink, it will solve nothing. It will make things worse between us."
"Drinking created other problems in my life, not just in my relationship."
"Me wanting to drink because of our fight, is just an excuse to return to drinking."
"Since I stopped drinking, our relationship has improved. It is not realistic for me to blame my drinking on her."
"I need to stop making excuses to drink."

E. **New Emotional Consequence or effect.**
Irritated (over the fight) but hopeful. Confidence in the ability to handle negative

Even slight changes can help. Research suggests talking (thinking?) in the third person can help (Kross et al., 2014). This approach can help with mood regulation and self-control (Bergland, 2017). For example:

First Person: "I do not think I can make it another day without using drugs." "I need to drink and cannot live without it."
Third Person: "Come on (your name), you can do this." "Get real (your name), you know you can do well without using, you have done it before."

Studies show thinking in the third person can also help us stay in charge of our emotions. Scientists tested this while measuring brain waves and discovered this technique can help reduce stress (Firger, 2017). It activates a part of our brain that moves us further away from what is stressing us out (Weintraub, 2015).

These additional suggestions may help address MAST:

- **Keep it short and simple.** When you are challenging these thoughts do not allow it to become a debate. The longer the discussion (negative self-talk) continues, the stronger the voice becomes.
- **Be consistent** and do not allow yourself to become complacent. MAST can sneak up on you even if you have been sober for a long time.
- **Reduce stress** as much as possible. Stress causes a more primitive part of your brain to activate (limbic system) which makes logical thinking more difficult.
- **Stay positive and fair.**
- **Accept feedback.** Allow other people to offer feedback on your thoughts. This could be a sponsor, a therapist, a family member, or a friend. These should be healthy and supportive people.
- **Practice patience.** These habits are hard to break and take time.
- **Balance self-reflection.** Allow yourself affirmations and take caution against overconfidence.

The key to challenging addictive thoughts is separating the inner voice from the sober one **(Figure 3.27)**. The naming of the voice assists in separating the two. This allows the addict to focus on getting out of the moment. Planning and expecting challenging moments can keep the voice quiet.

Figure 3.27

Thinking Error	Using Voice
Confirmation Bias: Referencing information that only supports our initial belief.	Everybody smokes pot, I may as well.
In-group Bias: The tendency to agree with a member of your own group.	I believe my (drinking) buddies and my wife is overreacting. I do not have a problem.
Gambler's Fallacy: If something happens more frequently than normal during a given period, it will happen less frequently in the future.	The last few times I was at the bar I drank too much. This time will be different. Won't happen again.
Observational Selection Bias: When we notice an item, we are more likely to notice it again.	I see people drinking all the time.
Status-Quo Bias: The current base line or situation is preferable. Change is seen as a loss.	I will lose so much if I give up using.
Negativity Bias: Tendency to pay more attention to bad news.	I will be miserable if I stop drinking. Everything stinks since I stopped using.
Projection Bias: We overestimate how many people are like us. We assume everyone thinks like us.	I like to have a few drinks at night. Everyone likes to unwind this way.
The Current Moment Bias: The desire to see things in the current moment, leaving pain for latter.	I am feeling uncomfortable now. I should use as it will make me feel better.
Anchoring Effect: Comparing things with only a limited set of information.	I was not successful in avoiding using on a couple of occasions. I cannot be successful in stopping use.

The environment also plays a role with thoughts. Having a sober and supportive network can aid in this fight against unsupportive emotions.

- It will allow you to better organize your thoughts.
- Improve self-discipline.
- Allow healing to start.
- Increase your confidence

Unsupportive or using surroundings will make it easier to give in to the voice. Once we recognize the voice, techniques such as mindfulness, progressive relaxation, and breathing exercises can help get you through the moment.

Mindfulness has been shown to strengthen immune functioning, improve sleep, and more effectively manage stress. Practicing mindfulness is helpful not just for recovery but also for good mental health in general. Associate Professor David Vago, PhD defines mindful awareness in this way: "paying attention that is continually watchful and discerning for what is arising in our minds and the passing world."

Substantial research has enabled us to understand the mechanisms behind addiction and how best to use the strategy of mindfulness to assist the alcoholic/addict to disrupt the craving-behavior cycle that occurs as part of the reward system in the brain. Professor Judson Brewer, MD, PhD describes how mindfulness works to drive a "wedge" between the craving and the addictive behavior. The result is a decoupling of the craving and the addictive behavior. He found that those individuals who most frequently practiced mindfulness when faced with a craving were able to reduce and eventually stop the addictive behavior. In fact, he has developed several apps to assist with decreasing cravings for addicts.

The research very clearly supports the use of mindfulness to improve awareness and wellness. Nearly 50% of our waking lives is spent in passive thought that has nothing to do with what we are currently doing, in short, daydreaming. Directing this untapped potential toward mindful practice helps you filter information not relevant in the present moment. For example, you attempt to breathe mindfully. While doing so, you notice your stomach gently rise and fall with your breathing. In the midst of your mindful breathing, you think "Oh, I forgot to turn off the television in the other room. My head hurts, and I'm a little sore from my workout yesterday." Let those thoughts go and return to the practice of breathing in and out. This is the starting point for mindfulness.

A couple of conditions must exist for mindfulness to be a successful intervention whether used to treat anxiety, depression, or addiction.

1.   Allow yourself to be completely aware in the present moment.
2.   Hold a non-judgmental attitude of yourself.

The difficulty and the most freeing part of mindfulness is the acknowledgement that we are never able to be perfect at anything. We recognize that there will be good, bad, or indifferent thoughts and we choose to turn our focus to being present in our here and now.

Dr. Shauna Shapiro explains that when one practices mindfulness, thanks to neuroplasticity, situations that are repeated cause cortical thickening. She notes that if we focus on judgment, impatience, and frustration, we will experience judgment, impatience, and frustration. If we focus instead on "cultivating kind attention even for the seemly unforgivable parts of our lives," we learn to be present with painful and difficult situations, but not be caught up in thinking and feeling them.

Many great resources exist to help develop the skills involved in mindful practice. It is recommended for both substance abusing individuals and family members to practice mindfulness. We have included a variety of resources below:

Brewer, J., & Kabat-Zinn, J. (2017). *The craving mind: From cigarettes to smartphones to love--why we get hooked and how we can break bad habits.* New Haven, CT: Yale University Press.

Brewer, J. (n.d.). Train your brain, change your habits. Retrieved from https://www.judsonbrewer.com/

Kabat-Zinn, J. (2013). *Full catastrophe living: Using the wisdom of your body and mind to face stress, pain, and illness* [Revised Edition]. New York City, NY: Bantam Books.

Kabat-Zinn, J. (2018). *Meditation is not what you think: Mindfulness and why it is so important.* New York City, NY: Hachette Books.

Dr. Shauna Shapiro, (n.d.). Retrieved from
http://www.drshaunashapiro.com/

Shapiro, S. L., & Carlson, L. E. (2017). *The art and science of mindfulness: Integrating mindfulness into psychology and the helping professions.* Washington, D.C.: American Psychological Association.

Vago, D. R. (n.d.). Starting a meditation practice. Retrieved from http://davidvago.bwh.harvard.edu/mindfulness-resources/starting-a-meditation-practice-retreat-centers-for-you/

Vago, D. R. (n.d.). Suggested reading list. Retrieved from http://davidvago.bwh.harvard.edu/mindfulness-resources/suggested-reading-list/

Chapter 29: Adolescence

Adolescence can be a joyous and memorable time for a lot of teens. Many positive events and experiences are created during the teen years. At the same time, brain development, social challenges, emotional changes, and hormonal activity create unique obstacles. If someone adds a mood-altering substance to the equation, it can add to the chaos of the teenage years, with the potential for deadly results. Not all teens who experiment or use drugs, even on a regular basis, wind up being lifetime users. In fact, most age out of substance use (Substance Abuse and Mental Health Services Administration, 2017b). However, introducing mood altering drugs to this age group can lead to serious consequences.

Intervening in youth substance abuse is an arduous task for adults. Parental involvement is often essential for the success of substance abuse therapy. They are, in most cases, the driving forces of therapy. Substance abusing teenagers however will usually not be invested in change if they are not presented with structure or accountability. Again, change often comes from within. It is important to keep in mind that the longer use continues, the more ingrained use becomes. Lifestyles become embedded with behaviors and peers that support this lifestyle. It becomes difficult to break away from these patterns. They may also lose out on learning important coping skills. Their emotional development could lag behind their age. Therefore, it is important to look at an adolescent's using history.

There are limitations to what parents can do. They can offer speed bumps to deter youth behavior, such as drafting a home contract to make all guidelines and expectations clear. We have included a home contract example (**Figure 3.28**). A more comprehensive one can be found on our website at www.myerscounseling.com. Each family is unique. Families should choose the areas they need to focus on most and can realistically address. It is important to let teens know positive changes can benefit them. We also recommend having a professional drug and alcohol counselor assist in the creation of these contracts.

Teens may stop their use for different reasons than their parents want them to stop. For example, most people under 17 years of age do not think a curfew is necessary. However, they may follow it because parents enforce the rule and there are consequences. Most parents, meanwhile, believe children should come home at reasonable hours on school nights. A proper night's rest is important, and nothing good happens after curfew. It is in the best interests of a child to have a curfew and parents to enforce one (value). Teens will follow a curfew to avoid consequences (behavior). If parents over present the value part of their message, their teen will tune them out. The value portion will come later in life when they can see this issue from outside their adolescent perspective. The behavior portion will create the desired change

There are many conversations we have had with parents who are frustrated that their child does not get the importance of something they are trying to convey. I will ask a parent how many times they have spoken to their child about a concern (value). Typically, the answer is "repeatedly." At this point it usually becomes a yelling match.

(Figure 3.28)
<u>HOME CONTRACT</u>

When filing out this contract it is important to be clear and concise to avoid misunderstandings. Each party has responsibilities in this contract. Once you commit to thee responsibilities, it is important that you adhere to them consistently. This contract is designed so that the teen will have choices as to what type of consequences (positive or negative) he/she chooses. It is also understood that this contract could be renegotiated once the child demonstrates a commitment to this and trust is reestablished in the family.

    I.   SCHOOL:

    1.   I will be on time to school. It is my responsibility to be at school on time.

    2.   If I choose not to make it to school on time my consequences will be:
    ____

    3.   If I choose to make it to school on time the privilege I will keep will be:
    ____

    4.   I agree to complete all my school assignments and turn them all in on time. Homework completed by ______ p.m. to be checked by:
    ____

    5.   If I choose not to do my school assignments my consequences will be:
    ____

    6.   If I choose to do my school assignments my privilege I get to keep will be:
    ____

    7.   In order to help structure my study habits, I will set aside the following hours to do my school work: Monday through Friday:
    _________________________ to _________________________

    8.   Saturday and Sunday: _________________________ to
    ____

Examples of Consequences	Examples of Privileges
1. Grounding 2. Loss of telephone/television/computer 3. Friends not allowed over 4. Loss of car 5. Loss of allowance	1. Extra chores to earn extra money 2. Extended curfew for special event 3. Concert attendance 4. Additional free time from home 5. Parent provided transportation

Teens may stop their use for different reasons than their parents want them to stop. For example, most people under 17 years of age do not think a curfew is necessary. However, they may follow it because parents enforce the rule and there are consequences. Most parents, meanwhile, believe children should come home at reasonable hours on school nights. A proper night's rest is important, and nothing good happens after curfew. It is in the best interests of a child to have a curfew and parents to enforce one (value). Teens will follow a curfew to avoid consequences (behavior). If parents over present the value part of their message, their teen will tune them out. The value portion will come later in life when they can see this issue from outside their adolescent perspective. The behavior portion will create the desired change

There are many conversations we have had with parents who are frustrated that their child does not get the importance of something they are trying to convey. I will ask a parent how many times they have spoken to their child about a concern (value). Typically, the answer is "repeatedly." At this point it usually becomes a yelling match.

The reality is that, emotionally and developmentally, teens will not see the world the same as an adult. There are too many factors involved for this to be an equal playing field. That is why society has adults making the decisions. If a parent is looking for their child to share the same values, they will be disappointed. It would be like putting a big piece of chocolate cake and a plate of vegetables side by side in front of a three-year-old. Then ask the child to choose the plate that is in his or her best interests. The three-year-old will choose the chocolate cake. Teenagers will make similar age appropriate choices. However, if we focus on a behavior instead of the value, that could yield better results. Telling a child, he cannot have the cake until he has vegetables focuses on a behavior (eating the right food) and consequence, as opposed to trying to explain the value of good nutrition. How many three-year-old children will choose the vegetables since vegetables are more nutritious?

Teens are less susceptible to consequences than adults. Teens will not see many of the consequences associated with adult substance abuse, or at least to the same magnitude. Having parents angry at you for using drugs or underage drinking differs from having a spouse threaten divorce for the same concerns. At age 16, employment is not as important as it is when you are 40 years of age and supporting a family. Consequences are less meaningful at this age.

Consequences need to come from either the teen's schools or parents. A school's enforcement will vary from school to school and state to state. Schools become involved only if a student violates their drug policy while at school, either on
Teens may stop their use for different reasons than their parents want them to stop. For example, most people under 17 years of age do not think a curfew is necessary. However, they may follow it because parents enforce the rule and there are consequences. Most parents, meanwhile, believe children should come home at reasonable hours on school nights. A proper night's rest is important, and nothing good happens after curfew. It is in the best interests of a child to have a curfew and parents to enforce one (value). Teens will follow a curfew to avoid consequences (behavior). If parents over present the value part of their message, their teen will tune them out. The value portion will come later in life when they can see this issue from outside their adolescent perspective. The behavior portion will create the desired change.

If use affects schoolwork, many districts will justify school involvement. School social workers will work with students within schools, however, there are limitations to how in-depth they can go. Their focus is usually on school-related issues. However, sometimes they can go beyond those parameters. School social workers can work with outside therapists and professionals to coordinate services. Also, some schools have groups that can address young adult needs. School counseling should complement but not replace substance abuse counseling. Some schools offer evaluations for students who have been caught on school property with substances or come to school impaired. Each school district has a different policy and approach to substance abuse issues. They should include these policies in the school handbook. In colleges, policies are set according to university guidelines. Students taking part in sports may have a separate set of rules.

Parents may need their own support and guidance during this time. A family or couple therapist can offer support and guidance. The family therapist and the individual therapist should not be the same person. Teens need to see their therapist as someone they can trust. A therapist who, in other sessions, encourages parents to impose consequences would not be viewed as a neutral third party by a teen. Likewise, a therapist who coaches parents to provide structure is often viewed unfavorably by the resistant substance-abusing teenager. For college students, tele-behavioral counseling and university counseling services can help maintain continuity of care.

Random drug screens can be used throughout therapy. We have included an explanation about drug screens (**Figure 3.29**). If a teen identifies him or herself as having to earn back trust, urinalysis is an excellent way to do that. Opposition to drug screens and counseling most likely shows the user is resistant to stopping. Rebuilding trust is something that takes time and results. We have also included information regarding urinalysis (**Figure 3.30**) If you are pursuing this course of action, it will be helpful to understand terminology and how it works.

Figure 3.29

	Urine	Hair	Oral Fluid
Drugs test for	THC, Amphetamines, Cocaine, Opiates, methamphetamines(MDMA), Phencyclidine(PCP)	THC, Amphetamines, Cocaine, Opiates, methamphetamines(MDMA) Phencyclidine(PCP)	THC, Amphetamines, Cocaine, Opiates, methamphetamines(MDMA), Phencyclidine(PCP)
Collection Method	Urine collected in cup. Witnessed or safeguards put in place. Sample temperature gauged.	Hair from scalp, body hair, underarm, leg or facial. Must be 1 ½ inches thick, 120 strands, size of pencil	Put strip in mouth. Wait 3-10 seconds.
Adulteration	Substitution, adding in, watering down, drinking a lot. Internet kits usually ineffective.	No known	No known
Detection Window	Depending on drug, 2 hours after use to 4 weeks (THC). Most fall within 2-5 days.	5th day and could go as far back as 3 months (for THC).	1-2 hours, falls within range of 24-36 hours.
Cut off levels of detection	Highest	Lowest threshold	Medium
Collection Ease	Most difficult. Most intrusive.	Moderate. Depends on person.	Easy
Confirmation test	Yes	Yes	Yes
Cost	Middle	High	Least

Figure 3.30

<u>ABOUT URINALYSIS</u>

When a urine sample is to be collected for testing, there are several important factors that individuals need to know. A **chain of custody** is required by the laboratory which will perform the actual testing. This means that the sample is required to be monitored during all aspects of the collection and testing. This necessitates a **witness** be present to observe the client providing the specimen and to ensure the sample is unaltered. Once the sample is collected, the witness must make sure the sample is sealed properly in the presence of the client and placed in a locked and refrigerated location until the laboratory courier is able to pick it up. Once at the lab, the specimen is handled with a strict chain of custody code requiring everyone who meets the specimen to sign for it. This safeguards against any tampering or alteration of the specimen. Courts and places of employment require proper chain of custody protocols to ensure reliable results that will hold up under court scrutiny.

Turn around time is the time it takes for the lab to test specimens and report the results (negative or positive). Usually it takes two to five working days for the results to be confirmed and reported. Factors that could influence time include what time of day the sample is collected, when the courier picks it up, when the laboratory receives and tests it, and how many confirmation tests need to be performed on the sample. Original specimens are tested with Emit testing. This is a less expensive testing procedure. The accuracy rate for Emit is approximately 95%. Each sample that initially tests positive is retested and sent through a more expensive and elaborate test (GCMS) that can detect specific amounts of the drug. GCMS has been gaged around 99% accuracy. The higher the number of nanograms per milliliter detected in the urine, the higher the concentration of the drug there is in the urine sample.

A **negative** result simply means that no substance was present in the sample in sufficient quantity to be detected by the test. It does <u>not</u> mean that the individual has not used illegal substances. The more testing that is performed, the surer one can be that a negative result means the individual is <u>currently</u> not using illegal substances. A **positive** result <u>does</u> mean that the individual has used that substance. A positive result does not necessarily mean that the individual was intoxicated at the time the sample was collected as there is no established relationship between amount of a drug in urine and level of intoxication. **High positive** or **low positive** readings could be interpreted several different ways. A high reading could mean that the individual used drugs or alcohol in large quantity or shortly before the sample was collected. There are some drugs that stay in the body longer, however, and may be detected by testing several days or weeks following their use. Concentration of substances in urine may also vary widely because of an individual's excretion patterns, metabolic rate, fluid intake, diet, and body weight. Each of these factors influences low positive readings also. Clearly then, the amount of a substance detected in a sample cannot be interpreted precisely. A more accurate gauge would be tests given on a regular basis which are better able to determine the extent of drug and alcohol use and patterns. Urinalysis should not be used as the sole criteria for determining substance use. It should be used as another tool in evaluating someone's drug and alcohol use.

Specimen integrity refers to whether a sample appears to be pure urine. Tests are run on the sample to determine if the specimen may have been adulterated. Possible means of adulteration are numerous, but proper witness protocol and chain of custody help to reduce these possibilities. A specimen may be altered intentionally or unintentionally. It is difficult at times to determine which has occurred. If the integrity of the specimen is in question, the general procedure is to request another sample as quickly as possible for a second test.

Passive inhalation refers to absorption of THC (active ingredient of marijuana) into the bloodstream of a non-smoker in close contact with others who are smoking marijuana. When THC is detected in the urine, the probability of passive inhalation is low. Research does not support the common occurrence of this phenomenon. A person who may test positive due to passive inhalation is probably deriving the effects of use without direct inhalation. However, as passive inhalation is a remote possibility, individuals would be wise to avoid contact with persons using marijuana. Courts and places of employment will not usually consider passive inhalation a reason for a positive result, if a person in such close proximity to the use of illegal substances would themselves be using those substances.

Random urinalysis refers to specimen testing at infrequent intervals to prevent an individual from being able to predict when a test will take place. This could mean that not all specimens would be sent to the lab, that specimens could be collected at intermittent time periods, or that specimens could be collected only when an individual is suspected of using. It is essential in random urine testing that clients provide specimens whenever requested, having the time period between the request and the actual sample collection be no more than a few hours. **Scheduled urinalysis** would require very frequent (at least three times weekly) sample collection as the person being tested would know the schedule and could adjust their pattern of use to avoid detection. In either random or scheduled urinalysis, the refusal to provide a specimen at the time it is requested must be considered by the agency collecting the sample as an admission of illegal substance use.

How a teen's substance abuse problem surfaces can help determine the course and direction of treatment. Illegal substance use can get someone in legal trouble. Underage drinking, dealing drugs, and poor decisions associated with teen substance use can create legal difficulties. If a legal issue presents itself and a teen winds up in the legal system, that can be helpful in creating accountability and structure. An external factor (legal system) can exert additional control and consequences. Continued use while involved in the courts can lead to court fines, visits to probation officers, and even incarceration. Adding additional consequences for their use can slow down or eliminate their use. These consequences cause using to become less appealing due to having to answer to a probation officer. There are limits to how much adults can rely on the court systems however. Most do not offer immediate consequences. It can be a lengthy process as well. It may be several months to over a year before the results of a court proceeding conclude (Butts, Cusick, & Adams, 2009).

Adolescents involved with the court system will likely have a substance abuse evaluation. This helps determine treatment options. Parents and caregivers are often conflicted in these situations. They want to protect their child. Parents often assist in obtaining a lawyer to assist the youth in the legal proceedings. But parents need to understand the difference between helping a child and enabling. Parents serve their child's best interests when they obtain an attorney who can look at a bigger picture than just getting their client off the charges. There are attorneys who will coach their clients (teens) on what to say during the substance abuse evaluation to avoid having a negative evaluation. Some parents pay lawyers to assist in avoiding legal consequences. The attorney who coaches a child through the evaluation is harming their client.

Through the court system, there is an agency called Treatment Alternatives to Safe Communities (TASC). This group has been around since 1976 and advocates for lenient sentencing with drug treatment. This serves as an alternative to incarceration. Not all states have this organization but that is something that your attorney should know. If not, the courts would know this information.

Depending on how long they were taking the substance, the drug, the frequency of use, and individual makeup of the child, they can experience withdrawal symptoms. These symptoms can present themselves in different ways. For certain drugs, there can be a serious medical reaction to stopping the drug. This requires medical supervision and can be life-threatening. Medical supervision is necessary. If you are working with an outpatient therapist, coordination of care is extremely important.

Withdrawal could present itself in other ways. It could create sleep challenges, moodiness, sadness, and more serious side effects such as depression. A teenager can have difficulties in adjusting to life without drugs, especially if they used them as a means to cope with life situations or their social connections are tied to a using group. Teens' dependence on friends and subsequent isolation may cause intense social disconnection that must be considered a serious treatment concern.

It is unknown what can surface once a youth stops using. Adolescents who have been physically or sexually abused have a higher rate of substance abuse. Teens, because of limitations in their emotional, physical, and brain development may not have a good understanding or insight into their emotions. Shame, embarrassment, and confusion can hamper teens and prevent them from fully disclosing what they are feeling or experiencing. Parents and professionals need to look for signs of these types of struggles.

Although adolescents may be reluctant to seek help on their own, parents can create an environment for change. They can find additional help through Families Anonymous, hospital run support groups, or agency support groups. These groups can supplement professional counseling. When considering levels of care, we recommend that you start at the least restrictive setting. The drug of choice, length of use, previous treatment history, and environmental factors are considerations to consider for higher or more intense levels of treatment. Start with an outpatient evaluation.

Even if sessions are only one time a month, therapy can be helpful. It will help keep everyone on track and prolong investment in recovery. Frequency and duration of therapy should be decided by all parties involved. The longer we are able to keep a substance abusing youth away from drugs the greater the possibility they may buy into abstinence. Longer term treatment should be considered if their current environment is not conducive to recovery. Some teens are so entrenched in their use, only a change in environment offers them the best shot at sobriety. The level of care should be decided by parents and professionals.

Chapter 30: Older Adults and Falling Trees

In our retirement years, we face special challenges in addressing substance abuse concerns. We are more vulnerable to abuse due to lifestyle changes, medical issues, and a decrease in social contact. For example, family may visit less frequently, retirement can create isolation, and prescription medication use increases at the same time mobility decreases. For those who turn to drugs and alcohol to cope, there are greater opportunities to conceal use (University at Buffalo, 2015). Widowers usually have even fewer people to answer to for their use. The more people involved in someone's life the greater the likelihood of a problem being detected. If someone is secluded and abusing substances, a tree falls in a forest but no one may hear it.

Oftentimes, a substance abuse problem is only identified following an accident or injury, particularly if the individual lives alone. A family member or caregiver may then notice a problem, or a professional (doctor) might identify a concern. There can be problems with relying on professionals to intervene in elderly substance abuse. If the professional is a doctor, he or she will rely on the information presented to them. An older adult can withhold information that would identify a problem. If the substance abuse problem results from medication or a medication/alcohol combination, the professional prescribing may not recognize the severity of the problem. This is especially the case if there is a lack of coordination in care with other professionals who are also prescribing medication..

Regardless of how we identify a substance abuse problem, it is important to address the following areas:

- Establish coordination of care with all health care providers.
- Complete a thorough history and list of all current medications, regardless of the drug of choice. Some medications can be redundant or interfere with other medications.
- Involve family members and friends in treatment. This does not mean all family members. This may overwhelm and confuse the communication between everyone. A designated spokesperson can talk with professionals and keep family members in the loop.
- Carefully monitor any medical detox from medication.
- Work on coping skills to help with pain management.

Therapists should be sensitive to the challenge's older adults face. Not only possibly the loss of family and friends but in some cases the loss in their place in society. We often tie our identity to our employment and retirement can feel like a tremendous loss of status or worth. This impacts self-confidence. For any addict, taking away medication or alcohol can also feel like another loss. If someone already feels isolated, taking away a drug of choice can intensify these feelings. It is helpful then to increase the level of social interactions and engagement. Church groups, community centers, and park districts can be helpful resources. If someone is in an adult care facility, it can be helpful to develop a relationship with a staff member who can encourage involvement in residential facility activities. Social activities are important aids in any recovery.

It is helpful to remember that physical and cognitive declines are inevitable at this stage in life. Some older adults may have more significant deficits than others. This does not mean at certain ages we no longer learn. Education about chemical dependency is important at any age. The counselor should include this as a component of therapy.

If transportation is an issue for the elderly, they can still connect with therapists. For individuals with limited resources, ride shares and knowledge of bus routes can help. This can promote a feeling of independence. That feeling is essential at this stage in life. Caregivers and family should direct discussions to seeking out available resources. Online counseling is an option most insurance companies allow. If they cannot access or use a computer, telephonic (phone) therapy can be an option (Medicare approves this in our experience).

The connection a client has with their counselor is essential in therapy. With seniors, this is particularly important. Include them in the process and encourage their input. A therapist experienced in working with older adults and substance abuse can be a case manager for all parties involved. Counselors should focus their therapeutic approach according to the needs and abilities of their clients.

For example, Jim struggled with retirement. He had worked long hours as a sales representative at a manufacturing company for 25 years. For a long time, he was looking forward to his retirement. His wife Ellie plans to retire in two years herself. They have two adult children who live out of town.

After he officially retired, Jim kept himself busy. After two months, he started sleeping later and spending more time at the local Legion Hall (he had been in the military). On some days, he would be there drinking even after his wife came home from work. Ellie and Jim started getting into arguments about his drinking. Even after spending the whole day at the hall, he would continue drinking when he got home.

Ellie expressed her concern numerous times, but Jim continued to ignore her requests. On one occasion, their arguing got heated and Jim struck Ellie. He had been drinking heavily and was able to vaguely recall hitting her. Jim was remorseful that he hurt Ellie and recognized that his drinking patterns were problematic. This incident motivated Jim to agree to go to counseling. Jim also admitted that his doctor on his last visit expressed concerns about his drinking. He acknowledged that he felt bored and unfulfilled since his retirement. Jim agreed to hold off on his drinking for a while to gain perspective and work on where he is at in this juncture in life. Jim spent less time at the Legion Hall and actively worked in therapy to redefine himself in retirement. He volunteered at a hospital and began to take long walks with his wife. He even chose to take a noncredit class at a local college. Jim was making an active choice to fill in the gaps that were created with his change in lifestyle.

Chapter 31: Family, Peers, and Leisure Pursuits

For individuals immersed in substance abuse, their lives revolve around their ability to continue to use drugs/alcohol. A chemically dependent person will find a social setting consistent with their substance abuse. They often become increasingly isolated or insulated from people who might create conflict to their substance use. This path offers less conflict, whereas other environments might require lying and hiding their use. They will find comfort and companionship in peers who support their lifestyle.

In this section, we will consider the role of an individual's surroundings, whether they are there by choice or by circumstance. If someone grows up surrounded by heavy drinking and drug use, this will seem normal. This will be their reference point for viewing the outside world. We have found environmental influences to be profoundly influential on children, teens and young adults. Although there is evidence leading to genetic factors influencing addiction, strong arguments have been made regarding environmental influences (KSU Alcohol and Other Drug Education Service, 2011; Jedrzejczak, 2015). At an early age they may have sensed something was wrong, but the family never mentioned or discussed the problem. In the substance abuse field, we refer to this as the elephant in the living room. The elephant (addiction) is sitting in the living room and everyone is ignoring its presence. Not all kids who grow up in high-use environments become users themselves of course, but they do often have a different frame of reference that they carry throughout their lives. This can of course create conflict with the outer world. What they see as normal others might see as out-of-control use. Waking up hung over, missing work because of a late-night cocaine binge, and blackouts may seem typical and normal behavior.

Once a person has stopped using, one of the first life changes they need to consider is their environment. This is especially true in early recovery. This can mean changing friend groups or even finding new employment. Recovery must be a priority, and all decisions should revolve around promoting sobriety. Resistance to these changes is to be expected. Stopping use is challenging enough, changing friends or altering the dynamics of relationships can seem overwhelming. Individuals may be reluctant to give up long-standing relationships and that is understandable. Friends who use may also push back about one's decision to seek substance abuse help. They may fear losing their using or drinking buddy, or it may make them reflect on their own use. Recovery often means turning away from friends (or friends turning away from you). Users also often have already burned bridges with friends and even family who may have given up on the substance abuser.

For teenagers, finding a new peer group can be even more challenging as fitting in is especially important for them. Peers can strongly influence decision making, and adolescents are more likely to take risks when around other peers (Chein, Albert, O'Brien, Uckert, & Steinberg, 2010). Having to change friend groups is an additional loss. Even a substance abusing youth committed to recovery will fight to keep their friends. They might believe that using friends could be convinced to be supportive, or that these friends will no longer get high or drink in their presence. At least that is what they will convince themselves.

Yet friends can also be a major asset in recovery, if they are the right friends. This is why sober support groups are so useful to individuals struggling with addiction. We cannot emphasize their importance enough. They can:

- Include motivation and support to continue abstaining (Hunter-Reel, McCrady, Hildebrandt, & Epstein, 2010)
- Include healthy peer pressure
- Eliminate or minimize the impulsive decisions to use
- Help overcome urges
- Present sober role modeling and reference points
- Lessen the anxiety associated with challenges in committing to abstaining
- Offer emotional rewards in continuing their decision to abstain from substance abuse
- Have a shared value in a sober lifestyle
- Provide nonjudgmental support recovery

Numerous studies support the importance of the environment to recovery. They have found social factors to be helpful in both our mental and physical health (Institute of Medicine and National Research Council, 2013, Chapter 6). Social engagement activates our reward system (Krach, Paulus, Bodden, & Kircher, 2010). This is the same neurological system activated by substance use. Individuals in positive sober lifestyles have a much greater chance of success in maintaining sobriety.

A good starting point for those who want to maintain relationships with using peers is committing to your goal of abstinence. If you make sobriety a priority, decisions about changing friends will come in time. You should actively evaluate situations that will put you at risk for relapse on a regular basis. Have contingency plans laid out to minimize risks of relapse. For example, if you are going to a friend's party where there is usually heavy drinking, it may help to arrive early and leave early before heavy drinking escalates, bring a partner (spouse or friend) who is supportive of your sobriety, rehearse responses to inquiries about your decision not to drink, and have a means to leave if the situation gets uncomfortable. It is important that your friend or spouse has your back in these situations. Their ability to abstain can support yours. For some, it will be like entering a lion's den. If these decisions will put anyone at risk, we strongly suggest avoiding these environments.

Keeping the same peer group or using environment is usually not successful. That does not mean it is impossible, but underestimating your environment often leads to relapse. For adolescents, they may need to experience how difficult it will be to maintain sobriety and keep the same peer groups. Parents should openly discuss concerns regarding their peer group and establish firm rules and consequences. Knowing they need to maintain sobriety can help motivate an adolescent to make healthy choices. For the more committed youth, finding new friends can be difficult. They may have to reestablish ties with former sober friends, join new clubs, get involved in religious groups, get involved in sports, or actively establish a sober social group.

School settings can also present challenges to maintaining sobriety. For some, this is a using environment. There are high schools that offer support groups for students in early recovery or who are returning from a treatment setting. Also, establishing contact with a school social worker can be helpful. Changing classes or schedules may also benefit the child. Discuss with your child's school counselor a plan of action as soon as possible.

There are many difficulties associated with recovery and having to redefine yourself is part of the challenge. This may mean creating a new identity by establishing new friends or activities. They can develop sober friends through some suggestions given in previous sections (exercise, support groups). Additional suggestions include:

- Sober bars
- Volunteer opportunities
- Religious organizations
- Meet up groups (meetup.com)
- Community volunteering or involvement
- Sport activities
- Noncredit college classes or workshops

Support is essential in recovery. Feeling isolated puts individuals at risk for relapse. There is an expression in the field that includes major risks for relapsing: **H**ungry **A**ngry **L**onely and **T**ired (HALT). Awareness of triggers and the right support are essential. Making this part of your action plan with your therapist or support group can really help.

Chapter 32: Runaway Trolley and Change

We end with our last thought puzzle: The Trolley Problem. Credited to British philosopher Philippa Foot, this moral dilemma asks the reader to imagine you are at the controls of a railway switch. Suddenly, you see a runaway trolley coming down the tracks, with no brakes. The track splits off and you can determine the direction of the out of control trolley. On one track there are five people, and on the other track there is one person. If you do nothing, the train will crash into the five people and kill them. If you flip the switch, it will go down the other track, killing the lone person. What do you do?

If you are choosing the track that has one person, you are imposing a decision of saving five people at the expense of one. You are actively intervening to kill the one person by switching the tracks. If you do nothing, five people die. Would your decision be any different if you knew the one person could discover the cure for cancer? Or two of the five people are murderers? No one would envy the track operator's choice here.

This ethical challenge is not an easy one. It is not meant to have a simple solution. Addicts face similar struggles. They are confronted with ethical, moral, and life-threatening decisions. Some of their decisions involve the lives of others, including family, friends, and coworkers. Users also make choices that conflict with their own value systems. The push and pull of addiction (costs and benefits) is a struggle that goes beyond logic and common sense. For some, this struggle can last a lifetime. Individuals who struggle with addiction understand they have a problem but can feel helpless in addressing the problem. They do not feel they are in the driver's seat of their life. They have turned those decisions over to substances. To escape, they will need to make difficult choices.

Understanding the challenges of stopping substances is not enough. Stopping use is just the beginning of reclaiming a healthy life. It is important not to underestimate the effort needed in recovery. Taking away the substances, although a healthy decision, can leave deficits to face. If we take away the rotting bricks from a building, we need to replace them with solid bricks, otherwise, the foundation can collapse.

We have touched on many aspects of addiction. Readers have gained a better understanding of how consuming addiction can be, not only for the chemically dependent but for their family and loved ones. Users turn choices over to addiction. They make decisions that seem baffling and confusing to those around them. Often these decisions are equally confusing for the addict. They do not completely understand why they keep doing the things they do. Stopping or cutting back is an option successfully exercised by some individuals. They see a conflict or a problem with their use and they quit. However, for many individuals, it's not that easy. Stopping means great efforts and sacrifices.

When a diabetic is initially informed by a medical professional of their diagnosis, they are informed of the lifestyle changes they will need to make to maintain their health. They will have to spend the rest of their lives adapting and adhering to a new lifestyle to accommodate their condition. This includes a change in diet, insulin shots if needed, and possibly other medication. They make these changes so they can live their lives in manageable ways. Failure to adhere to these adjustments is often life-threatening. We can say the same regarding addiction. Diabetics and substance abusers are not always successful in their attempts to stay healthy. The relapse rate is similar for both conditions, 30 to 50% for diabetes and 40 to 60% for substance abuse, yet public perception is quite different for diabetes than for substance abuse (NIDA, 2018b).

Those struggling with an addiction who are reluctant to make the necessary life changes will most often return to their use. A relapse is not a spontaneous event but a chain of events that lead up to a decision. Just as a diabetic may make poor diet decisions, an addict can deviate from their sobriety plan. These changes can lead to relapses, even small ones. Deciding to go to a bar after months of sobriety, going out with a friend you used drugs with, and changing your route home from work and passing an old drug hangout can steer you toward a relapse. Even changes in thinking can alter a path to abstinence ("maybe it is okay to have a drink now and then"). Those facing substance abuse may provide convincing arguments why their continued use is not a problem. Simply being aware of these risks and triggers, and recognizing MAST thoughts, is a major first step to keeping sober. It is our hope that this book has given you the tools to recognize and overcome destructive thoughts and triggers, and to make long-term, positive life changes.

The more you plan for in recovery, the more likely you will succeed. We have an included a checklist (**Figure 3.31**) to help you work toward creating a healthy balance in your life without substance use.

Figure 3.31

194

<table>
<tr><td colspan="4" align="center">Check List</td></tr>
<tr><td colspan="4">This checklist is not used an evaluative tool. The purpose is to identify potential problem areas for you in your recovery. Answering yes to any of these questions does not indicate a diagnosis. When you answer yes to a question, further attention should be given to this area. If you are seeing a therapist, have a Primary Care Provider, sponsor, or family member involved in your recovery, you can discuss with them a direction to pursue to address this area of concern. Resources provided in chapters specific for that challenge will also be helpful. Since many mental health symptoms overlap, a professional can help diagnosis the problem and suggest a course of action to address the problem(s). These problems should be addressed concurrently with your substance abuse recovery plan. Please circle yes if you agree with the statement and no if you disagree.</td></tr>
<tr><td>1</td><td>I feel bored</td><td>Y</td><td>N</td></tr>
<tr><td>2</td><td>I feel lonely</td><td>Y</td><td>N</td></tr>
<tr><td>3</td><td>I have difficulties concentrating</td><td>Y</td><td>N</td></tr>
<tr><td>4</td><td>I am forgetful</td><td>Y</td><td>N</td></tr>
<tr><td>5</td><td>I feel sad a lot</td><td>Y</td><td>N</td></tr>
<tr><td>6</td><td>I feel depressed</td><td>Y</td><td>N</td></tr>
<tr><td>7</td><td>I worry a lot</td><td>Y</td><td>N</td></tr>
<tr><td>8</td><td>My thoughts are racing</td><td>Y</td><td>N</td></tr>
<tr><td>9</td><td>I feel anxious</td><td>Y</td><td>N</td></tr>
<tr><td>10</td><td>I have difficulties sleeping</td><td>Y</td><td>N</td></tr>
<tr><td>11</td><td>I do not like the way I look</td><td>Y</td><td>N</td></tr>
<tr><td>12</td><td>I feel my diet is out of control</td><td>Y</td><td>N</td></tr>
<tr><td>13</td><td>I hate the way my body looks</td><td>Y</td><td>N</td></tr>
<tr><td>14</td><td>I have thrown up intentionally to lose or manage weight</td><td>Y</td><td>N</td></tr>
<tr><td>15</td><td>I feel isolated</td><td>Y</td><td>N</td></tr>
<tr><td>16</td><td>I have thoughts of hurting myself</td><td>Y</td><td>N</td></tr>
<tr><td>17</td><td>I do not have many friends</td><td>Y</td><td>N</td></tr>
<tr><td colspan="4">Recreational pursuits: 1,2,14, 15, 16, 17   Depression: 1,2,3,4,5,6,10,15   Anxiety: 7,8, 9,10 Eating Disorder: 11,12,13,14 Exercise: 1,2,11 Attention Deficit Hyperactivity Disorder: 3,4, Diet: 11,13</td></tr>
</table>

One last case study will serve to tie many of the issues covered here together with a reminder that, no matter the addiction, change is possible. Phil was a 22-year-old who sought out our services through the urging of his parents. They were concerned about his drinking and felt it had become a problem. Phil was also suffering from anxiety and was on medication prescribed by his primary physician. He was taking Xanax, a Benzodiazepine. When Xanax and alcohol are mixed, the effects of the alcohol will increase. His drinking started when he was 15. He quickly turned to into a heavy drinker. He had seen several therapists prior to seeing us. His parents informed him that if his drinking continued, he would be kicked out of the house. Phil had recently flunked out from college, which he was attending out of state.

The longest Phil had ever gone without drinking as an adult was a couple days. He was, for the most part, a daily drinker. His friend group was heavily involved in drinking as well. Phil was reluctant to stop his drinking. After several sessions, at the urging of his parents and girlfriend, he agreed to give abstinence a shot. There were several challenges for Phil. First, he was drinking daily, and we were not sure if he would go through alcohol withdrawal if he suddenly stopped drinking. His anxiety also played a role in this. He had been drinking to help when his anxiety spiked. He also had been taking Xanax for so long that immediately stopping could present withdrawal symptoms as well. He was not willing to change his friend group who encouraged his drinking. Lastly, he had a lot of idle time on his hands.

Our first course of action was to determine if he was at risk for withdrawal if he stopped drinking. When he was assessed at a hospital as recommended, he went through a medical detox. Phil agreed to this and spent 5 days in a detox unit. When he left the detox unit, he was motivated to stop drinking. We worked on his recovery plan. After some ups and downs, he reached 6 months sobriety. He did this by seeing us and going to Alcoholics Anonymous. It was difficult for him to find the correct medication dosage for his anxiety. He was finally able to get an additional medication added, which helped his anxiety.

Initially, he struggled with handling challenges. His usual coping mechanism was to drink. He had to learn how to deal with challenges without drinking. We were able to help him learn new coping skills and also identify his addictive voice. For example:

Phil: "I was having problems today with my mom yelling at me. It made me want to drink."

Mark: "It sounds like you had an argument with your mom, you felt stressed out because of it, and you had an urge to drink. These are all different entities. Your voice wants to associate everything together. This will make it more likely you will drink. You have had arguments before with your mom and other people and not drank. Your voice wants to convince you that they are all the same thing, but they are not. You want to drink because you want to drink. Nothing has changed if you return to drinking. Whatever you argued about will still be there when you are sober."

Phil: "Yeah, I really get it. I was just looking for an excuse to drink. It is hard sometimes."

Mark: "That, I am sure is true. However, how do you think going back to drinking will help."

Phil: "It won't. I have to keep remembering that."

Phil has been seeing us now for over 3 years. He has remained sober. He has also weaned off all the anxiety medication, finished his college degree, and eventually found new friends. He did this after realizing that he no longer shared any interests or connections with his friends since he stopped his drinking.

Phil is just one example of someone who turned their life around. We have worked with many individuals and families who steer themselves clear of the path of destruction that is addiction. Life offers many twists and turns that get us from point A to point B. These twists and turns can shape our lives. Who knew that a split-second decision made by a graduate student sitting on a bench in a Veterans Administration Hospital would set the course for his career path? And that that career would lead his wife and him to write a book? There are likewise many tipping points that lead individuals to seek help for substance abuse. Even after all these years working in the field, we often contemplate the seemingly chance circumstances that led someone to our office. If a woman waited an extra half-hour to start drinking, she would not been confronted by her child's coach about smelling of alcohol. Or a young professional who attends a company party, to be later confronted by his boss after having too many drinks. If he had missed that party, would he still be coming to see us?

We have seen the toll substance abuse takes on individuals and families. The choices that addicts and alcoholics make (or that substances make for them) cost them careers, families, and lives. We hope that you have learned that you have options and that overcoming addiction is possible. Choices define our character. The choices we make once we recognize a problem can literally mean life or death. Remind yourself that life may get worse before it gets better. Take slow consistent steps to change have the potential to improve our lives and the lives of those we love. Families of the chemically dependent have choices as well. It is important for families and those struggling with addiction, to turn to professionals to assist them in their journey in recovery.

The information presented in this book can empower individuals and families to take control of their lives. We hope that readers use this information to point themselves in a better direction, or to help someone who is struggling with addiction. Don't wait for the tree to fall to make a sound.

References

AddictionCenter, (2018, November 19). Sleeping pill addiction and abuse. Retrieved from https://www.addictioncenter.com/sleeping-pills/

Aerobic exercise may protect cognitive abilities of heavy drinkers, says CU study. (2013, April 16). Retrieved from https://www.colorado.edu/today/2013/04/16/aerobic-exercise-may-protect-cognitive-abilities-heavy-drinkers-says-cu-study

Albert, D., Chein, J., & Steinberg, L. (2013). Peer influences on adolescent decision making. *Current Directions in Psychological Science*, 22(2), 114-120. doi: 10.1177/0963721412471347

Alcohol & Drugs in the Workplace. (n.d.). Retrieved from https://www.facingaddiction.org/resources/alcohol-drugs-in-the-workplace

Alcohol and food equivalents. (n.d.). Retrieved from https://www.drinkaware.co.uk/alcohol-facts/health-effects-of-alcohol/calories/alcohol-and-food-equivalents/

Alcoholism: Clinical & Experimental Research. (2008, April 3). Alcohol alters prefrontal cortex activity through ion channel disruption. *ScienceDaily*. Retrieved from www.sciencedaily.com/releases/2008/04/080403183048.htm

Alzheimer's Association. (n.d.). Inside the brain: A tour of how the mind works. Retrieved from https://www.alz.org/alzheimers-dementia/what-is-alzheimers/brain_tour

American Association of Retired Persons. (2005). Prescription drug use among midlife and older Americans. Retrieved from https://assets.aarp.org/rgcenter/health/rx_midlife_plus.pdf

American College of Medical Toxicology. (2019). Cocaine. Retrieved from https://www.acmt.net/Cocaine.html#Q4

American Geriatrics Society. (n.d.). Why geriatrics? Retrieved from https://www.americangeriatrics.org/geriatrics-profession/why-geriatrics

American Psychiatric Association. (2013). *Diagnostic and statistical manual of mental disorders* (5th ed.). Arlington, VA: American Psychiatric Publishing.

American Society of Addiction Medicine. (2016). Opioid addiction 2016 facts & figures. Retrieved from https://www.asam.org/docs/default-source/advocacy/opioid-addiction-disease-facts-figures.pdf

Anderson, R. (2014, November 6). Pharmaceutical industry gets high on fat profits. Retrieved from https://www.bbc.com/news/business-28212223

Arkowitz, H. (2010, January 1). Why science tells us not to rely on eyewitness accounts. Retrieved from https://www.scientificamerican.com/article/do-the-eyes-have-it/

Arseneault, L., Cannon, M., Poulton, R., Murray, R., Caspi, A., & Moffitt, T. E. (2002, November 23). Cannabis use in adolescence and risk for adult psychosis: Longitudinal prospective study. *BMJ (Clinical research ed.), 325*(7374), 1212-1213. Retrieved from https://www.ncbi.nlm.nih.gov/pmc/articles/PMC135493/

Babson, K. A., Sottile, J., & Morabito, D. (2017, April). Cannabis, cannabinoids, and sleep: A review of the literature. *Current Psychiatry Reports, 19*(23). doi: 10.1007/s11920-017-0775-9

Bachai, S. (2013, July 10). 7 health benefits of drinking alcohol. Retrieved from https://www.medicaldaily.com/7-health-benefits-drinking-alcohol-247552

Bai, M. (2011, March 4). Can you cure yourself of drug addiction? Retrieved from https://www.scientificamerican.com/article/can-you-cure-yourself-of-addiction/

Barnea-Goraly, N., Menon, V., Eckert, M., Tamm, L., Bammer, R., Karchemskiy, A., Dant, C. C., & Reiss, A. L. (2005). White matter development during childhood and adolescence: A cross-sectional diffusion tensor imaging study. *Cerebral Cortex, 15*(12), 1848-1854. doi: 10.1093/cercor/bhi062

Beer by the numbers: Total alcohol consumption. (2016). Retrieved from https://www.nbwa.org/resources/total-alcohol-consumption

Beiter, R. M., Peterson, A. B., Abel, J., & Lynch, W. J. (2016, April 26). Exercise during early, but not late abstinence, attenuates subsequent relapse vulnerability in a rat model. *Translational Psychiatry 6*, e792. Retrieved from https://www.nature.com/articles/tp201658

Benezet, A. (1774). *The mighty destroyer displayed, in some account of the dreadful havock* [sic] *made by the mistaken use as well as abuse of distilled spirituous liquors* [Evans Early American Imprint Collection]. Retrieved from http://name.umdl.umich.edu/N32312.0001.001

Bengali, S., & Mostaghim, R. (2016, December 19). Iran's growing drug problem: 'No walk of society is immune.' Retrieved from https://www.latimes.com/world/la-fg-iran-drug-addiction-2016-story.html

Bergland, C. (2013, December 19). Why is the teen brain so vulnerable? Retrieved from https://www.psychologytoday.com/us/blog/the-athletes-way/201312/why-is-the-teen-brain-so-vulnerable

Bergland, C. (2017, July 28). Silent third person self-talk facilitates emotion regulation: Try using your own name during inner dialogues. Retrieved from https://www.psychologytoday.com/us/blog/the-athletes-way/201707/silent-third-person-self-talk-facilitates-emotion-regulation

Beyers, S. (2012, April 25). On the origins of ayahuasca [Blog post]. Retrieved from https://www.singingtotheplants.com/2012/04/on-origins-of-ayahuasca/

Bhatti, A. B., & Haq, A. U. (2017). The pathophysiology of perceived social isolation: Effects on health and mortality. *Cureus, 9*(1), e994. doi: 10.7759/cureus.994

Booth, S. (2015, April 29). Are your meds making you gain weight? Retrieved from https://www.webmd.com/diet/obesity/features/medication-weight-gain#1

Botanical Shaman. (2018, March 4). What religious rituals use psychoactive drugs? Retrieved from https://botanicalshaman.com/2018/03/04/what-religious-rituals-use-psychoactive-drugs/

Brecher, E. M., & the Editors of Consumer Reports Magazine. (1972). The Consumers Union Report on licit and illicit Drugs. Retrieved from http://www.druglibrary.org/schaffer/library/studies/cu/cu8.html

Brewer, J. (n.d.). Train your brain, change your habits. Retrieved from https://www.judsonbrewer.com/

Brewer, J., & Kabat-Zinn, J. (2017). *The craving mind: From cigarettes to smartphones to love--why we get hooked and how we can break bad habits.* New Haven, CT: Yale University Press.

Brown University. (2018, October 25). Just a few drinks can change how memories are formed. Retrieved from https://www.eurekalert.org/pub_releases/2018-10/bu-jaf101818.php

Bruce, R. D. (2010, March). Methadone as HIV prevention: High volume methadone sites to decrease HIV incidence rates in resource limited settings. *International Journal of Drug Policy, 21*(2), 122-124. doi: 10.1016/j.drugpo.2009.10.004

Bryner, M. (2010, July 29). How much alcohol is in my drink? Retrieved from https://www.livescience.com/32735-how-much-alcohol-is-in-my-drink.html

Budney, A. J., & Hughes, J. R. (2006, May). The cannabis withdrawal syndrome. *Current Opinion in Psychiatry, 19*(3), 233-238. Retrieved from https://www.ncbi.nlm.nih.gov/pubmed/16612207

Bushak, L. (2015, July 8). 8 strange addiction treatments used throughout history, from morphine to lobotomies. Retrieved from https://www.medicaldaily.com/8-strange-addiction-treatments-used-throughout-history-morphine-lobotomies-341740

Butts, J. A., Cusick, G. R., & Adams, B. (2009). Delays in youth justice [project funded by the National Institute of Justice]. Retrieved from https://www.ncjrs.gov/pdffiles1/nij/grants/228493.pdf

Carod-Artal, F. J. (2015, January-February). Hallucinogenic drugs in pre-Columbian Mesoamerican cultures. *Neurologia 30*(1), 42-49. doi: 10.1016/j.nrl.2011.07.003

Center for Behavioral Health Statistics and Quality. (2015). *Behavioral health trends in the United States: Results from the 2014 national survey on drug use and health.* (HHS Publication No. SMA 15-4927, NSDUH Series H-50). Retrieved from https://www.samhsa.gov/data/sites/default/files/NSDUH-FRR1-2014/NSDUH-FRR1-2014.pdf

Center for Prevention Research and Development. (2018). Illinois Youth Survey 2018 Frequency Report: State of Illinois. Champaign, IL: CPRD, School of Social Work, University of Illinois. Retrieved from https://iys.cprd.illinois.edu/UserFiles/Servers/Server_178052/File/state-reports/2018/Freq18_IYS_Statewide.pdf

Castaneda, R. (2017, January 9). What's the best diet for newly sober alcoholics and addicts? Retrieved from https://health.usnews.com/wellness/food/articles/2017-01-09/whats-the-best-diet-for-newly-sober-alcoholics-and-addicts

Cell Press. (2015, September 23). Adolescent brain may be especially sensitive to new memories, social stress, and drug use. *ScienceDaily*. Retrieved January 9, 2019 from www.sciencedaily.com/releases/2015/09/150923133517.htm

Center for Behavioral Health Statistics and Quality. (2015). *Behavioral health trends in the United States: Results from the 2014 national survey on drug use and health* (HHS Publication No. SMA 15-4927, NSDUH Series H-50). Retrieved from http://www.samhsa.gov/data/

Centers for Disease Control and Prevention. (2017, January 31). Alzheimer's disease and healthy aging. Retrieved from https://www.cdc.gov/aging/mentalhealth/depression.htm

Centers for Disease Control and Prevention. (2017, August 31). Annual surveillance report of drug-related risks and outcomes. Surveillance Special Report 1. Accessed from https://www.cdc.gov/ drugoverdose/pdf/pubs/2017- cdc-drug-surveillance-report.pdf

Centers for Disease Control and Prevention. (2018, October 19). Teen drivers: Get the facts. Retrieved from https://www.cdc.gov/motorvehiclesafety/teen_drivers/teendrivers_factsheet.html

Centers for Disease Control and Prevention. (2018, December 19). Opioid overdose: Understanding the epidemic. Retrieved from https://www.cdc.gov/drugoverdose/epidemic/index.html

Chein, J., Albert, D., O'Brien, L., Uckert, K., & Steinberg, L. (2010). Peers increase adolescent risk taking by enhancing activity in the brain's reward circuitry. *Developmental Science, 14*(2). doi: 10.1111/j.1467-7687.2010.01035.x

Cherry, K. (2018, September 21). How the fight or flight response works. Retrieved from https://www.verywellmind.com/what-is-the-fight-or-flight-response-2795194

Cherry, K. E., Walker, E. J., Brown, J. S., Volaufova, J., LaMotte, L. R., Welsh, D. A., Su, L. J., Jazwinski, S. M., Ellis, R., Wood, R. H., ... Frisard, M. I. (2011). Social engagement and health in younger, older, and oldest-old adults in the Louisiana Healthy Aging Study. *Journal of applied gerontology: the official journal of the Southern Gerontological Society, 32*(1), 51-75.

Child Welfare Information Gateway. (2014). Parental substance use and the child welfare system. Retrieved from https://www.childwelfare.gov/pubPDFs/parentalsubabuse.pdf

Chudler, E. H. (n.d.). Neuroscience for kids - Action potential. Retrieved from https://faculty.washington.edu/chudler/ap.html

Cicero, T. J., Ellis, M. S., Surratt, H. L., & Kurtz, S. P. (2014). The changing face of heroin use in the United States: A retrospective analysis of the past 50 years. *JAMA Psychiatry, 71*(7), 821-826. doi: 10.1001/jamapsychiatry.2014.366

Cleversley, K. (2002, January 1). Brugmansia aurea - Golden angel's trumpet. Retrieved from http://entheology.com/plants/brugmansia-aurea-golden-angels-trumpet/

Consumer Healthcare Products Association. (n.d.). *Statistics on OTC use.* Retrieved from https://chpa.org/marketstats.aspx

Crocq, M. A. (2007). Historical and cultural aspects of man's relationship with addictive drugs. *Dialogues in clinical neuroscience, 9*(4), 355-361. Retrieved from https://www.ncbi.nlm.nih.gov/pmc/articles/PMC3202501/

Crossen, J. (n.d.). The limbic system theory of addiction and the pre frontal cortex [PowerPoint slides]. Retrieved from http://jamescrossen.weebly.com/uploads/3/0/6/2/3062404/the_limbic_system.pdf

Crum, R. M., Ford, D.E., Storr, C.L., & Chan, Y. F. (2004, October). Association of sleep disturbance with chronicity and remission of alcohol dependence: data from a population-based prospective study. *Alcoholism: Clinical and Experimental Research, 28*(10), 1533-1540. Retrieved from https://www.ncbi.nlm.nih.gov/pubmed/15597086

Crum, R. M., Storr, C.L., Chan, Y. F., & Ford, D.E., (2004, July). Sleep disturbance and risk for alcohol-related problems. *The American Journal of Psychiatry, 161*(7), 1197-1203. doi: 10.1176/appi.ajp.161.7.1197

Curtin, S. C., Tejada-Vera, B., & Warner, M. (2017). Drug overdose deaths among adolescents aged 15 -19 in the United States: 1999–2015. NCHS Data Brief, No. 282.

Davis, K. (2018, June 25). Everything you need to know about barbiturates. Retrieved from https://www.medicalnewstoday.com/articles/310066.php

DEA Museum & Visitors Center. (n.d.). Cannabis, coca, & poppy: Nature's addictive plants. Retrieved from https://www.deamuseum.org/ccp/opium/history.html

Depra, D. (2015, March 13). Marijuana use in teen tears may lead to memory loss. Retrieved from https://www.techtimes.com/articles/39538/20150313/marijuana-use-in-teen-years-may-lead-to-memory-loss.htm

Depressants. (n.d.). Retrieved from https://www.drugfreeworld.org/drugfacts/prescription/depressants.html

Di Chiara, G., & Imperato, A. (1988). Drugs abused by humans preferentially increase synaptic dopamine concentrations in the mesolimbic system of freely moving rats. *Proceedings of the National Academy of Sciences of the United States of America, 85*, 5274-5278. doi: 10.1073/pnas.85.14.5274.

Drug policy of Portugal. (n.d.). In *Wikipedia*. Retrieved February 4, 2019, from https://en.wikipedia.org/wiki/Drug_policy_of_Portugal

Drug treatments for sleep problems. (2018, October 28). Retrieved from https://www.webmd.com/sleep-disorders/drug-treatments

East, A. (2018, March 27). Four common mental illnesses in the elderly: Learn the risk factors and symptoms to watch for. Retrieved from https://caringpeopleinc.com/blog/mental-illnesses-in-the-elderly/

The Editors of Encyclopaedia Britannica. (2018, April 27). Temperance movement. Retrieved from https://www.britannica.com/topic/temperance-movement

European Monitoring Centre for Drugs and Drug Addiction (EMCDDA). (2015). *European drug report: Trends and developments.* Luxembourg: Publications Office of the European Union. doi: 10.2810/084165

FECYT - Spanish Foundation for Science and Technology. (2018, March 15). The brain puts the memories warehouse in order while we sleep. *ScienceDaily.* Retrieved January 4, 2019, from www.sciencedaily.com/releases/2018/03/180315110640.htm

Feinman, M. (2018, February 24). Keeley gold cure for alcoholism brought thousands to Illinois. Retrieved from https://www.dailyherald.com/news/20180224/keeley-gold-cure-for-alcoholism-brought-thousands-to-illinois

Finney, J. W., Hahn, A. C., & Moos, R. H. (1996, December). The effectiveness of inpatient and outpatient treatment for alcohol abuse: the need to focus on mediators and moderators of setting effects. *Addiction, 91*(12), 1773-1796. Retrieved from https://www.ncbi.nlm.nih.gov/pubmed/8997760

Firger, J. (2017, July 28). Feeling stressed? Try talking to yourself, but in the third person. Retrieved from https://www.newsweek.com/stressed-talk-yourself-third-person-643628

Fontenot, B. (2011, September 8). Drinkers' poor diets. Retrieved from http://www.thedoctorwillseeyounow.com/content/addiction/art3429.html

Ford, D. E. & Kamerow, D. B. (1989, September 15). Epidemiologic study of sleep disturbances and psychiatric disorders. An opportunity for prevention? *JAMA 262*(11), 1479-1484. Retrieved from https://www.ncbi.nlm.nih.gov/pubmed/2769898

Formica, M. J. (2009, February 11). Primal Wiring, Survival and the Need to Be Loved. Retrieved from https://www.psychologytoday.com/us/blog/enlightened-living/200902/primal-wiring-survival-and-the-need-be-loved

Fottrell, Q. (2018, October 10). Nearly half of Americans report feeling alone. Retrieved from https://www.marketwatch.com/story/america-has-a-big-loneliness-problem-2018-05-02

Fraser-Thill, R. (2018, August 31). Myelination process and tween impulses. Retrieved from https://www.verywellfamily.com/myelination-process-3288324

Freeman, D. (2011, October 7). Recreational drug Ecstasy may bring better blood cancer meds. Retrieved from https://www.cbsnews.com/news/recreational-drug-ecstasy-may-bring-better-blood-cancer-meds/

Freeman, S. (2008, October 7). What happens in the brain during an orgasm? Retrieved from https://health.howstuffworks.com/sexual-health/sexuality/brain-during-orgasm2.htm

Friedmann, P. D., Herman, D. S., Freedman, S., Lemon, S. C., Ramsey, S., & Stein, M. D. (2003). Treatment of sleep disturbance in alcohol recovery: a national survey of addiction medicine physicians. *Journal of addictive diseases, 22*(2), 91-103. doi: 10.1300/J069v22n02_08

Fullerton, C. A., Kim, M., Thomas, C. P., Lyman, D. R., Montejano, L. B., Dougherty, R. H., Daniels, A.S., Ghose, S. S., & Delphin-Rittmon, M. E. (2014). Medication-assisted treatment with methadone: Assessing the evidence. *Psychiatric Services, 65*(2), 146-157. doi: 10.1176/appi.ps.201300235

Furman, T. (2017, June 6). A torture method developed to treat patients in mental hospitals: Hydrotherapy. Retrieved from https://onedio.co/content/a-torture-method-developed-to-treat-patients-in-mental-hospitals-hydrotherapy-16964

Gale, T. (2002). Hallucinogens and spiritual rituals. Retrieved from https://www.encyclopedia.com/medicine/medical-magazines/hallucinogens-and-spiritual-rituals

Gallagher, L., & Hetherington, A., (2005, November). Stone Age beer. Retrieved from http://discovermagazine.com/2005/nov/stone-age-beer/

Genes and addiction. (n.d.). Retrieved from https://learn.genetics.utah.edu/content/addiction/genes/

Getting Smart. (2015, May 8). The teenage brain: Scaffolding the brain for lifelong learning [Blog post]. Retrieved from https://www.huffpost.com/entry/the-teenage-brain-scaffol_b_7242344

Girodo, M., & Roehl, J. (1978, October). Cognitive preparation and coping self-talk: Anxiety management during the stress of flying. *Journal of Consulting and Clinical Psychology, 46*(5), 978-989. doi: 10.1037%2F0022-006X.46.5.978

Gold, M., & Adamec, C. (2011, April 17). Dr. Benjamin Rush and his views on alcoholism. Retrieved from http://www.health.am/psy/more/dr-benjamin-rush-and-his-views-on-alcoholism/

Grant, B. F., Chou, S. P., Saha, T. D., Pickering, R. P., Kerridge, B. T., Ruan, W. J., . . . Hasin, D. S. (2017). Prevalence of 12-Month Alcohol Use, High-Risk Drinking, and DSM-IV Alcohol Use Disorder in the United States, 2001-2002 to 2012-2013. *JAMA Psychiatry, 74*(9), 911. doi: 10.1001/jamapsychiatry.2017.2161

Groenewald, C., Palermo, T., & Rabbitts, J. (2018, March). Patterns and predictors of opioid use following adolescent spine surgery. *The Journal of Pain, 19*(3), S75. doi: 10.1016/j.jpain.2017.12.171

Guarnotta, E. (2018, December 7). Drug use in religions. Retrieved from https://www.recovery.org/addiction/religions/

Harbolic, B. K. (n.d.). Retrieved from https://www.medicinenet.com/alcohol_and_nutrition/article.htm#how_is_alcohol_metabolized

Harrison Narcotics Tax Act (n.d.). In *Wikipedia*. Retrieved February 4, 2019, from https://en.wikipedia.org/wiki/Harrison_Narcotics_Tax_Act

Hatfield, R. C. (Ed.). (2017, October 25). Barbiturates' side effects. Retrieved from https://drugabuse.com/library/barbiturates-side-effects/

He, W., Goodkind, D., & Kowal, P. (2016, March). *An aging world: 2015 – International population reports.* United States Census Bureau. Retrieved from https://www.census.gov/content/dam/Census/library/publications/2016/demo/p95-16-1.pdf

Hedegaard, H., Miniño, A. M., & Warner, M. (2018, November). Drug overdose deaths in the United States, 1999-2017. Retrieved from https://www.cdc.gov/nchs/products/databriefs/db329.htm

Hickman, T. A. (2018). Keeping secrets: Leslie E. Keeley, the gold cure and the 19th-century neuroscience of addiction. *Addiction, 113*, 1739-1749. doi: 10.1111/add.14222

Hill, S. Y., Mendelson, W. B., & Bernstein, D. A. (1977). Cocaine effects on sleep parameters in the rat. *Psychopharmacology, 51*(2), 125-127. doi: 10.1007/bf00431727

History of Cocaine. (n.d.). Retrieved from https://cocaine.org/history-of/

History.com Editors, (2018, August 21). War on drugs. Retrieved from https://www.history.com/topics/crime/the-war-on-drugs

Horvath, A. T., Misra, K., Epner, A. K., & Cooper, G. M. (n.d.). Stress regulation and withdrawal: Addictions' effect on the hypothalamus. Retrieved from https://www.centersite.net/poc/view_doc.php?type=doc&id=48377&cn=1408

How addiction hijacks the brain. (2011, July). Retrieved from https://www.health.harvard.edu/newsletter_article/how-addiction-hijacks-the-brain

How heroin affects sleep. (2018, August 25). Retrieved from https://theoakstreatment.com/blog/how-heroin-affects-sleep/

Howard, J. (2018, October 3). Here's how much fast food Americans are eating. Retrieved from https://www.cnn.com/2018/10/03/health/fast-food-consumption-cdc-study/index.html

Hser, Y., Grella, C. E., Hubbard, R.L., Hsieh, S-C., Fletcher, B. W., Brown, B. S., & Anglin, M. D. (2001). An evaluation of drug treatments for adolescents in 4 US cities. *Arch Gen Psychiatry, 58*(7), 689-695. doi: 10.1001/archpsyc.58.7.689

Hunter-Reel, D., McCrady, B. S., Hildebrandt, T., & Epstein, E. E. (2010, November). Indirect effect of social support for drinking on drinking outcomes: the role of motivation. *Journal of Studies on Alcohol and Drugs, 71*(6), 930-937. Retrieved from https://www.ncbi.nlm.nih.gov/pubmed/20946752

Hyman, S. E. (2005). Addiction: A disease of learning and memory. *American Journal of Psychiatry, 162*(8), 1414-1422. doi: 10.1176/foc.5.2.foc220

Informed Health Online. (2017, August 10). Using medication: What can help when trying to stop taking sleeping pills and sedatives? Retrieved from https://www.ncbi.nlm.nih.gov/books/NBK361010/

Institute of Medicine and National Research Council. (2013). *U.S. Health in International Perspective: Shorter Lives, Poorer Health.* Washington, DC: The National Academies Press. doi: 10.17226/13497.

Ireland, K. (n.d.). How does junk food affect the way you concentrate? Retrieved from https://www.livestrong.com/article/461051-how-does-junk-food-affect-the-way-you-concentrate/

Is alcohol disrupting your sleep? (n.d.). Retrieved from https://www.chronobiology.com/is-alcohol-disrupting-your-sleep/

James, M., Charnley, J., Flynn, J., Smith, D., & Dayas, C. (2011). Propensity to 'relapse' following exposure to cocaine cues is associated with the recruitment of specific thalamic and epithalamic nuclei. *Neuroscience, 199*, 235-242. doi: 10.1016/j.neuroscience.2011.09.047

Jaslow, R. (2012, March 9). LSD should be considered for alcoholism treatment, study says. Retrieved from https://www.cbsnews.com/news/lsd-should-be-considered-for-alcoholism-treatment-study-says/

Jedrzejczak, M. (2005, August). Family and environmental factors of drug addiction among young recruits. *Military Medicine,170*(8), 688-690. Retrieved from https://www.ncbi.nlm.nih.gov/pubmed/16173210

Jones, A. (2015, September 30). A good night's sleep? The truth about using marijuana and alcohol as sleep aids. Retrieved from https://bigthink.com/ideafeed/a-good-nights-sleep-the-truth-about-using-marijuana-and-alcohol-as-sleep-aids

Kabat-Zinn, J. (2013). *Full catastrophe living: Using the wisdom of your body and mind to face stress, pain, and illness* [Revised Edition]. New York City, NY: Bantam Books.

Kabat-Zinn, J. (2018). *Meditation is not what you think: Mindfulness and why it is so important.* New York City, NY: Hachette Books.

Kann, L., Kinchen, S., Shanklin, S. L., Flint, K. H., Hawkins, J., Harris, W. A., Lowry, R, O'Malley Olsen, E., McManus, T., Chyen, D., Whittle, L. Taylor, E., Demissie, Z., Brener, N., Thornton, J., Moore, J., & Zaza, S. (2014). Youth risk behavior surveillance - United States, 2013. *Morbidity and Mortality Weekly Report: Surveillance Summaries, 63*(4), 1-168. Retrieved from https://www.cdc.gov/mmwr/pdf/ss/ss6304.pdf

Kantor, E. D., Rehm, C. D., Haas, J. S., Chan, A. T., & Giovannucci, E. L. (2015, November 3). Trends in prescription drug use among adults in the United States from 1999-2012. *Jama, 314*(17), 1818-1830. doi: 10.1001/jama.2015.13766

Kell, J. (2017, February 7). 3 signs the U.S. liquor business had a great 2016. Retrieved from http://fortune.com/2017/02/07/liquor-industry-strong-sales-2016/

Khan Academy. (n.d.-a). The synapse. Retrieved from https://www.khanacademy.org/science/biology/human-biology/neuron-nervous-system/a/the-synapse

Khan Academy. (n.d.-b). Homeostasis. Retrieved from https://www.khanacademy.org/science/biology/principles-of-physiology/body-structure-and-homeostasis/a/homeostasis

Konkel, L. (2015, October 16). What is GABA? Retrieved from https://www.everydayhealth.com/gaba/guide/

Krach, S., Paulus, F. M., Bodden, M., & Kircher, T. (2010, May 28). The rewarding nature of social interactions. *Frontiers in behavioral neuroscience, 4*(22). doi:10.3389/fnbeh.2010.00022

Kross, E., Bruehlman-Senecal, E., Park, J., Burson, A., Dougherty, A,. Shablack, H., Bremner, R., Moser, J., & Ayduk, O. (2014). Self-talk as a regulatory mechanism: How you do it matters. *Journal of Personality and Social Psychology, 106*(2), 304-324. doi: 10.1037/a0035173

KSU Alcohol and Other Drug Education Service. (2011, Spring). Alcoholism: Nature vs. Nurture [Newsletter]. Retrieved from https://www.k-state.edu/counseling/student/aodes_news/sp11vol54.pdf

Kuerbis, A., Sacco, P., Blazer, D. G., & Moore, A.A. (2014, August). Substance abuse among older adults. *Clinics in Geriatric Medicine, 30*(3), 629-654. doi: 10.1016/j.cger.2014.04.008

Lambert, N. M., Gwinn, A. M., Baumeister, R. F., Strachman, A., Washburn, I. J., Gable, S. L., & Fincham, F. D. (2013). A boost of positive affect: The perks of sharing positive experiences. *Journal of Social and Personal Relationships, 30*(1), 24-43. https://doi.org/10.1177/0265407512449400

Laskowski, E. R. (2018, December 14). How much should the average adult exercise every day? Retrieved from https://www.mayoclinic.org/healthy-lifestyle/fitness/expert-answers/exercise/faq-20057916

Laudet, A. B., Savage, R., & Mahmood, D. (2002). Pathways to long-term recovery: a preliminary investigation. *Journal of Psychoactive Drugs, 34*(3), 305-311. doi: 10.1080/02791072.2002.10399968

Lebel, C., & Beaulieu, C. (2011). Longitudinal development of human brain wiring continues from childhood into adulthood. *Journal of Neuroscience, 31*(30), 10,937-10,947. doi: 10.3410/f.12934956.14228054

Lerner, M. (n.d.). Unintended consequences. Retrieved from http://www.pbs.org/kenburns/prohibition/unintended-consequences/

Li, W., Li, Q., Zhu, J., Qin, Y., Zheng, Y., Chang, H., Wang, H., Wang, L., Wang, Y., & Wang, W. (2013). White matter impairment in chronic heroin dependence: A quantitative DTI study. *Brain Research, 1531*, 58-64. doi: 10.1016/j.brainres.2013.07.036

Liappas, J. A., Lascaratos, J., Fafouti, S., & Christodoulou, G. N. (2003, May). Alexander the Great's relationship with alcohol. *Addiction, 98*(5), 561-567. Retrieved from https://guides.libraries.psu.edu/apaquickguide/intext

Lipari, R. N., & Hughes, A. (2017, January 12). *How people obtain the prescription pain relievers they misuse.* Center for Behavioral Health Statistics and Quality, Substance Abuse and Mental Health Services Administration. Retrieved from https://www.samhsa.gov/data/sites/default/files/report_2686/Short Report-2686.html

Lipari, R. N., & Van Horn, S. L. (2017, August 24). Children living with parents who have a substance use disorder. Retrieved from https://www.samhsa.gov/data/sites/default/files/report_3223/Short Report-3223.pdf

List of countries by alcohol consumption per capita. (n.d.). In *Wikipedia.* Retrieved February 4, 2019, from https://en.wikipedia.org/wiki/List_of_countries_by_alcohol_consumption_per_capita

Logan, R. W., Seggio, J. A., Robinson, S. L., Richard, G. R., & Rosenwasser, A. M. (2010). Circadian wheel-running activity during withdrawal from chronic intermittent ethanol exposure in mice. *Alcohol, 44*(3), 239-244. doi:10.1016/j.alcohol.2010.02.011

Mahfoud, Y., Talih, F., Streem, D., & Budur, K. (2009, September). Sleep disorders in substance abusers: How common are they? *Psychiatry, 6*(9), 38-42. Retrieved from https://www.ncbi.nlm.nih.gov/pmc/articles/PMC2766287/

Malnutrition. (2005, January, 6). Retrieved from https://healthengine.com.au/info/malnutrition

MarketWatch. (2014, June 3). The 10 drunkest nations on Earth. Retrieved from https://www.marketwatch.com/story/10-countries-where-people-drink-the-most-2014-05-30

Mather, M. (2016, January 13). Fact sheet: Aging in the United States. Retrieved from https://www.prb.org/aging-unitedstates-fact-sheet/

Matthews, G. A., Nieh, E. H., Vander Weele, C. M., Halbert, S. A., Pradhan, R. V., Yosafat, A. S., . . . Tye, K. M. (2016). Dorsal raphe dopamine neurons represent the experience of social isolation. *Cell, 164*(4). doi:https://doi.org/10.1016/j.cell.2015.12.040

Mattson, M., Lipari, R. N., Hays, C., & Van Horn, S. L. (2017, May 11). *A day in the life of older adults: Substance abuse.* Substance Abuse and Mental Health Services Administration, The CBHSQ Report. Retrieved from https://www.samhsa.gov/data/sites/default/files/report_2792/Short Report-2792.html

Mattyasovszky, M. (2018, September 28). Top 10 cocoa producing countries. Retrieved from https://www.worldatlas.com/articles/top-10-cocoa-producing-countries.html

Mayo Clinic Staff. (2018, January 30). Prescription sleeping pills: What's right for you? Retrieved from https://www.mayoclinic.org/diseases-conditions/insomnia/in-depth/sleeping-pills/art-20043959

Mayo Clinic Staff. (2018, February 6) Over-the-counter weight-loss pills Retrieved from https://www.mayoclinic.org/healthy-lifestyle/weight-loss/in-depth/weight-loss/art-20046409

Mayo Clinic Staff. (2018, November 6). Alcohol: Weighing risks and potential benefits. Retrieved from https://www.mayoclinic.org/healthy-lifestyle/nutrition-and-healthy-eating/in-depth/alcohol/art-20044551

McLeod, S. (2009). Eyewitness testimony. Retrieved from https://www.simplypsychology.org/eyewitness-testimony.html

Mechelmans, D. J., Strelchuk, D., Doñamayor, N., Banca, P., Robbins, T. W., Baek, K., & Voon, V. (2017). Reward sensitivity and waiting impulsivity: Shift towards reward valuation away from action control. *International Journal of Neuropsychopharmacology, 20*(12), 971-978. doi:10.1093/ijnp/pyx072

Mental Health America. (2018, May). Evidence for peer support. Retrieved from http://www.mentalhealthamerica.net/sites/default/files/Evidence%2 0for%20Peer%20Support%20May%202018.pdf

Mersy, D. J. (2003, April 1). Recognition of alcohol and substance abuse. *American Family Physician, 67*(7), 1529-1532. Retrieved from https://www.aafp.org/afp/2003/0401/p1529.html

Miller, W. R., & Hester, R. K. (1986). Inpatient alcoholism treatment: Who benefits? *American Psychologist, 41*(7), 794-805. doi: 10.1037/0003-066X.41.7.794

Miron, J., & Zwiebel, J. (1991, April). Alcohol consumption during prohibition. *American Economic Review, 81*, 242-247. doi: 10.3386/w3675

Morabia, A., Fabre, J., Ghee, E., Zeger, S., Orsat, E., & Robert, A. (1989). Diet and opiate addiction: A quantitative assessment of the diet of non-institutionalized opiate addicts. *Addiction, 84*(2), 173-180. doi:10.1111/j.1360-0443.1989.tb00566.x

Mudaliar, A. (2018, April 20). Summary and significance of the Harrison Narcotics Act of 1914. Retrieved from https://historyplex.com/summary-significance-of-harrison-narcotics-act-of1914

Nader, M. A., Czoty, P. W., Nader, S. H., & Morgan, D. (2012). Nonhuman primate models of social behavior and cocaine abuse. *Psychopharmacology, 224*(1), 57-67.

National Alliance on Mental Illness. (n.d.). Mental health by the numbers [Multiple graphs visualizing statistics provided by the National Institute of Mental Health]. Retrieved from https://www.nami.org/getattachment/Learn-More/Mental-Health-by-the-Numbers/childrenmhfacts.pdf

National Institute on Aging. (n.d.). *How the aging brain affects thinking.* United States Department of Health & Human Services. Retrieved from https://www.nia.nih.gov/health/how-aging-brain-affects-thinking

National Institute on Alcohol Abuse and Alcoholism. (1993, October). Alcohol and nutrition. Retrieved from https://pubs.niaaa.nih.gov/publications/aa22.htm

The National Institute on Drug Abuse Blog Team. (2017, March). Prescription stimulant medications (amphetamines). Retrieved from https://teens.drugabuse.gov/drug-facts/prescription-stimulant-medications-amphetamines

National Sleep Foundation. (n.d.-a). How alcohol affects the quality - and quantity - of aleep. Retrieved from https://www.sleepfoundation.org/sleep-topics/how-alcohol-affects-sleep

National Sleep Foundation. (n.d.-b). What is circadian rhythm? Retrieved from https://www.sleepfoundation.org/sleep-topics/what-circadian-rhythm

Neuroscience News. (2016, February 26). How drugs and alcohol can hijack your brain. Retrieved from https://neurosciencenews.com/addiction-amygdala-striatum-3739/

Neuroscientifically Challenged. (2014, May 17). Know your brain: Prefrontal cortex. Retrieved from https://www.neuroscientificallychallenged.com/blog/2014/5/16/know-your-brain-prefrontal-cortex

Newman, K. (2017, September 1). Study: Millennials less likely to use opioids to treat pain. Retrieved from https://www.usnews.com/news/national-news/articles/2017-09-01/millennials-not-as-likely-to-reach-for-opioids-to-treat-pain-study-says

The New York Times. (2010, July 16). Are sleeping pills addictive? Retrieved from https://consults.blogs.nytimes.com/2010/07/16/are-sleeping-pills-addictive/

News-Medical.net. (2009, September 1). Alcohol consumption disrupts circadian rhythm in humans. Retrieved from https://www.news-medical.net/news/20090901/Alcohol-consumption-disrupts-circadian-rhythm-in-humans.aspx

NIDA. (n.d.). Brief Screener for Alcohol, Tobacco, and other Drugs. Retrieved from https://www.drugabuse.gov/ast/bstad/#/

NIDA. (n.d.). Older Adults. Retrieved from https://www.niaaa.nih.gov/alcohol-health/special-populations-co-occurring-disorders/older-adults

NIDA. (2016, May 6). Cocaine. Retrieved from
https://www.drugabuse.gov/publications/research-reports/cocaine

NIDA. (2017, March 23). Health consequences of drug misuse. Retrieved
from https://www.drugabuse.gov/related-topics/health-
consequences-drug-misuse

NIDA. (2017, April 24). Trends & statistics. Retrieved from
https://www.drugabuse.gov/related-topics/trends-statistics

NIDA. (2017, September 26). MDMA (Ecstasy) abuse. Retrieved from
https://www.drugabuse.gov/publications/research-reports/mdma-
ecstasy-abuse

NIDA. (2018, January 17). Misuse of prescription drugs. Retrieved from
https://www.drugabuse.gov/publications/research-reports/misuse-
prescription-drugs

NIDA. (2018, January 17). Principles of drug addiction treatment: A
research-based guide (Third Edition). Retrieved from
https://www.drugabuse.gov/publications/principles-drug-addiction-
treatment-research-based-guide-third-edition

NIDA. (2018, July). Commonly Abused Drugs Charts. Retrieved from
https://www.drugabuse.gov/drugs-abuse/commonly-abused-
drugs-charts

Nida-Rümelin, M. (2009, November 23). Qualia: The knowledge
argument. Retrieved from https://plato.stanford.edu/entries/qualia-
knowledge/

Nicholson, A. N., Turner, C., Stone, B. M., & Robson, P. J. (2004, June).
Effect of Delta-9-tetrahydrocannabinol and cannabidiol on
nocturnal sleep and early-morning behavior in young adults.
Journal of Clinical Psychopharmacology, 24(3), 305-313.
Retrieved from https://www.ncbi.nlm.nih.gov/pubmed/15118485

Oakford, S. (2016, April 19). Portugal's example: What happened after it
decriminalized all drugs, from weed to heroin. Retrieved from
https://news.vice.com/en_us/article/59eqgk/ungass-portugal-what-
happened-after-decriminalization-drugs-weed-to-heroin

Oaklander, M. (2017, July 27). New hope for depression. Retrieved from
http://time.com/4876098/new-hope-for-depression/

Odum, A. L. (2011). Delay discounting: I'm a k, you're a k. *Journal of the experimental analysis of behavior, 96*(3), 427-39. doi: 10.1901/jeab.2011.96-423

OECD. (2015, December 5).Tackling harmful alcohol use: Country note - Ireland. Retrieved from https://www.oecd.org/ireland/Tackling-Harmful-Alcohol-Use-Ireland-en.pdf

Painkillers driving addiction, overdose. (n.d.). Retrieved from https://www.webmd.com/pain-management/news/20170731/doctors-still-overprescribing-opioids-in-us#1

Parekh, R. (2017, January). What is addiction? Retrieved from https://www.psychiatry.org/patients-families/addiction/what-is-addiction

Park, S. (2014, October 16). 5 areas of brain damage caused by obstructive sleep apnea [Blog post]. Retrieved from https://doctorstevenpark.com/5-areas-of-brain-damage-caused-by-obstructive-sleep-apnea

Parmet, S. (2013, August 29). Alcohol breaks brain connections needed to process social cues. Retrieved from https://today.uic.edu/alcohol-breaks-brain-connections-needed-to-process-social-cues

Patten, A. R., Sickmann, H., Hryciw, B. N., Kucharsky, T., Parton, R., Kernick, A. & Christie, B. R. (2013). Long-term exercise is needed to enhance synaptic plasticity in the hippocampus. *Learning & Memory, 20*, 642-647. doi: 10.1101/lm.030635.113

Peri, C. (2014, February 13). 10 things to hate about sleep loss. Retrieved from https://www.webmd.com/sleep-disorders/features/10-results-sleep-loss#1

Perkins, S. (2018, December 27). Can alcohol deplete the body of nutrients? Retrieved from https://healthyeating.sfgate.com/can-alcohol-deplete-body-nutrients-9335.html

Peters, B. (2017, May 30). The critical effects of sleep deprivation on your body and health. Retrieved from https://www.verywellhealth.com/what-are-the-physical-effects-of-sleep-deprivation-3015079

218

Peters, R. H., Wexler, H. K., & Lurigio, A. J. (2015, March). Co-occurring substance use and mental disorders in the criminal justice system: A new frontier of clinical practice and research. *Psychiatric Rehabilitation Journal, 38*(1), 1-6. doi: 10.1037/prj0000135

Powers, T. (2015, September 13). Recognizing the stages of Alcoholism: The Jellinek Curve. Retrieved from https://www.thefix.com/history-behind-jellinek-curve

Prescription Drug Abuse in the Elderly. (n.d.). Retrieved from https://familydoctor.org/condition/prescription-drug-abuse-in-the-elderly/

Prochaska, J. O., & DiClemente, C. C. (1983, June). Stages and processes of self-change of smoking: toward an integrative model of change. *Journal of Consulting and Clinical Psychology, 51*(3), 390-395. Retrieved from https://www.ncbi.nlm.nih.gov/pubmed/6863699

Prochaska, J. O., DiClemente, C. C., & Norcross, J. C. (1992, September). In search of how people change. Applications to addictive behaviors. *American Psychological Association, 47*(9), 1102-1114. Retrieved from https://www.ncbi.nlm.nih.gov/pubmed/1329589

Prochaska, J. O., Norcross, J. C., & DiClemente, C. C. (1995). *Changing for good*. New York: Avon Books.

Project MATCH (Matching Alcoholism Treatment to Client Heterogeneity): rationale and methods for a multisite clinical trial matching patients to alcoholism treatment. (1993, December.) *Alcohol Clin Exp Res., 17*(6), 1130-1145. Retrieved from https://www.ncbi.nlm.nih.gov/pubmed/8116822

Pullar-Strecker, H. (1945, July). The use of insulin in the treatment of alcoholism and alcoholic addiction. *The British Journal of Inebriety, 43*(1), 14-27. doi: 10.1111/j.1360-0443.1945.tb05437.x

Reilly, G. (2011, July 12). Alcohol-related deaths on the rise in Ireland. Retrieved from https://www.thejournal.ie/alcohol-related-deaths-on-the-rise-in-ireland-175243-Jul2011/

Roan, S. (2009, November 16). You can cut back on alcohol. Retrieved from https://www.latimes.com/health/la-he-alcohol16-2009nov16-story.html

Roos, D. (2019, January 14). How Prohibition put the 'organized' in organized crime. Retrieved from https://www.history.com/news/prohibition-organized-crime-al-capone

Root, T. L., Pinheiro, A. P., Thornton, L., Strober, M., Fernandez-Aranda, F., Brandt, H., Crawford, S., Fichter, M. M., Halmi, K. A., Johnson, C., Kaplan, A. S., Klump, K. L., La Via, M., Mitchell, J., Woodside, D. B., Rotondo, A., Berrettini, W. H., Kaye, W. H., & Bulik, C. M. (2010). Substance use disorders in women with anorexia nervosa. *The International journal of eating disorders, 43*(1), 14-21. doi: 10.1002/eat.20670

Roots of Prohibition. (2011). Retrieved from http://www.pbs.org/kenburns/prohibition/roots-of-prohibition/

Salz, A. (2014, December). CPE monthly: Substance abuse and nutrition. *Today's Dietitian, 16*(12). 44. Retrieved from https://www.todaysdietitian.com/newarchives/120914p44.shtml

Sansgiry, S. S., Bhansali, A. H., Bapat, S. S., & Xu, Q. (2016). Abuse of over-the-counter medicines: a pharmacist's perspective. *Integrated pharmacy research & practice, 6*, 1-6. doi: 10.2147/IPRP.S103494

Santolaria-Fernández, F. J., Gómez-Sirvent, J. L., González-Reimers, C. E., Batista-López, J.N., Jorge-Hernández, J.A., Rodríguez-Moreno, F., Martínez-Riera, A., & Hernández-García, M. T. (1995, April). Nutritional assessment of drug addicts. *Drug Alcohol Depend., 38*(1), 11-18. Retrieved from https://www.ncbi.nlm.nih.gov/pubmed/7648992

Scourboutakos, M. J., Semnani-Azad, Z., & L'Abbe, M. R. (2013). Restaurant meals: Almost a full day's worth of calories, fats, and sodium. *JAMA Intern Med., 173*(14), 1373-1374. doi: 10.1001/jamainternmed.2013.6159

Selemon, L. D. (2013, March 5). A role for synaptic plasticity in the adolescent development of executive function. *Translational Psychiatry, 3*(3). doi:10.1038/tp.2013.7

Seltzer, L. F. (2015, July 8). Trauma and the freeze response: Good, bad, or both? Retrieved from https://www.psychologytoday.com/us/blog/evolution-the-self/201507/trauma-and-the-freeze-response-good-bad-or-both

Senay, I., Albarracín, D., & Noguchi, K. (2010). Motivating goal-directed behavior through introspective self-talk: The role of the interrogative form of simple future tense. *Psychological science, 21*(4), 499-504. Retrieved from https://www.ncbi.nlm.nih.gov/pmc/articles/PMC3626423/

Dr. Shauna Shapiro, (n.d.). Retrieved from http://www.drshaunashapiro.com/

Shapiro, S. L., & Carlson, L. E. (2017). *The art and science of mindfulness: Integrating mindfulness into psychology and the helping professions.* Washington, D.C.: American Psychological Association.

Shuttleworth, M. (2008, February 23). Asch experiment. Retrieved from https://explorable.com/asch-experiment

Shuttleworth, M. (2008, June 22). Stanford prison experiment. Retrieved from https://explorable.com/stanford-prison-experiment

Siddiqui, S. V., Chatterjee, U., Kumar, D., Siddiqui, A., & Goyal, N. (2008). Neuropsychology of prefrontal cortex. *Indian journal of psychiatry, 50*(3), 202-8. doi: 10.4103/0019-5545.43634

Siegel, D. J. (2014, February 4). Pruning, myelination, and the remodeling adolescent brain. Retrieved from https://www.psychologytoday.com/us/blog/inspire-rewire/201402/pruning-myelination-and-the-remodeling-adolescent-brain

Simonson, M. (2014, February 15). Experiment to treat inebriates began 150 years ago. Retrieved from https://www.thedailystar.com/opinion/columns/experiment-to-treat-inebriates-began-years-ago/article_423f67db-ed84-58db-8363-378cd1bd9f61.html

Sinha, R., Fox, H. C., Hong, K. I., Hansen, J., Tuit, K., & Kreek, M. J. (2011). Effects of adrenal sensitivity, stress- and cue-induced craving, and anxiety on subsequent alcohol relapse and treatment outcomes. *Archives of general psychiatry, 68*(9), 942-952. doi: 10.1001/archgenpsychiatry.2011.49

6 health problems linked to lack of sleep. (2012, March 18). Retrieved from https://abcnews.go.com/Health/Sleep/health-problems-linked-lack-sleep/story?id=15930879

Smith, L. P., Ng, S. W., & Popkin, B. M. (2013). Trends in US home food preparation and consumption: Analysis of national nutrition surveys and time use studies from 1965-1966 to 2007-2008. *Nutrition journal, 12*, 45. doi: 10.1186/1475-2891-12-45

Smith, O. (2017, October 19). Mapped: The world according to cocaine consumption. Retrieved from https://www.telegraph.co.uk/travel/maps-and-graphics/cocaine-consumption-by-country/

Sohn, E. (2013, December 6). Lack of sleep: What it does to your brain. Retrieved from https://mashable.com/2013/12/06/lack-of-sleep/#oP004cmBtgq5

Srikameswaran, A. (2011, April 1). Cocaine causes memory drain. Retrieved from https://www.futurity.org/cocaine-causes-memory-drain/

St-Onge, M. P., Keller, K. L., & Heymsfield, S. B. (2003, December). Changes in childhood food consumption patterns: a cause for concern in light of increasing body weights. *The American Journal of Clinical Nutrition, 78*(6), 1068–1073. doi: 10.1093/ajcn/78.6.1068

Stannard, L. (n.d.). What is dopamine & norepinephrine? Retrieved from https://www.livestrong.com/article/17497-dopamine-norepinephrine/

Statistica. (n.d.). U.S. pharmaceutical industry - Statistics & facts. Retrieved from https://www.statista.com/topics/1719/pharmaceutical-industry/

Structure and function of the brain. (n.d.) Retrieved from https://courses.lumenlearning.com/boundless-psychology/chapter/structure-and-function-of-the-brain/

Substance Abuse and Mental Health Services Administration. (2014, September). *Results from the 2013 national Survey on drug use and health: Summary of national findings.* U.S. Department of Health and Human Services - Substance Abuse and Mental Health Services Administration Center for Behavioral Health Statistics and Quality. Retrieved from https://www.samhsa.gov/data/sites/default/files/NSDUHresultsPDFWHTML2013/Web/NSDUHresults2013.pdf

Substance Abuse and Mental Health Services Administration. (2016, November). *Facing Addiction in America: The Surgeon General's Report on Alcohol, Drugs, and Health*. Office of the Surgeon General (US). Washington (DC): US Department of Health and Human Services. Retrieved from https://www.ncbi.nlm.nih.gov/books/NBK424859/

Substance Abuse and Mental Health Services Administration. (2017). *Key substance use and mental health indicators in the United States: Results from the 2016 National Survey on Drug Use and Health* (HHS Publication No. SMA 17-5044, NSDUH Series H-52). Retrieved from https://www.samhsa.gov/data/

Substance Abuse and Mental Health Services Administration, Center for Behavioral Health Statistics and Quality. (2017). National Survey on Drug Use and Health (NSDUH), Appendix I. Retrieved from https://www.cdc.gov/nchs/data/hus/2017/050.pdf

Swanson, J. (2014, July 8). Nutrition for addicts: Healing the body. Retrieved from https://www.addiction.com/3446/nutrition-for-addicts/

Szalavitz, M. (2009, April 26). Drugs in Portugal: Did decriminalization work? Retrieved from http://content.time.com/time/health/article/0,8599,1893946,00.html

Talukder, G. (2013, March 20). Decision-making is still a work in progress for teenagers. Retrieved from https://brainconnection.brainhq.com/2013/03/20/decision-making-is-still-a-work-in-progress-for-teenagers/

Tardanico, S. (2014, April 15). Is social media sabotaging real communication? Retrieved from https://www.forbes.com/sites/susantardanico/2012/04/30/is-social-media-sabotaging-real-communication/#2bc7ac4e2b62

Thomas, K., &, Schmidt, M. S. (2012, July 2). Glaxo agrees to pay $3 billion in fraud settlement. Retrieved from https://www.nytimes.com/2012/07/03/business/glaxosmithkline-agrees-to-pay-3-billion-in-fraud-settlement.html

Thompson, D. (2017, July 31). Doctors still overprescribing opioids in U.S. Retrieved from https://www.webmd.com/pain-management/news/20170731/doctors-still-overprescribing-opioids-in-us#1

Tracy, K., & Wallace, S. P. (2016). Benefits of peer support groups in the treatment of addiction. *Substance abuse and rehabilitation, 7,* 143-154. doi: 10.2147/SAR.S81535

Transform. (2014, July 14). The success of Portugal's decriminalisation policy – in seven charts [Blog post]. Retrieved from https://www.tdpf.org.uk/blog/success-portugal%E2%80%99s-decriminalisation-policy-%E2%80%93-seven-charts

Travis, A. (2014, October 30). Punitive drug law enforcement failing, says Home Office study. Retrieved from https://www.theguardian.com/society/2014/oct/30/punitive-drug-laws-are-failing-study

Trickey, E. (2018, January 4). Inside the story of America's 19th-century opiate addiction. Retrieved from https://guides.libraries.psu.edu/apaquickguide/intext

Twining, C. M. (1916, January 1). The preparation of serums and antitoxins. *Journal of the American Pharmaceutical Association, 5,* 21-29. Retrieved from https://play.google.com/store/books/details?id=uVM9AQAAMAAJ&rdid=book-uVM9AQAAMAAJ&rdot=1

The Understood Team. (2017). 3 areas of executive function. Retrieved from https://www.understood.org/en/learning-attention-issues/child-learning-disabilities/executive-functioning-issues/3-areas-of-executive-function

United States Food & Drug Administration. (2015). *Information for consumers (drugs): The impact of direct-to-consumer advertising.* Retrieved from https://www.fda.gov/Drugs/ResourcesForYou/Consumers/ucm143562.htm

University of Bristol. (2016, February 19). Best to sleep on it: Brain activity patterns during sleep consolidate memory. *ScienceDaily.* Retrieved December 31, 2018, from www.sciencedaily.com/releases/2016/02/160219134813.htm

University at Buffalo, State University of New York, (2015, Fall). Substance abuse in older adults: A hidden problem. Retrieved from https://www.buffalo.edu/content/dam/www/ria/PDFs/ES16ElderlySubAbuse.pdf

University of Texas at Austin. (2018, August 7). Socially isolated rats are more vulnerable to addiction, report researchers. Retrieved from https://news.utexas.edu/2013/01/23/socially-isolated-rats-are-more-vulnerable-to-addiction-report-researchers/

U.S. Department of Health and Human Services and U.S. Department of Agriculture. (2015, December). *2015 – 2020 Dietary guidelines for Americans* (8th ed). Retrieved from https://health.gov/dietaryguidelines/2015/guidelines/

Vago, D. R. (n.d.). Starting a meditation practice. Retrieved from http://davidvago.bwh.harvard.edu/mindfulness-resources/starting-a-meditation-practice-retreat-centers-for-you/

Vago, D. R. (n.d.). Suggested reading list. Retrieved from http://davidvago.bwh.harvard.edu/mindfulness-resources/suggested-reading-list/

Valjak, D. (2017, January 16). Sigmund Freud recommended cocaine for treatment of many physical and mental issues. Retrieved from https://www.thevintagenews.com/2017/01/16/sigmund-freud-recommended-cocaine-for-treatment-of-many-physical-and-mental-issues/

Vastag, B. (2009, April 7). 5 years after: Portugal's drug decriminalization policy shows positive results. Retrieved from https://www.scientificamerican.com/article/portugal-drug-decriminalization/

Villa, L. (2018, September 20). Mental health and drug abuse. Retrieved from https://drugabuse.com/library/mental-health-and-drug-abuse/

Vimont, C. (2013, July 26). Sleep problems and substance use disorders: An often overlooked link. Retrieved from https://drugfree.org/learn/drug-and-alcohol-news/sleep-problems-and-substance-use-disorders-an-often-overlooked-link/

Volkow, N. (2014). Drugs, brains, and behavior: The science of addiction. Retrieved from https://www.drugabuse.gov/sites/default/files/soa_2014.pdf

Wake Forest University Baptist Medical Center. (2008, April 7). Subordinate monkeys more likely to choose cocaine over food. Retrieved from www.sciencedaily.com/releases/2008/04/080406153354.htm

Warner, J. (2008, July 1). U.S. leads the world in illegal drug use. Retrieved from https://www.cbsnews.com/news/us-leads-the-world-in-illegal-drug-use/

Watkins, M. (2018, November 29). How drugs affect the brain and central nervous system. Retrieved from https://americanaddictioncenters.org/health-complications-addiction/central-nervous-system

Weiner, B., & White, W. (2007, January). The Journal of Inebriety (1876-1914): history, topical analysis, and photographic images. *Addiction, 102*(1),15-23. Retrieved from https://www.ncbi.nlm.nih.gov/pubmed/17207119

Weintraub, P. (2015, May 4). The voice of reason. Retrieved from https://www.psychologytoday.com/us/articles/201505/the-voice-reason

Weir, K. (2012, April). The pain of social rejection. *American Psychological Association, 43*(4), 50. Retrieved from https://www.apa.org/monitor/2012/04/rejection.aspx

Wemm, S. E., & Wulfert, E. (2017). Effects of acute stress on decision making. *Applied psychophysiology and biofeedback, 42*(1), 1-12. doi: 10.1007/s10484-016-9347-8

What is Moderation Management? (n.d.). Retrieved from https://www.moderation.org/about_mm/whatismm.html

White, B. (2014, May 9). Brain surgery as addiction treatment? [Blog post]. Retrieved from http://www.williamwhitepapers.com/blog/2014/05/brain-surgery-as-addiction-treatment.html

Wilson, W., Marshall, T. R., Clarke, J. P., Swanson, C. A., Bryan, N. P., & Clark, C. (1914). *Harrison Narcotics Tax Act, 1914.* Retrieved from https://www.naabt.org/documents/Harrison_Narcotics_Tax_Act_1914.pdf

Winkelman, J. W., Buxton, O. M., Jensen, J. E., Benson, K. L., O'Connor, S. P., Wang, W., & Renshaw, P. F. (2008). Reduced brain GABA in primary insomnia: preliminary data from 4T proton magnetic resonance spectroscopy (1H-MRS). *Sleep, 31*(11), 1499-1506. Retrieved from https://www.ncbi.nlm.nih.gov/pmc/articles/PMC2579978/

Wlassoff, V. (2015, April 3). The dope on pot – How marijuana affects sleep and dreams. Retrieved from http://brainblogger.com/2015/04/03/the-dope-on-pot-how-marijuana-affects-sleep-and-dreams/

Wong, M. M., Robertson, G. C., & Dyson, R. B. (2015, January 16). Prospective relationship between poor sleep and substance-related problems in a national sample of adolescents. *Alcoholism: Clinical and Experimental Research, 39*(2), 355-362. doi: 10.1111/acer.12618

Worbe, Y., Savulich, G., Voon, V., Fernandez-Egea, E., & Robbins, T. W. (2014). Serotonin depletion induces 'waiting impulsivity' on the human four-choice serial reaction time task: Cross-species translational significance. *Neuropsychopharmacology, 39*(6), 1519-1526. doi:10.1038/npp.2013.351

The World Health Organization (WHO). (n.d.) The ICD-10 classification of mental and behavioural disorders: Clinical descriptions and diagnostic guidelines. Retrieved from https://www.who.int/substance_abuse/terminology/ICD10ClinicalD iagnosis.pdf?ua=1

Yurgelun-Todd, D. (n.d.). Inside the teenage brain [Interview]. Retrieved from https://www.pbs.org/wgbh/pages/frontline/shows/teenbrain/intervie ws/todd.html

Zimmermann, K. A. (2017, June 6). Medical marijuana: Benefits, risks & state laws. Retrieved from https://www.livescience.com/24554-medical-marijuana.html